MAKE BELIEVE IN FILM AND FICTION

Make Believe in Film and Fiction

Visual vs. Verbal Storytelling

Karl Kroeber

MAKE BELIEVE IN FILM AND FICTION
© Karl Kroeber, 2006.
Jacket image: *Scarf Dance*, both sculpture and photo, by Jean T. Kroeber.

First published in 2006 by
PALGRAVE MACMILLAN™
175 Fifth Avenue, New York, N.Y. 10010 and
Houndmills, Basingstoke, Hampshire, England RG21 6XS
Companies and representatives throughout the world.

PALGRAVE MACMILLAN is the global academic imprint of the Palgrave Macmillan division of St. Martin's Press, LLC and of Palgrave Macmillan Ltd. Macmillan® is a registered trademark in the United States, United Kingdom and other countries. Palgrave is a registered trademark in the European Union and other countries.

ISBN-13: 978–1–4039–7279–8
ISBN-10: 1–4039–7279–6

Library of Congress Cataloging-in-Publication Data

Kroeber, Karl, 1926–
    Make believe in film and fiction : visual vs. verbal storytelling / Karl Kroeber.
        p. cm.
    Includes bibliographical references and index.
    ISBN 1–4039–7279–6 (alk. paper)
    1. Motion pictures and literature. 2. Narration (Rhetoric)
3. Film adaptations. I. Title.

PN1995.3.K76 2006
791.43′6-dc22   2005056648

A catalogue record for this book is available from the British Library.

Design by Newgen Imaging Systems (P) Ltd., Chennai, India.

First edition: May 2006

10 9 8 7 6 5 4 3 2 1

6242120

This book is dedicated to my daughter, Katharine, who taught me to appreciate the genius of Buster Keaton, and my cat, Mr. Underfoot, who by volunteer services as paperweight and keyboard cover made certain that none of this book was written with unseemly haste.

Contents

ACKNOWLEDGMENTS

Much in this book originated with the Columbia students who participated in my seminars *Nineteenth-Century Novels and Twentieth-Century Films*, but among the many from whom I learned, I'll mention only the two now geographically most distant: Adeline Yeo in Singapore, and Ricardo Hernandez Anzola, now teaching film courses in Venezuela. Among professional colleagues who did what they could for my dubious project, I am most grateful to Martin Meisel, less for critiquing substantial portions of the manuscript than for the years of friendship during which he has incalculably enriched my mind with his wisdom about literature, history, science, painting, and the subtleties of academic administration. To a much younger colleague, Jason Stevens, I am indebted, beyond his reading of some chapters, for his sharing with me his extraordinary knowledge of film history. Kathy Eden is the kind of office-neighbor who keeps one intellectually alert, and to her I also owe the quotation which is the final sentence of this book, in her ingenious translation, since I found I could not improve on it. I have depended on the enthusiastic encouragement and practical wisdom of Marilyn Gaull in achieving a publishable book, but I am even more grateful to her as a long-time ebullient friend generous in sharing both the range of her interests and the depth of her commitment to humanistic scholarship. Finally there is the continuing debt for which no words are adequate to the artist in residence, who this time had to serve as wound-dresser as well as the usual car-parker, household handy person, and four-star chef.

Chapter 1

Brutal Beginnings: Imagining Murder/ Watching Murder

Charles Dickens was the first famous novelist to commit murder for profit. Three decades after he made Bill Sikes bludgeon the prostitute Nancy to death in *Oliver Twist*, a Russian admirer introduced fiction's most celebrated double murderer, Rodion Raskolnikov. Moviemakers have always delighted in murders, and among the most notorious is the killing of Marion Crane in Hitchcock's *Psycho*. Naked Marion appears to be slashed in a blur of splashing water, spattering blood, and flapping shower curtain. The curtain, water, and bloodily convulsive action disguise the details of the knifing as well as the identity of her maniacal killer. Dostoyevsky is more explicit, slow moving, and carefully gruesome.

> He pulled the ax out all the way, raised it up in both hands, hardly aware of what he was doing, and without effort, almost automatically, he brought the blunt side down on her head. . . . The old woman was bareheaded as usual. Her scant, gray-flecked hair, as usual greasy and streaked with oil, was in a rat's tail plait, fastened by a piece of broken horn comb that stuck out at the nape of her neck. She was short, and his blow struck her on the very top of her head. She cried out feebly. Then all at once she slumped in a heap to the floor, even as she managed to raise both hands to her head. One hand still held his pledge. He struck again, and then again, with all his strength, on the top of her head with the blunt side of the ax. The blood poured out as from an overturned glass, and her body collapsed backward. He stepped back as she fell, and he bent over her face. She was dead. Her eyes were staring as if leaping out at him. Her forehead and her face were convulsively contorted. (1:7)[*]

[*] Because all the novels I discuss exist in a variety of popular editions, my citations are simply to chapters, or, as here, to parts and chapters. Except where otherwise indicated I am responsible for the translations.

Differences in how Marion Crane and the old pawnbroker are murdered illustrate how novelists and filmmakers inflame our imaginations by different forms of make believe. The differences should stir our recognition that motion pictures were the first art to make possible genuine visual storytelling. And appreciation of the distinctions between the imagining evoked by film and fiction should increase the pleasure and profit we derive from excellent storytelling in each form—even the pleasures of seeing or imagining horrifying murders.

The sensationalism of the *Psycho* shower murder takes the first-time viewer by surprise: visual narrative centers attention on the unpredictable. Exciting events often occur unexpectedly in ordinary life, and our visual perceptual system is spectacularly efficient at registering what we could not have anticipated. Confronted with startling violence, our attention (both physiological and psychic) concentrates, excluding everything except the immediate sight. Reading the murder in *Crime and Punishment* is a slower, more diffuse, process. This murder horrifies by enacting what we and Raskolnikov have fearfully anticipated. And parts of Dostoyevsky's narrative carry out minds away from details of the killing. The novel is less sensational because it enables us not to *see* the murder but to *imagine* it.

Seeing and imagining are entirely distinct. Watching *Psycho*, we see what appears to be a murder; reading *Crime and Punishment*, we see black marks, letters, on a white page. Reading fiction is facilitated by *shutting out* sensory impressions. We ignore the physical shape of the letters on the page so as to imagine minute details, such as the broken comb at the nape of the pawnbroker's neck. But the words also provoke imagining of what is *not* part of the immediate scene, for instance, the reference to the woman's hair being arranged "as usual," and the description of the blood pouring from her head "as from an overturned glass." The oddity of this simile—when was the last time you saw a glass full of blood?— displays how unfettered is verbal make believe by sensory verisimilitude. As surprising and more disturbing is our imagining aroused by Raskolnikov's bringing down on the pawnbroker's head the *blunt* side of his ax. During *Psycho*'s murder, we are not made to think about the difference between the edge and the point of the killer's knife. But by specifying the blunt side of the ax, Dostoyevsky incites us to imagine its opposite, the ax's edge, the *possibility* of what might have happened had Raskolnikov used the "appropriate" striking part of the ax. Raskolnikov's murder is peculiarly revolting because it stimulates us to imagine how it could have been done "better."

Dostoyevsky's technique here is now called "side-shadowing," narrative that invokes readers' underconsciousness of how events might have happened otherwise than they did, or even not have happened at all (Morson, 1994; 1998). This technique is unavailable to movies, which cannot display what is never visible. Raskolnikov's second murder, however, seems more like the killing of Marion Crane because it is unexpected. He had not anticipated Lizaveta's return to the apartment, nor had first-time readers of the novel. Yet when she appears all readers instantly understand why—remembering that Raskolnikov overslept and came to the pawnbroker's apartment later than he had planned. Our imagination has no difficulty flashing back to, and instantaneously returning from, events long before the current moment, even though the narrative has just maneuvered us into imagining from inside Raskolnikov's mind. We share his shock of startled fear as, fumbling through the pawnbroker's possessions, he suddenly hears the sound of movement in the room where there should be only a bloody corpse. As Raskolnikov pauses, we pause with him, feeling his bewildered fear. When he rushes out and confronts Lizaveta, we realize why she is here, as he may or may not. For at this moment the narrative carries us away from imagining through Raskolnikov's mind and back to an "objective" imagining perspective as he again raises the ax. We imagine him striking without sharing in his perceptions and feelings as he kills. This shifting of *how* we imagine, one instant inside the murderer's mind, the next outside his subjectivity, is such an easy operation for our mind that we probably don't even notice its activity. But the shift in imaginative position affects our response, in part because it creates a formal parallel/contrast between this narration and that of the first murder making the specificity of the second killing more hideous. We now imagine Raskolnikov facing his victim, pathetic and innocent Liza, whom he sees seeing his terrible purpose, pitiably half-holding up one hand, and deprived of the power of speech, whereas the pawnbroker was turned away from him, her head bent, muttering over the pledge. And the second time Raskolnikov strikes with the edge of the ax.

What Dostoyevsky imagined is accessible to any reader because it is carefully *structured* imagining. Such formalizing is the salient feature of all powerful verbal make believe, which never allows the *order* of events as they would occur in actuality to interfere with the most effective *structuring* of the imagining process created by the storyteller. The key feature of this formalizing is continuous associating of what we *are* reading and *are* imagining with what we *have* read and *have* imagined.

In the *Psycho* shower scene, nothing distracts our attention from visible movements—and the episode is constituted entirely of movements of knife, bodies, curtain, and cascading water. The very indistinctness of the murderer's face (which of course is essential to the plot) contributes to our concentration on the action. We focus on the knifing, more than on killer or on victim. The violent episode thus manifests in miniature the structure of the entire film, which allows nothing to impede its actions. Physical activity dominates visual narrative, of which the central feature is perceptible motion. This is why lots of movies are crudely melodramatic. But when intelligently organized, a narrative of physical movements can be as intellectually compelling as emotionally exciting.

The key to understanding visual make believe is the fundamental paradox in this scene from *Psycho*: we *imagine* we see Marion Crane being murdered. This paradox has become the focus for all the most sophisticated critics of motion picture artistry—especially those philosophically inclined, like Gregory Currie (1996), Kendall Walton (1990), and Noël Carroll for more than two decades. The paradox arises because our imagining of the shower murder is evoked by entirely normal processes of visual perception. We see the knife directed by Norman Bates's hand in the same way we see knives used in everyday life, as when our spouse slices a loaf of rye bread. At *Psycho* we know we are watching a movie, not least because our eyes are registering simultaneously both the actions and the screen on which they are projected. But watching a movie we use our visual perceptions almost exactly as we use them all day every day. Contrarily, when we imagine Raskolnikov's murders these perceptions are in abeyance except for the print on the page. Raskolnikov's actions are entirely and forever imaginary; they never had and they never will have any perceptible existence.

Awareness of this fundamental distinction can increase our enjoyment of the related yet different experiences of visual and verbal make believe, even though forcing us to reconsider some of our preconceptions about how we see. My sight of the knife in Norman Bates's hand is essentially identical with my sight of the knife in my wife's hand as she cuts open a peach. This sight in itself carries no ethical charge—and neither does the *sight* of Norman knifing Marion. There is no *moral* difference between *seeing* a knife penetrating a peach or a woman's body. We, the spectators, add emotional and ethical valences to what we see. The ethical "innocence" of all sights as sights moviemakers exploit, especially by making it difficult for us *not* to believe we are seeing in the movie things as they "really" are, uncontaminated by either the moviemakers' cleverness or our own preconceptions, prejudices, biases, or psychological peculiarities. Contemporary critics have taken to repeating endlessly that such presentation and perception is illusory, and we know it is, but that doesn't matter when in a movie theater we watch Marion Crane being slaughtered. The killing "looks real," because we seem to perceive its events exactly as we perceive the events of real life. This exposes the fundamental difficulty faced by every moviemaker—concealing the deceptiveness that is the essence of his art. Unlike Dostoyevsky, who increases the effectiveness of his narrative by making its structure discernible, a moviemaker like Hitchcock must *appear* never to distort the "natural" order of actions. If he succeeds, his movie can strike with devastating power, because then the emotional and moral significance of events created by their spectators appear "naturally" embodied in vividly visible realities.

How movies lure us into investing "objective" sights with ethical as well as emotional meaning is displayed by the appalling conclusion of the Oscar-winning film from Yugoslavia, *No Man's Land*. This shows multitudes of supposedly concerned people abandoning a dangerously wounded Bosnian lying on a mine that cannot be defused, and that, if he is lifted off it, will explode to destroy everything within thirty yards. Spectators are thus finally left with nothing in the fading light of the setting sun but the sight of the injured man deserted by the people who have swarmed around him, a few because they care for him, more pretending to care, pretending to sympathize, pretending they can and will help him. The ethical impact of this scene is conveyed most powerfully by its utter clarity. Thanks to the moviemakers' skill in arranging its "reality," we see with a precise distinctness every substantial detail of this physical embodiment of moral horror. We see, with our vision cleansed of prejudices, preconceptions, and comforting illusions, the brutal insanity of war.

The perspicuousness that a movie forces upon its spectators may be, paradoxically, of confusion or indistinctness—as in the *Psycho* murder. Hitchcock's genius in this scene is making us imagine we have seen what in fact he does not literally show, the knife entering Marion's body. This cleverly concealed omission intensifies the shock of the killing, because *we* imagine its climax—which happens in our mind. Simultaneously the obscured concealment sustains the scene's fundamental terror: a personal attack whose violence is bewildering in its total unexpectedness. *That* we feel powerfully because the visual clarity (even of its confusingness) of the crime wipes out the psychological protections with which we guard ourselves against traumatic sensations. And we can enjoy Hitchcock's brutal murder because there is in vision an indestructible defense against being psychically injured by what we see: distancing. "Sight is the most distancing sense" (Ong: 1977, 138). We literally cannot see anything except at some distance, and to see something is to recognize its separateness from us. This is why we cannot really share sights. An appeal to "come look at this" invites someone to see *what* we see, to have a perception only *like* ours, just as physically different perspectives produce different sights. Everybody in the theater sees the same events in *Psycho* and *No Man's Land*, but each sees in her own idiosyncratic fashion, as well as from a singular perspective. So far as movies are primarily visual experience, a film may drive apart those who gathered together to watch it. Verbal make believe is utterly different. We read for the meaning, not the perceptible actuality of the words on the page, and that meaning takes form entirely within our mind. We cannot be separated from what we read because it is totally in our mind. We read alone, but we are not distanced by reading from what we read. We are always aware that we are reading, but our engagement with what we read can become very intimate. We realize the intimacy of reading when we pick up a novel written in a language in which we are not fluent, and find ourselves blocked from the familiar processes by which our mind enters—and is entered by—another's consciousness.

These are the distinctions that will be the basis of all the discussions in the following pages. Although there have been plenty of comparisons between novels and movies, none to my knowledge has attempted such an extended and detailed contrasting of visual and verbal make believe. Nor have other critics founded their analyses so consistently as I will on the experiences of *rereading* and *reseeing*. This concentration explains my choice of exemplifying texts: nineteenth-century "classic" novels and twentieth-century "classic" movies. These are stories that reward reexperiencing. Analyzing films or novels as if they were read or seen only once, or as if there were no significant differences between first encounters and subsequent ones obscures exactly what makes fine fiction and movies worth rereading and reseeing—again and again. And there are illuminating differences between rereading a novel and reseeing a film. Seeing *Psycho* a second time is a radically different experience from a first viewing, whereas differences between a first and second reading of *Crime and*

Punishment are far more complex and difficult to specify, even though not so obvious.

This suggests another fundamental distinction that requires the strongest possible emphasis. A sight is immediate, whereas language requires time. The difference Vladimir Nabokov defines in *Lolita* when Humbert Humbert apologizes for his account of his wife's death when struck by an automobile: "I have to put the impact of an instantaneous vision into a sequence of words; their physical accumulation on the page impairs the actual flash, the sharp unity of impression" (60). Visual perceptions are always of the present, and are always pressing future-wards, always following the arrow of time, leading toward new sights. Visual make believe, because built on sensory perceptions, must respect this dominating directionality The most distinctive characteristic of verbal make believe, to the contrary, is its freedom from confinement to temporal sequence. If we examine the finest novels, we discover that their telling of new events also reevokes what has already been told. The experience of reading a novel is a continuously recursive process. Thus in *Crime and Punishment*, to cite a blatant instance, near the end of the novel Svidrigailov dreams that someone has given wine to a little girl who suddenly changes into a prostitute. This will remind even a first-time reader that early in the novel Raskolnikov followed a drunken girl down a St. Petersburg street and drove off a predatory "gentleman" pursuing her, shouting at him, "Hey, you! You Svidrigailov! What are you up to" (1:4). Such back-allusiveness exploits a quality of language that is never in abeyance and affects every element in all verbal discourse. All languages consist of a relatively limited number of words continuously being used and reused. As Mikhail Bakhtin most famously insisted, every word we speak or write carries traces of earlier uses by ourselves and others. There are virtually no "original" words—neologisms either disappear rapidly or as quickly become part of the heavily repeated word pool. A skillful novelist (or the composer of an epic, for that matter) deliberately *exploits* such historical "contaminations" to intensify the recursive potency of his narrative. This characteristic assures that the verbal storyteller's language can be continuously self-reevaluating. Verbal storytelling is thus especially suited for subtle stimulation of changes in self-awareness. An equivalent function for visual narrative is not easy to establish, but it seems worth searching for, since I do not believe that watching excellent movies is merely a way of killing time.

CHAPTER 2

MOVING SCULPTURE FOR MOVING EYES

To understand how motion pictures evoke imagination we must recognize that *only* movies tell stories visually. What are called "narrative paintings" are not really narratives. This truth embarrasses me, because some years ago I published criticism of what I called "narrative paintings." I now realize that paintings by Giotto and Vermeer inspire us to remember or to invent stories, but they do not actually *tell* stories as do movies. Seeing a movie is a different experience from seeing a painting—or even a still photograph. That is why more people go to movie theaters than to art galleries. Paintings (or still photographs, any pictorializations that don't move) never appeal, as movies do, to what our eyes do best and most easily—perceive motion.

If there is a more difficult subject than the science of visual perception, I don't want to know about it, yet to talk usefully about our experiences of seeing movies we need some idea of how our eyes actually function, and to abandon antiquated ideas about seeing, such as that ancient "phantom of optics, the retinal image" (Sparshott, 213). Most helpful for this are the principles of ecological visual perception pioneered by a remarkable scientist, J. J. Gibson, not least remarkable for writing on very complicated topics with elegant clarity. Gibson is responsible for the method by which for more than sixty years visually guided airplanes have made their landings. This contribution resulted from Gibson's being asked at the beginning of World War II for advice in training airplane pilots. This work brought to sharp focus Gibson's recognition that *normally* seeing depends on humans moving their eyes while their heads and bodies are also moving within an environment that is itself *never* static (Gibson, 53). This mobility of our visual perceptual system enabled navy pilots to accomplish almost routinely what always struck me as an amazing feat: guiding a plane buffeted by shifting winds to a successful landing on an aircraft carrier pitching and rolling in the ocean.

Gibson showed that the human perceptual system evolved to be effective when we are moving and is beautifully adapted to specifying the significance of movements in our environment. As total organisms we continuously interact with the sea of energy in which we live as Raymond Williams noted, "new facts about perception" make it "a determining relation between neural and environmental electrons" (20). Gibson distinguishes between our perceptual systems and our senses—the latter being reactive and basically passive, while the former are proactive processes for entering into the environment, orienting ourselves, exploring, investigating, seeking. Visual perception involves the entire organism, eyes alertly moving in a mobile head attached to an active body all of which is unceasingly affecting and being affected by its surroundings. The part of the environment most important for vision is the circumambient optic array, the ever-changing light that encircles us, always offering complex information, not mere signals.

This light array is heterogeneous, unbounded, and never empty; it always envelops any real site in ecological space that could be occupied by an observer. Our eyes continually seek to specify invariants in this restless environment. Because the earth spins 1,000 miles an hour as it races around the sun, every instant the light conditions of our seeing are shifting. Eyes that were not well adapted to scanning changing conditions would be less useful than our wonderful organs of sight. It is by following their *path of observations* that we can most efficiently distinguish variations and nonvariations in the perpetually dynamic ambient array surrounding us (Gibson, 72–75). When we identify normal visual perception in terms of a path of observations (rather than a fixed perspective point), we will not forget that seeing always occurs in time as well as space. An old problem of optics has been to explain how we see a tabletop, for example, as rectangular, when it is demonstrable that, except in the unusual circumstance of looking down at it perpendicularly, the tabletop must appear trapezoidal (Peacock, 385). Gibson's ecological approach reformulates the problem by noting that we see the tabletop from many different positions (because we exist in time and our bodies move). Looking at the tabletop, we see different trapezoids but always with the same relations between angles and proportions, and these "invariant" relations specify visual perception of the table's rectangularity. We see the table as rectangular because we do not see it once from a single position but as changing as we move (body, head, eyes) along our path of observations in shifting relations to it. Our vision is splendidly adapted to be effective in our dynamic spatio*temporal* world.

This is why we may see "better" when moving than when stationary. It appears that the parts of our eyes that recognize color evolved later than the parts that recognize motion, and that when there is conflict, movement-perception overrides color-perception: it is more useful to know whether the lion is coming at you than its color (Anderson and Anderson, 1996, 358). Registering movements with acuity facilitates our exploring of our environment, actively entering into reciprocal engagement with it. We foster this reciprocity by continually shifting our perspective on the physiological as well as the cognitive level to participate proactively in the never ceasing activity of the world. The most common and ingrained mistake about our perceptual systems is to think of them as passive, as mere receptors. Gibson's most famous experiment with splendid simplicity demonstrated the opposite. He tested the ability of people blindfolded to identify the shape of various common cookie cutters when these were pressed by the palm of the hand. If the cookie cutter was pressed against a passive hand, seldom was the shape of the cutter correctly identified, whereas if the subjects were allowed to press their hands on to the cutters, they almost always identified the unique shape correctly (Harré, 134–142). This orientation of our visual perception system to proactive discovery makes it susceptible to improvement. We can learn to see better by seeing in different ways in different situations. I believe that movies honor and reward our powers of vision and enable us to learn to use our eyes better: "film teaches the eye about reality" (Arnheim, 73).

An airplane pilot, the driver of a car, or a pedestrian perceives simultaneously with the layout of the environment through which each is traveling the movements of the traveler's own body, because self-perception and perception of environment are inseparably complementary (Gibson, 182). In Gibson's phrase, "perceiving the world entails co-perceiving of where one is in the world" (200). Perceiving is neither simply a mental nor simply a bodily act, but a psychosomatic one. These facts determine our experiences watching a motion picture—the only visual art that literally displays movements. Gibson gave some attention to the visual arts, most of that are unmoving, although "the eye developed to register change and transformation" (293). He observed that because visual perception is never merely receiving input from outside but always includes proactive scanning into the environment, we normally have no difficulty determining whether we are seeing a picture or reality. Our eyes are equipped to enable us to distinguish swiftly between the surface *of* a picture and the surfaces *in* a picture, whether still or moving. Physiologically as well as cognitively we register what is represented *as* a representation. Someone who mistakes a painting or photograph for actual reality is distorting the normal workings of her visual perceptive system. Recent studies demonstrate how entirely noncognitive, purely neurological processes underlie and precede cognitive input into our seeing. This is exemplified in the "Vanishing Dot" experiment (Ramachandran and Antis, 104).

On the left are illustrated what our eyes see when two dots are projected one above the other on a screen and then displaced to the right. Even viewers who know what is happening see the dots "moving" to the right, that is, our eyes "automatically" (without cognitive input) register both as "moving" right. If the lower dot in the second frame is excised (as in the middle set), our eyes register a converging movement of the lower dot toward the upper. At the far right is illustrated what happens when tape is fixed over the *place* of the lower dot in the second frame. Our eyes register the lower dot now as "moving" horizontally to "hide" itself under the tape, even when we know there is no such concealment. Our perceptual system has evolved to "assume" (i.e., to function automatically as if) objects observed remain in continuous existence, and if moving follow relatively straight lines, and that objects are integral (all their parts move together), so that a moving object will sequentially cover and uncover parts of the background against which it is seen. The Andersons observe that "such processing is carried out at a low level in the visual system by neurons that programmatically excite and inhibit other neurons independent of cognitive activities," and exemplify with simple imagery the evolutionary utility of this physiology (1996, 359). If we see a leopard running across a field, when the animal disappears behind a bush our eyes "assume" that the leopard emerging from the other side of the bush is the same leopard. If one catches sight of a few spots of the leopard's coat leaping through high grass, our eyes assume the rest of the leopard is there leaping too. When it stalks through shorter grass, the grass will disappear at the edge of the animal's head and shoulders, and our eyes "expect" the grass to reappear at the edges of the leopard's hind legs and tail. If our neuronal system makes us vulnerable, as the dot experiment shows, to "illusions," the vulnerability is valuable for our survival in the real world.

This experiment reminds us that visual experience is always constituted by an *interplay* between perceptual processes and brain processes that is more continuously nuanced than is suggested by the popular metaphor of "nerves sending messages." This interplay in watching movies differs from that of viewing still pictures of any kind, drawings, paintings, photographs (for simplicity I refer only to paintings here). With both movie and painting, our eyes register *both* the surfaces of what is depicted and the screen or canvas supporting the depictions. But there is something unusual in how we focus our gaze intently on the fixed painting. The strain in such concentration as our eyes continuously scan the picture is suggested by the desire most of us have not only to stand still in front of a painting, but also to walk about it, to look at it from different distances and angles. The power of fixed concentration is not unnatural, but it requires special effort. Apparently the areas of the brain that process information from the central part of the retina are larger than those that handle inflow from the peripheries. But concentration follows what is *triggered* by peripheral vision, and is only one part of the diverse kinds of "eye shiftings" and "brain sequencings" that constitute ordinary seeing.

Normally our eyes continuously search around, our attention most often caught by movements upon which we then concentrate, interpreting these dynamic variations in the visual array. Watching a movie may be closer to this common use of our eyes than looking at a painting—perhaps one reason that movies have been welcomed in every culture. Of course we watch a lighted screen from a position of darkness and without moving our head much or walking about—which is not the ordinary way in which we use our eyes. Indeed, watching a movie might seem close to an inversion of normal seeing in a natural environment—and there is no doubt that we are always aware of the artificiality of the experience. But the film presents us with more significant movements than are likely in our ordinary environment, and we watch the movements with a concentration equal to that we apply to the still painting. Also we watch a flat screen only in front of us, whereas in natural circumstances the visual array is circumambient. The limitation of watching only a flat screen certainly reinforces our awareness of the artifice, but it is one that offers food for our eyes of the kind they feast on eagerly.

In telling a story, a movie superimposes a cognitive discourse structure—a plotted narrative—on a mode of pictorial representation fitted to reward the processes of visual perception that stimulate brain activity (Turner, 61–108). The proactivity of visual perception and its intrinsic temporality make it fit to be the carrier of story. Because our thinking about the visual arts is built upon centuries of attention only to what is static, pictures and statues that don't move, we tend to forget that seeing movements is seeing in time. Actions constitute events, which take time to occur. Movies and movies alone among visual arts are capable of displaying events that constitute narratives.

We need also to consider what we do *not* see in movies. Our environment always offers an overabundance of sensations, more "information" than any organism can use. Perceptual systems are selective systems, separating out for an organism the tiny fraction of available information most useful to its particular needs. Movies offer us a preselection to select from. The making of a movie is a laborious screening out, making a lot of things invisible, so that movie viewers see only what the moviemakers wish them to see, and only from pre-determined perspectives, yet seeing with hyper-acuity the meaning-fulness of all that they are allowed to perceive. Now all stories, verbal as well as visual, are created by acts of selection. The great storytellers are those who know what to leave out—as Homer excised 99 percent of the Trojan War in *The Iliad*. In this respect movies and novels are similar. But there is a decisive difference in what can and cannot be omitted from each mode of storytelling—as becomes apparent when one examines films adapted from novels.

When Jane Austen in *Pride and Prejudice*, for example, tells of Darcy's first proposal to Elizabeth, she concentrates on the emotions precipitated—the proposal of marriage makes the two furiously angry. The colloquy takes place in a room that is undescribed, except that a mantelpiece is mentioned, and Elizabeth is seated—on something unidentified. The filmmaker adapting the novel, however, has to decide whether Elizabeth is sitting on a chair or a sofa, what other furniture may be in the room, what the mantelpiece is made of and looks like, and, if there is a window, what it looks out upon. A room has walls that have to be shown, so how they are decorated the film-maker must decide. All these necessary decisions "distort" Austen's presentation, because she *chose* to omit these matters the filmmaker has no choice but to present to his audience.

Moviemakers' omissions differ radically from those of verbal storytellers, because they can do what Jane Austen's couldn't, even when she chose to describe. They can enable us to see (not "just" imagine seeing) the unfolding of events in a manner very close to how we normally witness actions in real life. A consequence of this power, however, is that moviemakers must be careful in preselecting what is displayed, or spectators will notice omissions and to feel they are seeing a falsification. On the contrary, we seldom notice what the novelist leaves out, because it never comes into existence for our imagining. Among several dozen critical commentaries discussing Darcy's proposal to Elizabeth, for example, I found not a single reference to the room in which it occurs. The wallpaper that most probably was there simply does not exist in the novel, nor, in fact, do the room's walls. Precisely because movies present visual reality approximately as we ordinarily perceive it, we are quick to notice when something, an object, a gesture, a play of light, is not shown that "ought to be there." Part of the success of Carl Dreyer's highly stylized film *Joan of Arc*, for instance, derives from the seeming appropriateness of its extremely austere setting. The action is confined to a religious trial court in which only the participants' faces attract the eye; the result is a powerfully "realistic" effect—although the immediate cause for this stylization was lack of money. The art of visual narrating requires disguising the rigorously meticulous shaping of what is shown so that it appears complete and completely "natural." It is important viewers do not become aware of the moviemaker's controlling purposes, his artistry in selecting. Verbal narrative, to the contrary, can be quite arbitrarily selective in what it tells without the reader noticing the stylizing. Reader and writer share in novelistic imagining. In part we don't notice what the author chooses to omit because her choice has also partly become our own. This helps to explain why many popular novels are unabashedly told by a narrator who is pretty much indistinguishable from the author. These novels can, as is often said, change our lives, one reason being that for a time they enable us partly to *be* a genius, Leo Tolstoy, George Eliot, Jane Austen, Gustave Flaubert, and the like.

The nature of filmic stylizing may be highlighted by a contrast with what we see in stage sets. The most opulent stage set a theatergoer perceives and "masters" within a few seconds, thereafter concentrating not on it but on the human actions of the play. This is why most good plays can be successfully performed either with elaborate sets or on a bare stage with few props. Sets play a vastly different role in movies—indeed, in its French form *mise-en-scène*, staging, has become one of the primary terms of movie criticism. Interior scenes in movies require special care for angles, vistas, and light effects, otherwise interior spaces will appear not as a movie *mise-en-scène* but as what they really are, stage sets, and the movie will seem "stagy"— damning criticism of a film. Outside in the natural world with its superabundant visual phenomena, on the other hand, stage designers are disadvantaged and moviemakers liberated. If a movie shows a young girl running through a field of tall grass waved by the wind, even such a smarmy shot may be effective because viewers feel they are seeing normally. They forget that the moviemaker prearranged and preselected to make visible in the scene the peculiar complexities with which in fact wind moves the tall grass.

Movies are unique in their effectiveness at showing motion in the world to be continuously various and ever ongoing. No art displays better than movies the livingness of the natural world with panoramic sweeps of changing weather or focusing on slow, minute processes of transformation. But central for every moviemaker are the movements of human beings. Nearly a century ago Vachel Lindsay, the first important American critic of movies, suggested they be regarded as "moving sculpture" (84–96). He had been impressed by the curious phenomenon that the figures on the silver screen, although no more than flickering images of light, often convey a surprising sense of solidity, seeming not like silhouettes but massive. It is true, as several critics have pointed out, that movies, unlike stage plays, may attain powerful effects without any human figures on the screen. But no film holds our interest very long without introducing people (or people-like figures, since robots, aliens, and talking animals nowadays clutter multiplexes). Lindsay's linking of movies with sculpture, the art that has most persistently concentrated on the human body, is correct: we go to the movies to watch people.

Which is probably not our reason for going to an exhibition of modern art, where the ordinary human body has become rather rare. It is a historical fact

> that at the same moment that twentieth-century painting was girding itself to make a complete break with representationalism, the "representational" movies came into being . . . A Mondrian or late Rothko, purified of figure and primarily "inactive," remains pure design. . . . its pretension to being art rather than mere decoration is based on a quite simple idea: an aesthetic image need not be a statement concerning

something external to itself . . . this theoretic position has animated the practice of pure-abstract art from the beginning when Kandinsky, Mondrian, Pevsner, Gabo, Malevich, and Delaunay . . . advocated a new "realism." (Tyler, 137, 139)

Such art can be affiliated with other movements such as Braque's cubism, and even Picasso's, so far as his virtually exclusive attention to human subjects almost always involves some form of "distortion." Tyler goes on to identify painting's shift at the beginning of the twentieth century as a reaction against the complacent sterility of nineteenth-century academic art—just at the moment when motion pictures appeared to rivet hyper-acute vision on realistically imaged human behavior.

> Film is the art . . . where the finished "form" is the most easily soluble into raw "content." . . . Classic Western art evolved through the aesthetic desire to come as close to nature (or "content") as possible while in the same act "idealizing" it. (Tyler, 138)

This observation on the movies' reinvigoration of a fundamental principle of Western art may explain the success of early movie improvisations, whose unselfconsciousness, illustrated by Mack Sennett's cheerful "we weren't making art, we were making money as fast as we could" (85) helped recovery of "realistic" aspirations just at the moment when other visual arts were abandoning those ideals. Early moviemakers were willing to try anything from the cheapest melodrama to a new "spectacular" (and often ludicrous) rendering of some classic drama, opera, or historical event because they had what seemed the perfect medium for representing in a fashion exactly in accord with the commonest, even the most vulgar, conception of what constituted "reality." The provocativeness of Lindsay's concept of "moving sculpture" becomes increasingly attractive when we consider the historical circumstances in which motion pictures exploded into Western art.

Movies are unsurpassed at showing human beings in action because they can show these actions continuously engaged with a total animate environment. This strength makes movie criticism difficult, because critical analysis stops action: movie criticism often focuses on a single frame. This falsifies the continuousness essential to the visual experience of movie seeing. The reader of a verbal narrative can stop at any time, flip the pages back, or lay the book down and start doing something entirely different. Novelists may also at any point halt the action of their narrative to comment on what is happening, speculate on what might have happened, indulge in philosophizing, and so forth. It is both easy and often effective for a novelist to call attention to the manner of her telling, but this is a difficult and risky maneuver for visual storyteller. Our visual perceptive system, to which movies primarily appeal, is built on "assumptions" physiological as well as cognitive that any current action is in the process of producing a subsequent action. All the elaborate preparing of the scene and adjustments of camera and lighting and angles, followed up by painstaking editing, that moviemakers engage themselves in are to sustain the spectators' sense of normal vision, which is distinguished by continuous forward movement. As many have observed, spectators automatically assume that what comes on the screen after a fade out, wipe, or any break is subsequent to what was previously seen. If this essential reality of the continuity of normal seeing is sustained by a movie, its display of quite unlikely sequences of events will seem "real," and quite ordinary events may be endowed with intense significance.

Effective visual narrative therefore tends to be self-concealing. The highest skill of a film editor's cutting lies in making the cuts invisible, so the audience never notices there has been excising and joining. All such forms of concealment are of little or no concern to verbal storytellers, whose stories are completely hypothetical, not tied to sensory actuality except for the printed text that we ignore to enjoy imagining. On these grounds, J. R. R. Tolkien suggested that fantasy could be fully successful only in verbal stories (70). That judgment clearly was in the mind of Peter Jackson, director of the move trilogy *The Lord of the Rings*, when he explained his aim in filming the most fantastic parts of the story was necessarily a paradoxical one— to make the fantastic as real as possible.

The root of the difficulty for a movie director of fantasy is that imagining in movie watching must be treated as a secondary activity. The same is true, of course, for painting and sculpture, but, "[C]inema makes more demands on our senses and nerves and fewer demands on our imaginations than another other art" (Mast, 1977, 106). It is, after all, impossible to imagine what one is actually perceiving, to imagine the sunset we are watching or to imagine the sound of a bell that is really ringing in our ears. Visually, there is no conditional tense, only the present moving into the future, whereas novelists are often happiest writing in a past subjunctive. Such contrasts may assist us in understanding the unique power of movies. Too often this is explained in terms of viewer "identification" with characters—an explanation that tends to confuse more than clarify. A movie such as Buster Keaton's *The General*, for example, would fail if we simply identified with its protagonist, Johnny Gray. We *sympathize* with him, but that is very different from identifying with him (Bordwell, 1996, 16–17). Visual perception involves a separation of self from what is seen, and we are always aware of seeing Johnny in action, usually at some distance. This movie, like all fine films, arouses sympathy, partisanship, "rooting" for or against characters that we perceive are not ourselves.

The terrific emotional energy aroused by movies is somewhat like that aroused in impassioned spectators at a sporting event. This analogy was first proposed by Vachel Lindsay, when he suggested movie audiences were similar to baseball fans—in the bleachers, not in the box seats (227). The comparison was given systematic intellectual articulation by a philosopher of history, W. B. Gallie. Gallie pointed out that game and story alike promise a definite but uncertain outcome to spectators following them. That promise enables audiences to savor contingencies as contingencies when they arise, knowing that they are contributing to a final "meaning," the ultimate outcome of their interplay, the not-yet- determined final score. One savors the contingent events because one fully appreciates that they are not predetermined or inevitable but are in as yet unknown ways contributing to an ultimately intelligible whole that will bestow on them, retrospectively, a significance that may be suspected when they occur but cannot be surely known until the unique total pattern of the game/story completes itself (Gallie, 22–50). We fear the shortstop's error in the seventh inning may be fatal to our side, not realizing that an inning later it will force our evil opponents to pinch-hit for their pitcher who is stymieng our guys (this must be a National League game). On the literary side, on first reading one hardly expects the violence with which Elizabeth rejects Darcy's proposal to intensify his love for her, but when we find later that it has, that unexpected development confirms our faith in the intensity of his affection for her. The analogy of course breaks down because good stories get better with each rereading, whereas TV-replayed games do not. The difference is that the game (we trust) is not "fixed," whereas we know the story is—the teller knows the outcome before we do. The story's accidents have been purposefully selected and placed. The teller "plays" on the audience—which may become resentful if made aware of being manipulated, as happens in poor fiction.

Gallie urged his analogy on the ground that we "follow"—understand and appreciate—both game and story best when our emotions of sympathy and antipathy are strongly evoked. His point is profoundly important. The "intelligibility" of excellent narrative is as much a matter of emotional as of intellectual coherence. Gallie's analogy is especially apt for visual narrative (of which we are literally spectators) because the imagining evoked by both game and movie is primarily conjectural. When watching a game or a movie, if we are emotionally involved we become very busy imaginatively anticipating the probable results of particular events we now see. The movie's highly controlled, and intensely prefocused sights enhance this responsiveness, intensifying our seeing along a path of observations, as we obviously do when we hike through the woods or drive our car across town. Even when we are not moving through space we are ineluctably caught up in the forward flow of time, just as the light of our spinning earth changes every instant. We are always seeing "freshly," seeing differently from the way we saw a moment before, and therefore continuously reconstruing our perceptions of the mobile visual array constituting our environment. A movie, unlike a still picture, offers entrance into this dynamic process because it is constructed of a continuous succession of transient sights. In the movie theater we do not move from our seat, but we do see—literally see—a story, see "the unpredictable and the predetermined unfold together to make everything the way it is" (Stoppard, 47), the structure of cognitive narrative adding meaning to each new sight even as it reinforces that meaning with the strength of sensory perception.

Movies provoke anticipatory imagining that differs from the associative imagining aroused by novels, which continuously bring the past into the present and—as is manifest in ironic passages—consistently evoke what is not said by what is said. All verbal texts contain subtexts. The difference is dramatized by motion pictures' two super-realistic innovations in visual art: the "panoramic" shot and the close-up. Paintings even of vast landscapes never portray motion. Movies can depict movement not only *in* such landscapes, the horseman riding across the desert, but also movement *of* landscape, rivers, wind-blown trees, the shifting of light. A movie can display not merely a sunrise but the sun rising—and as with the actual phenomenon as a natural percept without inherent subtext. As important, a moviemaker with a mobile camera can move viewers into or out of a scene. This is a very common way of using our eyes, walking closer to an object to see it more clearly, but until the movies such motions had played only a tiny role in visual art (Meisel, 61–63). Long-shot moving panoramas offer the viewer an orienting possibility of seeing differently, seeing something else, seeing what might be seen in the next moment from another position. As Gibson observed, being oriented in an environment means seeing one's location in terms of other possible locations one could be in. A sense for this interplay of self and encompassing environment movies uniquely evoke: they alone can make the *dynamics* of distance and surroundings a significant dimension of narrative.

The close-up even more sensationally distinguishes the art of motion pictures. We can, of course, walk very close to a painting, a portrait face, for example, and even examine it with a magnifying glass. But that is very different from the movie in which the face "magnifies itself." And such magnification is a uniquely powerful narrative device. Dimensional change intensifies for an audience the interactivity of physiological and cognitive scanning , particularly when, as is usually the case, what is visible on the screen is drastically reduced as the entire field of vision is filled with a single object, especially if it is a human face. The "double-take" (which only movies can fully exploit through close-ups) best illustrates these effects. Buster Keaton's celebrated blink in *The General* when the railroad car he thought he had sidetracked appears in front of his engine exemplifies the experience of not believing what we see. It is not unusual in ordinary life suddenly to realize that we have misperceived or misanticipated, but normally the experiences are so transient and trivial we instantly forget them. Our system of visual perception functions well because it is capable of almost instantaneous self-corrections, and these are the dramatic mini-stories intrinsic to every double-take. In fact, the double-take illustrates how movies tell stories by manipulating normal processes of seeing, including the ability to adjust and readjust with lightening speed — in the blink of an eye. But double-takes are difficult to imagine: they play no role in verbal narrative. Try telling somebody about a movie double-take you enjoyed.

But the double-take is only a special feature of the common close-up, the most distinctive innovation introduced into visual art by the motion picture. It would not be difficult to write an interesting essay on close-ups of hand movements, or of physical objects. Close-ups of objects are especially fascinating, because such shots are usually not merely descriptive; through the sheer fact of close focus they endow the object with symbolic potency even while affirming its sheer perceptible existential beingness. But the facial close-up is of course most powerful and complex, as is suggested by this description.

> Asta Nielsen once played a woman hired to seduce a rich young man. The man who hired her is watching the results from behind a curtain. Knowing that she is under observation, Asta Nielsen feigns love. She does it convincingly: the whole gamut of appropriate emotion is displayed in her face. Nevertheless we are aware that it is only play-acting, that it is a sham, a mask. But in the course of the scene Asta Nielsen really falls in love with the young man. Her facial expressions show little change; she has been "registering" love all the time and done it well. How else could she now show that this time she was really in love? Her expression changes only by scarcely perceptible and yet immediately apparent nuance—and what a few minutes before was sham is now the sincere expression of a deep emotion. Then Asta suddenly remembers that she is under observation. The man behind the curtain must not be allowed to read her face and learn that she is now no longer feigning, but really feeling love. So Asta now pretends to be pretending. Her face shows a new, by this time threefold, change. First she feigns love, then she genuinely shows love, and as she is not permitted to be in love in good earnest, her face again registers a sham, a pretense of love. but now it is this pretense that is a lie. Now she is lying that she is lying. And we can see all this clearly in her face. (Balázs, 64)

When I first read this description, I had not seen the film Balázs describes, and I suspected that he might be "reading into" Nielsen's face what she could not have in fact displayed. I thought he might have imagined what no other observer would see. Yet I also wondered whether he was better equipped by his historical circumstances to see more in the close-up than I can. The doubt arose from my reading early commentators on movies, all of whom were impressed by close-ups. They dwell on facial expressions they seem to have watched with a concentration missing from comments of recent film critics. In any event, we need to remember that movie watching, like novel reading, is a socially conditioned activity: what we see depends to some degree on when, historically, we see it (and the same is true for imagining), even as one can trace changing directorial styles of representing facial expressions (Smith, 13–15).

When we watch a movie even though we seem fixed in our seats, we are psychically very active. Using one's eyes, however, is entirely different from using one's camera, which "is a caricature of imagination" (Barfield, 73). The mechanical instrument can be physically moved, but its "eye" is not, like ours, vitally exploratory. It is not perpetually self-readjusting and continuously reciprocally interactive with its environment: A hand-held movie camera is likely to produce jumpy, wobbly pictures, whereas we leap over and scramble through rough terrain without ever once having our eyes wobble or jump. The camera is useful for reducing our visual environment to a flat screen in front of us. We may be rewarded by results of filmmakers' purposeful concentration, but if too much of our normal freedom of seeing is sacrificed the movie bores or irritates. This is one reason movie plots are more consistently directed to what comes next than novel plots, and employ flashbacks sparingly. Movie flashbacks are usually most effective when exceedingly brief, which brings them close to normal visual processes (Bordwell, 1989, 72). The forwarding pressure of visual perception, however, can powerfully reinforce the emotional-intellectual development of a movie's story line. Verbal storytelling, contrarily, is intrinsically "past directed" (Lukács, 130). Even as we distinguish words their sounds die in our ears. Verbal telling of events automatically places them in the past, even if the tense used is the present.

What the Hell Happened to the Sound Track?

Musical backgrounds and sound tracks are scarcely mentioned in this book, not because I think them insignificant but because they are of enormous importance to the total experience of watching motion pictures. To deal adequately with the issues they raise would jeopardize two of my central purposes—to increase appreciation that movies are the *only* form of visual storytelling, and that the representation of human movement is the essential feature of film artistry. I develop contrasts between the make believe of twentieth-century motion pictures, created by manipulation of audiences' normal visual perceptions, and the make believe of nineteenth-century novels, created by evocations of imagining made possible by readers' almost total suppression of sensory input. To take account of the complexities brought into play by either the sound track or the musical score of motion pictures would obscure the insights I can attain by concentrating on the fundamental opposition between perceptible movement and direct imagining.

I hope to follow this work with a study doing justice to all aspects of sound movies, because only when we take account of the union of photography with sound track and musical score can we appreciate the synaesthetic totality that constitutes the full aesthetic uniqueness of motion pictures. But the essential feature of motion picture art is visual representation, and that is the focus of attention here. And despite the thirty years of silent films, we tend to overlook the importance of silence in films with sound tracks. Very often, I am tempted to say always, the most important segments of good movies contain no dialogue, and frequently are without music. In many films there are substantial scenes in which no words are spoken and there is no musical background—the robbery sequence in *Rififi* being merely a celebrated example. Because so much of a good sound movie is silent, very brief and simple speeches, often only a word, can be invested with enormous emotional and moral power. But because movies employ relatively little speech (when contrasted to stage plays), non-speech sounds are often important in films, less at climactic moments (as they are on the stage) than as a continuous ongoing accompaniment or background to the action. Many if not most conversations in movies include background noises whose irrelevance to what is being said enhances the authenticity of the actors' words and gestures. In fact, much of the "realistic" effect of movies derives from their offering the commonplace sounds of life—the crunching of snow underfoot, the tearing sound of a paper being ripped, the overlapping noises of an urban street, the buzz of flies, the clink of dishware—all these *as* ordinary background noise. This continuousness of the unimportant sounds of life is of course absent from fiction. To make us imagine sounds, novelists must use words to refer to them, and thereby falsely advance them from the background to the foreground of our attention.

Movie music presents even more wonderfully complex issues. It has long been recognized that no experience is more difficult to discuss profitably than that of listening to music—and movies offer two kinds. Critics call one "diegetic music," music that is created within the film, when a band plays, a character strums a guitar, somebody turns on a radio, or the star of a musical opens her mouth so we can hear somebody else's voice. More significant in its effects is the background music that we hear coming from the theater amplifiers, but which is totally ignored within the movie and whose source is never explained. At movies that are any good we normally don't think about who is playing this music, where they may be playing, and why they use these particular instruments. But unquestionably the mysterious music has tremendous influence in shaping our experience of watching a movie. There is no equivalent to this "unaccountable" phenomenon in any other art.

Our acceptance of background music, moreover, is clearly a matter of aesthetic convention: to most contemporary moviegoers, for example, the background music of thirties and forties Hollywood films (which ultimately derived from practices of stage melodrama) often seems obtrusive and too insistently obvious in its emotional orientations. Yet it might be argued, for example, that the background music to the 1940 *Wuthering Heights* adds compelling strength to the sentimental interpretation of the novel presented in that adaptation. Or that Korngold's music is crucial in establishing the balletic quality of Errol Flynn's *Robin Hood* that endows the movie with its surprisingly enduring charm. Or one might ask, in what ways have the changes in auditory and visual conventions interacted, since any answer would be illuminating of the total viewing experience offered by particular films.

One could also consider that background and diegetic music are not always distinct, and assess the effects of such interpenetrating, as when, for simple instances, the background music of *Casablanca* later repeats parts of the *Marseillaise* first played by Sam and sung by the patrons in Rick's bar, just as the background music at the end of *The Bridge on the River Kwai* echoes "Colonel Bogey's March" that the British prisoners entered whistling. In *La Strada*, the background melody associated with Gelsomina is sung *in* the film by the woman hanging out the laundry—with stunning effect. Another kind of visual-auditory interplay is illustrated by *High Noon*, justly famous for using as its sole background music the Western ballad written for the film by Dimitri Tiomkin (which became a best-selling single record). Although I discuss the movie at some length, I ignore the effective reinforcement (in part through heavy cello orchestrations) this background music provides to the film's intense concentration, beginning with its making the time of the action coincide with the real time of the movie's length. To take up such issues would double the length of this book, and so, regretfully, I ignore them. I am encouraged in my choice because recently the study of movie music has advanced impressively—among the best of the newer critics I would cite especially Giorgio Biancorosso (2002, 2004), who brings to his criticism an unusual combination of thorough training as a musicologist with extensive knowledge of motion picture practices, accompanied by a sound understanding of philosophical issues posed by commentators on musical experience such as Roger Scruton and Theodore Adorno.

CHAPTER 3

INSIDE AND OUTSIDE SOMEBODY ELSE'S FANTASY

There aren't any novels that are more frequently reread than those of Jane Austen, so none better exemplify how verbal stories become "classics." Austen's novels began as modest commercial successes, continuing popular enough after the break through of cheap publications in the 1830s to be reprinted throughout the nineteenth century (St. Clair, 578–580). Sales increased markedly after World War I, when Austen fans became known as Janeites, a term popularized by a story of Rudyard Kipling's. Soon critics were discovering in her fiction qualities to which she had humorously laid claim a century before in *Northanger Abbey*, where she describes a good novel as

> a work in which the greatest powers of the mind are displayed, in which the most thorough knowledge of human nature, the happiest delineation of its varieties, the liveliest effusions of wit and humor are conveyed to the world in the best chosen language. (Chapter 5)

But even accelerating critical admiration for Jane Austen's fictions hasn't adequately explained why her novels are so rereadable. One possibility is that they exploit "side participation," that D. W. Harding suggested, long while ago, is important both in novels and in the experience of reading them. He calls attention to those parts of life spent in looking at what others are doing, or listening to someone tell others about events in which one has not been directly engaged. A side participant is admirably situated to pass judgment on what others say and do. Indeed, side participating is *always* evaluative, because the listener-in or looker-on does so with an attitude necessarily either welcoming or aversive, however weakly—otherwise she wouldn't listen or watch at all. And side participating can certainly extend our patterns of interest and sentiment and judgment—think of a girl watching a mother care for an infant. Such "side-attended events" may be even more formative of our behavior and value systems than events in which we are primary actors.

The varieties of side participation in fiction are legion (Gaylin). Sometimes characters speak to one another in the presence of others with more interest in having an effect on a sideparticipant than on the person directly addressed. This occurs in *Pride & Prejudice* (2:8) when Elizabeth sits at the piano with both Darcy and his cousin attending her closely. This positions readers to judge why and to what effect she responds to Darcy by addressing not him but his cousin, Colonel Fitzwilliam. We recognize that she has found polite means of rebuking Darcy (whom she strongly dislikes) for his failures of politeness, and for not making proper use of his natural gifts and educational advantages. We also perceive, as she does not, that this adroitness increases his unwelcome admiration for her.

> "Perhaps," said Darcy, "I should have judged better, had I sought an introduction, but I am ill qualified to recommend myself to strangers."
>
> "Shall we ask your cousin the reason of this?" said Elizabeth, still addressing Colonel Fitzwilliam. "Shall we ask him why a man of sense and education, and who has lived in the world, is ill qualified to recommend himself to strangers?"
>
> "I can answer your question," said Fitzwilliam, "without applying to him. It is because he will not give himself the trouble."
>
> "I certainly have not the talent which some people possess," said Darcy, "of conversing easily with those I have never seen before. I cannot catch their tone of conversation, or appear interested in their concerns, as I often see done."

At this point Elizabeth shifts the indirectness of her response by apparently speaking abstractly.

> "My fingers," said Elizabeth, do not move over this instrument in the masterly manner which I see so many women's do. . . . But then I have always supposed it to be my own fault—because I would not take the trouble of practicing."

The conclusion of this scene rearranges the characters' roles, when as Elizabeth resumes playing Lady Catherine joins Darcy standing at the piano and with an offensive condescension, meant to warn off

Elizabeth, remarks to him, knowing Elizabeth will hear:

> "Miss Bennet would not play at all amiss, if she practiced more, and could have the advantage of a London master . . . though her taste is not equal to Anne's."

Sometimes a side participant is affected by a speech in ways of which the speaker and addressee are unaware, as when Elizabeth overhears Darcy's denigrating comment about her to Bingley—indeed, this accidental overhearing launches the plot of the novel. Austen exploits a wide variety of side participations, often to dramatize not only what is talked about but also *how* it is spoken about—the importance of such tonalities being familiar to all of us from having as children listened in on our parents' conversations. Harding proposed that side participating even extends into the *origins* of fictionalizing, since conversation may consist in suggestions about what *may* or *might* happen— "Imagine that." Yet his approach does not do any justice to the imaginative engagement evoked by superior verbal make believe. Mature readers become contributory creators of the make believe they read even as they critically evaluate it. They imagine constructively, because their imagining does not require any surrender of their respect for the practical exigencies of real life. We stop reading make believe properly when the tension of dual responsibilities of psychic engagement and detachment degenerate into self-indulgent personal fantasizing.

Part of the complexity of novel reading arises from the instability of roles of both characters in a novel and its readers, what Wolfgang Iser has discussed under the rubric of the "wandering viewpoint." "The relation between text and reader," he observes, "is quite different from that between object and observer: instead of a subject-object relation [as with a movie], there is a moving viewpoint which travels along *inside* that which it has to apprehend" (108). Novel readers, besides following transformations in the characters' roles, shift their relations to the evolving story in accord with changes in how it is told, when, for instance, they are addressed directly by its narrator. Such "wanderings" inevitably produce evaluations of emotional relationships. Illustrative is Harding's example of the exclamation, "I'd like to kill that bastard" to illustrate how language facilitates interfusing emotion and judgment. The exclamation gives shape and direction to an anger probably not satisfiable by direct action and addressed to a "third" party, not the object of the speaker's hostility. In this case what may have been a side participant becomes the addressee of an expression of anger toward someone else, a position that calls for some judgment of the "validity" of the emotion. And if in this instance the addressee is a character in a novel, the reader "outside" can hardly escape estimating the rightness or wrongness of the addressee's judgment. This response of the reader, furthermore, is likely to be vulnerable to a future reassessment, first as the story develops, and later in any rereading of the novel.

Novelistic conversations plainly reveal how readers not merely "listen in" but become actively engaged in the development of characters' interacting thoughts and feelings (Young; Tandon). A conversation at Netherfield in chapter 10 of *Pride and Prejudice* also suggests why novelistic dialogue often loses vitality and cogency when spoken by actors in a movie or on stage. "Conversation" in a novel is totally imagined; we do not hear the characters actually speak, as we do at a movie or play. We imagine the words being heard and we *also* imagine them *being spoken*. We imaginatively participate in the saying as well as in the listening. Thus in the Netherfield conversation when Bingley speaks to his sister—"that will not do for a compliment to Darcy, Caroline, . . . because he does not write with ease. He studies too much for words of four syllables"—imaginatively we share in Bingley's verbal teasing of his friend as he speaks to his sister as fully as we share in the acts of hearing his words by others in the room. This is a cause for the common reference to "identifying" with the characters in novels. Such "identifying," however, never excludes simultaneous critical assessment of the nature and purpose of the speech that we imagine making *with* the speaker. Even as we imagine ourselves saying Bingley's words, we perceive that he is making a joke at his friend's expense *and* that the joke articulates Bingley's judgment of the difference in personality between the two men. The judgment at once affirms for us Bingley's more outgoing amiability, while implying recognition of his friend's superior intellectual powers.

The imaginative process of reading manifested here is what Bakhtin called "living into" or "live entering." This is distinct from "identifying" or empathy, experiencing from another's position. Morson explains that in "living into" (Russian *vzhivaiu*)

> one enters another's place *while still maintaining one's own place*, one's own "outsideness" with respect to the other. "I actively live into an individuality, and consequently do not, for a single moment, lose myself completely, or lose my singular place outside that other individuality." Later in his life . . . Bakhtin was to rethink this concept in dialogic terms as "creative understanding." Dialogic response . . . depends on

the irreducibility of both participants. . . . Respecting the author's "outsideness" and "otherness," the reader "lives into" the text and lives alongside the text. (1989, 11)

The conversational complications produced by Charles Bingley's remark exemplify the validity of Bakhtin's insistence that in imaginatively "entering into" the speech of novel characters readers maintain their separate individuality. Bingley's jibe at Darcy is countered by his sister, who hopes to become Darcy's wife and is ready to denigrate anybody, even her brother, in order to flatter his friend:

> "Charles writes in the most careless way imaginable. He leaves out half his words, and blots the rest."
> "My ideas flow so rapidly that I have not time to express them—by which means my letters sometimes convey no ideas at all to my correspondents."

Elizabeth responds to Bingley's self-deprecating good humor, by observing that his humility "must disarm reproof." But Darcy ripostes both to his friend and to Elizabeth by replying;

> "Nothing is more deceitful . . . than the appearance of humility. It is often only carelessness of opinion, and sometimes an indirect boast."
> "And which of the two do you call *my* little recent piece of modesty?"
> "The indirect boast;—for you are really proud of your defects in writing, because you consider them as proceeding from a rapidity of thought and carelessness of execution, which if not estimable, you think at least highly interesting."

Readers enjoy and learn from these exchanges because they *both* participate in the friendly antagonists' personal motives shaping their speech and the diverse effects (both intended and unintended) of what they say upon their hearers, *and* because they retain their "outsideness" even as they imagine not merely hearing the words spoken but also speaking them. It is this dual relation to the text that permits readers to appreciate fully both Bingley's pleasant but mildly egocentric personality and Darcy's more penetrating understanding of psychological motivations, the basis of his harsher judgments upon the limitations of the sociable good humor that makes Bingley a more readily likable yet more superficial person.

All excellent fiction stimulates our imagination into rapid, flexible, and comprehensive activity founded on our simultaneous engagement with and "objective" judgment of the characters we imagine. Second-rate fiction is unsatisfying because it does not so strenuously exercise this double capacity of taking on another's consciousness even while assessing its powers and limits. In the Netherfield scene, Elizabeth, present only because of the accident of her sister's illness, and in fact hostile to Darcy, is shrewdly perceived by Miss Bingley as a potential rival, because Darcy, to his own troubled surprise, is finding himself attracted to Elizabeth despite her social inferiority. The ethical dimension of the verbal exchanges is produced by this particularized diversity in the characters' social and emotional relationships that result in moral conflict. This happens when Darcy illustrates Bingley's indirect boasting by citing the falsity of his claim that if he ever decided to leave Netherfield he would depart in five minutes. By so boasting to Elizabeth's mother, Darcy tells his friend, he intended

> a sort of panegyric, of compliment to yourself—and yet what is there so very laudable in a precipitance which must leave very necessary business undone, and be of no real advantage to yourself or anyone else?

Bingley replies that at least he truly believed, and still believes, what he said of himself to be true, so that he was not showing off. Darcy retorts,

> I dare say you believed it; but I am by no means convinced that you would be gone with such celerity. Your conduct would be quite as dependent on chance as that of any man I know; and if, as you were mounting your horse, a friend were to say, "Bingley, you had better stay till next week," you would probably do it, you would probably not go— and, at another word, might stay a month.

Most significant in this passage is Darcy's making forceful his condemnation of Bingley's instability of character by inventing a little story. This turn of conversation into a small piece of make believe is almost inevitable when there are differences of opinion about behavior's moral implications. Indeed, this conversation exemplifies the psychologist Jerome Bruner's assertion that storytelling, the fundamental form of make believe, is the primary fashion by which

> human beings, in interacting with one another form a sense of the canonical and ordinary as a background against which to interpret and give meaning to breaches in and deviations from "normal" states . . . Such narrative explications have the effect of framing the idiosyncratic in a "lifelike"

fashion that can promote negotiations . . . a system concerned not solely with sense and reference but with "felicity conditions"—the conditions by which differences in meaning can be resolved by invoking mitigating circumstances that account for divergent interpretations of "reality." (67)

Make believe is a primary means for human beings to explore ethical issues, because, besides offering "felicity conditions," it fosters negotiation through the concretizing of issues instead of generalizing about them. The make believe story displays for joint engagement and evaluation specific manifestations of behavior interesting because focusing attention on its particular moral implications.

In the Netherfield conversation the unique personality of each character is imaginatively evoked for us by their judgments on particular social behavior revelatory of their moral commitments. The novelist thus makes it possible for readers to participate imaginatively in ethical conflicts, not as metaphysical or ideological abstractions, but as specific acts in "canonical" interpersonal relationships. Thus Elizabeth's inverts Darcy's "moral" of his story:

> "You have only proved by this," says Elizabeth to Darcy, "that Mr. Bingley did not do justice to his own disposition. You have shown him off now much more than he did himself."

But Bingley emphasizes the conflict of their evaluations of his behavior by pointing out that Darcy "would certainly think better of me, if under such a circumstance I were to give a flat denial and ride off as fast as I could."

> "Would Mr. Darcy then consider the rashness of your original intention as atoned for by your obstinacy in adhering to it?"

Both Bingley and Elizabeth have entered into Darcy's little make believe (just as we have entered into Austen's encompassing one), but Bingley at this point withdraws, saying he is unable to untangle the moral complexity, and asking Darcy to explain himself. The four-way conversation is reduced to a confrontation between Darcy and Elizabeth. Yet even in that contraction of focus Austen's text refines our understanding of all the characters and the complexity of their interrelations. By confessing his inadequacy, Bingley manifests an attractiveness—his genuine humility (in contrast to the false humility we will find in Mr. Collins). He is able to tease Darcy because Bingley (unlike his sister) respects his friend less for his wealth and position than for his emotional energy, his honesty, and his clarity and strength of mind. In judging Darcy a worthy guide, he anticipates Elizabeth's final judgment. Because Bingley can so unashamedly admit Darcy's personality is stronger and more complex than his own, the two can be genuine friends without being equals. And that the younger man's modest amiability is not mere weakness gives dramatic force to Elizabeth's taking from him the burden of argument about Darcy's narrative.

> "You must remember, Miss Bennet," Darcy says, "that the friend who is supposed to desire his return to the house, and the delay of his plan, has merely desired it, asked it without offering any argument in favour of its propriety."
>
> "To yield readily—easily—to the *persuasion* of a friend is no merit with you."
>
> "To yield without conviction is no compliment to the understanding of either."
>
> "You appear to me, Mr. Darcy, to allow nothing for the influence of friendship and affection . . . in general and ordinary cases between friend and friend where one of them is desired by the other to change a resolution of no very great moment, should you think ill of that person for so complying with the desire, without waiting to be argued into it?"

Darcy responds by saying that to pursue the debate meaningfully they will have to specify with precision the importance of the request and the degree of intimacy between Bingley and his fictitious friend. To sustain the make believe that is enabling them to debate politely but productively a real ethical dilemma, they will have to create something rather like *Pride and Prejudice*. Darcy's burgeoning narrative centers on questions of friendship, integrity, affection, intimacy, persuasion, and prejudice—precisely the central issues of Austen's novel. This structural micro-macro relation exemplifies how nineteenth-century novelistic make believe aims not forever to resolve moral problems but to evoke them as recurrently vital issues of ordinary life. Jane Austen, neither a philosopher or a ideologue (thank God!), enables us to imagine *processes* of personal interrelating as activities which—at their best—may be productive of valuable moral questioning. In this she is exemplary. Excellent verbal make believe consistently evokes imagining of distinctive personalities within determinate social circumstances whose specific moral orientations are valuable because their conflict animates both our minds and our feelings. Tobin Siebers, in the most thoughtful and informed analysis I know of this fundamental aspect of Jane Austen's narrative art, insists on its antagonism to philosophic moralizing.

> Plato wanted to expel conflict from his republic, and it is no accident that he identifies literature with conflict because storytelling is the principal means by which we confront disputes. It is a form of argument in which we try to hear the particulars about situations which trouble us. . . . It may never be clear how useful stories are for solving real problems. . . . But we do face problems by telling stories about them. (150–151)

The Netherfield conversation illuminates vividly a fundamental characteristic of all verbal make believe, because Austen does not describe the tonalities of voice, nor the physical position nor movements of the speakers, excluding all the external circumstances in which the conversation take place. She allows nothing to interfere with our imagining of acts of speaking and hearing. The seemingly casual and trivial conversation carries complex meaningfulness because it focuses our imagining so completely on the interplay of morally inflected motives and responses as they "spontaneously" emerge in commonplace talk. Austen offers her readers an opportunity to learn to recognize dynamic processes of moral conflict that are in fact an undercurrent of all serious conversations—especially those that are carefully polite.

Yet, in considering the novel as a whole, such learning does not quite explain my experience (which I judge from Austen's ever-widening popularity is not idiosyncratic) that on every rereading of *Pride and Prejudice* I find it more important that Darcy and Elizabeth marry. My response derives not merely from a sharpening understanding, for example, of the difficulty posed by their social circumstances, but more from the intensifying of my ethical/emotional *approval* of an event I know from previous readings is inevitable. This suggests how far beyond Harding's observations we must go to understand what psychic processes are involved in our "entering into" verbal make believe. A helpful description of this remarkable process developed by a critic ignorant of Bakhtin's earlier analyses is that of the French critic Georges Poulet explaining the extraordinary effect on him of *Madame Bovary*.

> As soon as I replace my direct perception of reality by the words of a book, I deliver myself to the omnipotence of fiction. I am someone who

has as objects of his own thought thoughts which are part of a book I read, and which are therefore the cogitations of another. I am thinking the thoughts of another. I am a self who is granted the experience of thinking thoughts foreign to him. My consciousness behaves as though it were the consciousness of another.

What happens when I read a book? I feel sure that as soon as I think something, that something becomes in some indefinable way my own. Whatever I think is part of my mental world. And yet here I am thinking a thought which manifestly belongs to another mental world, which is being thought in me.

Reading is the act in which the subjective principle which I call I, is modified in such a way that I no longer have the right to consider it as my I. To understand a literary work, then, is to let the individual who wrote it reveal himself to us in the work. The annexation of my consciousness by another in no way implies I am the victim of any deprivation of consciousness. Everything happens as though, from the moment I become a prey to what I read, I begin to share the use of my consciousness with this being who is the conscious subject ensconced at the heart of the work. He and I, we start having a common consciousness.

I am a consciousness astonished by an existence which is not mine, but which I experience as though it were mine. This astonished consciousness is the consciousness of a being who is allowed to apprehend as its own what is happening in the consciousness of another being. (55–56)

Poulet's "consciousness sharing," like Bakhtin's of "entering into," focuses on a paradoxical condition of reading in which one participates in the activities of another mind without diminishing the integrity of one's own subjectivity. Poulet's account, however, needs to be clarified in one respect. He might seem to represent the reading experience as merely an interpenetration of the author's and the reader's consciousness. In fact, the author's consciousness in fiction comes to us primarily through the consciousness of his or her fictive characters (which often of course includes a narrator). In reading novels, our consciousness is "astonished" in *multiple* ways. In *Madame Bovary*, for example, our consciousness intersects not only with Flaubert's but also with his protagonist's. We imaginatively share in Emma Bovary's experience—but without ever surrendering our own consciousness, without ever merely "identifying" with her, without losing the capacity to assess critically as it happens what she and we experience. Reading a novel, we *add* to our self-awareness the self-awareness not just of another but of others. In novel reading we do not surrender any portion of our self-consciousness as we open it to (or enter into) interactivity not alone with the novelist but also with the characters he has imagined. Indeed, we can fully share in Flaubert's consciousness *only through* our participation in his creation of imaginary consciousnesses such as Emma Bovary's.

What is true of Flaubert's novel is true of all excellent fiction—it enables a more profound interpenetration of human consciousnesses than is available in any other mode of discourse. This is why novel reading can be such a fantastic learning experience. Bakhtin's and Poulet's approach also opens the way to understanding why rereading can be a more, rather than less, intense experience than a first reading. In rereading it is possible both to share more deeply in the now "familiar" consciousnesses of author and characters, even while, because we know the full arc of their histories, more rigorously evaluating them and their acts.

Poulet's and Bakhtin's depictions of the imaginative process by which we read a novel also inadvertently highlight why watching movies is so different an experience. First we literally witness, then from what we witness we conjecture, and it is through conjecturing that our imagination comes into play. In reading a novel, to the contrary, we begin by imagining. The "sensations" we experience in reading are all imagined, never actual. The "sensation" in a novel of seeing a mountain involves, as Gilbert Ryle observed, "missing just what one would be due to get, if one were seeing the mountain" (255). The "sensation" in the novel is in fact an *imagining* of the sensation of seeing the mountain, which Ryle describes as "a more sophisticated operation" than actual perception (256).

This difference helps to explain why direct narrative sequentiality in movies tends to be more important than direct narrative sequence in novels. The Russian Pudovkin's recommendation that directors should structure their scenarios in terms of a series of questions and answers may be good advice for a movie director, but is too simple for a novelist. The imagining evoked by verbal fiction moves easily in any and every direction temporally as well as spatially, and it is never confined to unidirectional sequentiality. Each of our visual perceptions, however, is immediately displaced by another. This is one reason it is so distressing to be in an environment that is visually uniform and unchanging (Meister). An effective movie exploits this perceptual drive forward, whereas effective novels exploit the power of imagination to move instantaneously any whichway in either time or space. It is fair if surprising, then, to judge that narrative in its simplest sense may be more important in movies than in novels.

Furthermore, although novels are founded on the possibility of consciousness sharing, central to the movie experience are the facts that we always see only surfaces and that visual perception begins in—and always requires—separation of spectators from what they see. In the visual narrative of a movie, there cannot be the immediate psychic interpenetrating Bakhtin and Poulet identify as the foundation of novel reading. This "limitation" of movies, however, is simultaneously a source of their unique power. By intensifying normal modes of vision, a movie by improving our visual capacities may strengthen the cognitive effects of what we see. Only in movie watching is our conjectural imagining's full power realized—to the point of recognizing its limitations.

These differences reflect absolute differences between the creation of visual and verbal make believe. Moviemaking has to be a collaborative process. What the spectator finally sees has been laboriously constructed and minutely controlled in every detail—a task that can be carried out only through conjoined efforts of many people—despite the claims of some *auteur* theorists. These err in the fashion Tolstoy detected in military historians who thought that because a general was officially in command he controlled all an army's actions. Tolstoy's point emphatically is not that the quality of a general (or a movie director) is unimportant. Tolstoy insists, instead, that the best general (or director) is the one who understands the limitations on his personal ability to determine what will happen, because a battle (like a movie) is too large and complex an event to permit such management by any individual. Which can produce surprising benefits. The uncertainty of the moviemaking process, Kurosawa observed,

> is similar to that of a pot being fired in a kiln. Ashes . . . can fall onto the melted glaze during firing and cause unpredictable but beautiful results. Similar unplanned but interesting effects arise in the course of directing that I call "kiln changes." (Goodwin, 63)

Moviemakers will take the right visual effects any way they can get them. In moviemaking the end always justifies the means. Moviemakers don't give a damn how actions are performed, only how they will appear on the screen. The novel we read, however, is essentially what the novelist wrote, the fiction writer's performance and the fiction we read being indistinguishable. A good novelist is of course always alert to the effects she wishes her words to produce, but she has only words to evoke these effects. There are no trick shots in novel writing—whereas in a sense every movie is entirely composed of trick shots. The novelist, because engaged in a consciousness-sharing mode of discourse, cannot (and would not want to) so systematically exploit discrepancies between execution and effect. The writer, moreover, is unusually aware of the polysemous character of words. She knows very well that her control of the interpretation of her language is severely restricted. When she writes, "the glass of red wine," she recognizes that her readers are going to imagine different kinds of glasses, different shades of red, perhaps even different kinds of wine. Her skill as a novelist lies in knowing how to make most productive imaginative use of these inevitable but uncontrollable *diversities* of response. The moviemaker, to the contrary, attempts to control as completely as possible what *everybody* in the audience will see. And at a movie we all do see the same thing—however widely our *interpretations* of what we have seen may differ. So filmmakers choose a particular glass as the only one precisely appropriate to the dramatic situation, the drinker, the historical epoch, and so forth. And they may as well be concerned with the particular shade of red—which probably means disgusting actors by filling the glass with something that isn't wine. Of course different interpretations of the resulting movie scene are not merely possible but certain, and even likely to be violently opposed, because intelligent moviegoers are active spectators. But the interpretive differences are about determinate (because physically verifiable) visual facts. There are no perceptible facts in novels, only indivuated imaginings. Novels are in this regard constituted of specifically focused and purposefully meaningful indeterminacies (Casey, 123). The diverse shapes of glasses are finite but fairly extensive: what was the shape of the glass from which the blood poured in *Crime and Punishment*? Or the word "red": exactly what color is that? to pose a famous linguistic/philosophic conundrum. A reader may imagine a glass shaped differently from the one Dostoyevsky had in mind, and may imagine a shade of red different from what the novelist fantasized. Such variations are the conditions that allow the consciousness of different readers actively to enter into the processes of Dostoyevsky's imagining. Verbal make believe makes room for everybody's power of fantasy.

As Bakhtin and Poulet admit, it is not easy to describe precisely the processes by which we share someone else's make believe. Besides the paradox of simultaneously entering into another's subjectivity while retaining the integrity of our own, our minds function with incredible swiftness, and each imaginative act is unique. The nature and rewards of these operations are exemplified with unusual clarity in Chapters eight and nine of Part two of Tolstoy's *Anna Karenina*, a segment that provides a vivid stylistic complement to both *Madame Bovary*, which was the text Poulet concentrated on in developing his insights, and Dostoyevsky's fiction, Bakhtin's principal inspiration. These chapters, furthermore, constitute a critical juncture in a story about problems of love, marriage, family relations, and adultery in the lives of ordinary people—these problems being central to most of the best nineteenth-century fiction (Tanner).

Anna's husband, Alexei, returns home alone "having found nothing improper or peculiar in his wife sitting at a separate table with Vronsky having an animated conversation . . . but he had seen that to others in the drawing room it appeared something peculiar and improper, and therefore he, too thought it improper." He decides he should speak of this to Anna when she returns. He reads in his study until one in the morning, his usual hour for preparing for bed. Instead of going to bed, he begins pacing back and forth through the dining room, drawing room, Anna's dressing room, deciding what he will say to her. We follow the workings of Alexei's psyche as he transforms himself from a man convinced that jealousy is a shameful feeling into a man overcome by unadmitted jealous passions. Tolstoy's narrative permits us to share in this psychic reversal, as violent as any physical action yet not physically perceptible, for its only external manifestation is Alexei's repeated pacing through the house, always turning back at the door of the bedroom. What Tolstoy's words provoke us into imagining includes a negativity, blockage of the normal functioning of Alexei's mind:

> When Karenin had decided to speak with his wife, that had seemed easy and simple, but now, thinking about how to do this, it seemed complicated and difficult.

Here the story's narrator offers readers an opinion about the Alexei's ideas and emotions.

> Now, although his persuasion that jealousy is a shameful feeling . . . had not been demolished, he felt he was confronting something stupid and illogical, and he did not know what to do. Karenin was facing life—the possibility that his wife loved somebody else, and this was incomprehensible to him, because it was real life. He had lived and worked all his life in bureaucratic spheres, which engage only with reflections of life. . . . He now experienced what a man might feel when carelessly

crossing a bridge over a chasm who suddenly sees that the bridge is collapsing and he is about to fall into the abyss. The abyss was real life.

The metaphor in this passage provides readers means for judging the validity of the narrator's judgment. A reader not only shares in Alexei's subjective life but must also decide whether to accept the narrator's assessment of his psychological condition. Nothing obliges us to agree with the narrator's opinion as to the *cause* of Karenin's distress—and the metaphor gives us a specific basis for making our own judgment, since any verbal trope succeeds only so far as readers are willing to accept its aptness.

The difficulty in imagining here for a reader such as myself is that Tolstoy (like Dostoyevsky, Dickens, Flaubert, Jane Austen, and the rest) is so damn perceptive and intelligent, and such a persuasive writer, that I am tempted to accept instantly what his narrator says as *the* truth. But it is not. Only a lazy reader concurs in the judgment without testing it. That this "covert" (Chatman, 1978, 117) or "undramatized" narrator (Booth, 1987, 273). is not infallible is demonstrated by the famous first sentence of the novel, which asserts an invariable difference between happy and unhappy families for which no one has ever offered the slightest factual evidence, and which is an odd beginning for a story in which every family experiences unhappiness (Alexandrov, 112–133). This opening sentence alerts us to an opinionated narrator with whom we may at times disagree even though he is often convincing. The cogency of the narrator's opinion is established only when having asked ourselves is that true, we thoughtfully answer, yes. Often we may make that judgment in a flash, so it is difficult to recognize that we have indeed judged, not passively accepted. Recognizing the nature of our response is also difficult because verbal make believe such as Tolstoy's is continuously stimulating our mind in a variety of ways. Here, for example, we are questioning how firm was Alexei's conviction that a man who does not trust his wife degrades himself even more than her—even though we know, as he does not, that his jealousy is justified—that Anna *is* unfaithful to him. Intelligent reading of excellent fiction is an incredibly strenuous psychic activity.

In following the development of Alexei's feelings, readers simultaneously share his subjective understanding of his situation even as they pass judgment on it, and share in—while assessing—the narrator's opinion as to why and with what consequences Alexei's self-awareness is incomplete. When Anna returns, the story becomes even more complex, because now readers also share her subjectivity. "Anna, I must talk with you," says Alexei, to which she responds:

> "With me?" she answered with surprise. . . . "What is it? What about?" she asked, sitting down. "Well, let us talk then if it is so important. But it would be better to go to bed."
>
> Anna said what came into her mind and hearing her own words was amazed at her skill at lying. How simple and natural her words were; they really sounded as if she were just sleepy.

In empowering us to imagine Anna hearing her own words as well as her surprised judgment of them, the passage simultaneously arouses an evaluative counter-understanding, because we evaluate Anna's lying in a fashion she does not.

> "Anna, I must warn you," he said.
>
> "Warn me?" she asked; "what about?"
>
> She looked at him so naturally and cheerfully, that someone who did not know her as her husband did would have noticed nothing unusual in what she said or how she spoke. But for him, who knew her—knew that when he was a few minutes late going to bed, she noticed, and wanted to know the reason—knew that she had always told him at once all her pleasures and sorrows—for him her refusal to pay attention to his state of mind, or to say a single word about herself, told him everything. He saw that her soul, before always open, now was closed to him. And he knew from her tone that she was not embarrassed by this. . . . He now felt like a man who comes home to find his house locked against him.

Even in imagining this clash of personalities we are simultaneously enabled to conceive years of Alexei and Anna's *previous* life together. Specific details of this life are not specially germane to the situation, but, because the confrontation provokes a break in repeated patterns of behavior that have constituted a texture of relationship, they arouse our sympathy for Alexei's response to Anna's words as a response of which no other person is capable. We thus experience the uniqueness of a not uncommon event, the emergence of an emotional division between long-married husband and wife. The paragraph's closing simile, reminding us that someone other than Alexei or Anna is telling us what happened, frees us from confinement in either Alexei's or Anna's subjectivity, and enables us to understand this quarrel as the shattering of long-established relations of mutual trust, devastating in different ways to both parties, who equally refuse to admit that it is a catastrophe.

> "He doesn't really care!" she said to herself; "But other people noticed, and that upsets him" "You are not well, Alexei Alexandrovich!" she said, as she rose, and was about to leave the room, but he stepped forward as if wishing to stop her.
>
> She had never seen his face look so gloomy and ugly. Anna stopped, threw back her head, bent it to one side, and with her quick fingers began to take out her hairpins.
>
> "Well, I'm listening. What comes next?" she said calmly and ironically. "I am listening with special interest, because I want to understand what this is all about."

As she spoke she wondered at her coolly natural tone and her skillful choice of words. Here our attention focuses simultaneously on the efficacy of Anna's preventing any real interchange between herself and her husband and on her awareness of her own duplicity, thus complicating our judgment of her behavior. Anna is certainly behaving very badly. Yet her assessment of the source of Alexei's emotion is in accord with the narrator's—that her husband was affected not by his feelings toward Anna but by the feelings of others. And as we are allowed to experience her wonder at her intuitive skill in play-acting we cannot but to some degree sympathize with her. Which exacerbates our pain at her change when Alexei "mildly" urges her:

> "Anna, for God's sake don't talk that way! . . . I am you husband, and I love you."
>
> For a moment her face fell and the mockery in her eyes faded away, but the word "love" aroused her again. "Love!" she thought. "As if he could love! If he had never heard other people talk about love, he would never have found that word. He does not know what love is."

Here again, because we believe Anna *does* know what love is (even what Alexei recalls of her interest in him and the former freedom of her speech to him proves that she did once love him), we are compelled to sympathize with the vitality that has led to her attachment to Vronsky, the real life of which Alexei is frightened (Sankovitch, 100–101). We cannot simply condemn Anna even as her falsity and her refusal to meet Alexei's efforts to be affectionate crystallize our understanding of how destructively and self-destructively she is behaving. Concurrently we feel there is justice in her effort to escape from Karenin's imprisoning of her and himself within social conventions that deny the reality of life itself. Yet we do not forget that Anna's joy in her vitality is perniciously falsifying her life and the life of others.

This analysis may suggest something of the dynamics of imagining evoked by verbal make believe of lives of people not extraordinary—except insofar as our participation in their consciousnesses makes us intimately aware of their personalities in a fashion we seldom attain with real people. Our entering into Alexei and Anna's crisis teaches us much about self-misunderstanding in personal relationships, but even more valuable is the opportunity for tremendous psychic exertion offered by Tolstoy's make believe. No Olympic gymnast puts his body through more complexly organized exercises of controlled violence than a quiet reader of this passage demands of her imaginative capabilities. Any careful reader of this make believe increases the strength and subtlety of her conscious mind.

Two characteristics of this psychic refining and fortifying deserve emphasis. First, the continuity of the activity. Our consciousness when we are awake is always working. Language through its intrinsic self-referentiality activates the productiveness of that continuity, enhancing awareness of the temporal interconnectedness of what we experience. Second, the exercise arouses our evaluative capacities—because consciousness *is* a search for the meaningfulness of phenomena: "every man who knows the law of gravitation draws a moral from it" (Frye, 254). Associative imagining empowers us to decide what is truly real (the hidden causes of events, for example), and on the basis of that decision we try to shape, reorganize, and perfect the actual things or relations constituting our environment. Enhancement of this persistent, proactive impulse to affect reality distinguishes adult make believe from daydreaming, in which there is no sharing of consciousness. The value of make believe is its energizing productively the consciousness of others, not that of its creator alone. The large decision we make that Tolstoy's personal fantasy, *Anna Karenina*, is worth reading and rereading is a judgment with practical consequences: the experience improves the efficacy of our self-conscious powers, the only powers enabling any individual to distinguish between existing thoughtlessly by habit and deciding to live what she decides is a *good* life No form of discourse is more helpful in making that momentous distinction than verbal storytelling.

CHAPTER 4

MAKE BELIEVE IS ALWAYS A STORY

"Imagining" as we normally use the term refers to fantasy that either invokes something not perceptually present, such as an absent person—"Imagine what Helen is doing today in Venice"—or invokes something not known to exist, highly improbable or impossible—as is implied in "You're just imagining things." Imagining in this commonplace sense is the foundation of all make believe, which Gilbert Ryle thought "of a higher order" than ordinary belief (250), and which more recently has been usefully examined by Kendall Walton in his *Mimesis and Make Believe*. But whereas Walton seeks to identify how imagination operates in the same fashion in both movies and literature, I am identifying differences between the make believe of novels and the make believe of films. Of course there are important similarities—without these, meaningful contrast would be impossible. Ultimately, however, if we are fully to appreciate both kinds of make believe we must distinguish between the imagining in which movies and novels originate and with which they are experienced by their audiences.

The original and still primary meaning of "story" (the essential form of both verbal and visual make believe) is a *verbal* account. To tell a story means to speak, and to be told a story means to listen to words. When we say a movie tells a story we are using "tells" metaphorically, because our language has not yet absorbed the concept of purely visual narrative. The point needs advertisement, because it is easy to misapply to motion picture narrative criteria appropriate only to verbal storytelling. The novels I concentrate on are chosen to emphasize through contrast the innovativeness of storytelling by moving pictures. *Pride and Prejudice, Wuthering Heights, Madame Bovary, Great Expectations, Crime and Punishment*, and *Anna Karenina* are among the finest accomplishments of nineteenth-century fiction, the period just before the appearance of movies. In the course of the twentieth-century, movies supplanted novels as the most popular form of entertainment. This usurpation was not merely the result of unexpected technological accidents (e.g., that the film which makes motion pictures possible was a by-product of manufacturing celluloid collars), but was also a culmination of a long development in Western culture toward increasing emphasis upon the visual: "hypervisualism is the mentality fostered by the modern world" (Ong, 1977, 124). Although differences between the imagining in novel reading and movie watching are rooted in physiology (differences between seeing and hearing), they are also manifestations of historical processes (Darnton).

Movies alone among the visual arts make possible storytelling that is entirely pictorial (Currie 1990, 7–9) not requiring any use of words, or dependence on verbal narratives that precede them. Every story is an artifact, and is always recognized by its audiences as a human construct. A story is *about* things that happened (or may have happened or might happen). We always know this when we are being told a story. We attend to it in full awareness that what we are reading—or hearing or seeing—is some human being's fabrication, not physical events and phenomena in themselves. Some stories, of course, are true, and some are not, but there is no "sharp grammatical or lexical distinction between true stories and imagined ones," (Bruner, 52) and I argue that there is equally no imagistic distinction between true and imagined movie stories. More important than its truth or falsity is the simple fact that a story is always recognized by its audience as an artifact. Much more interesting than the question of how one distinguishes between true and false stories, is the question of why do human beings so thoroughly enjoy stories they know to be literally untrue? Millions of people have been doing that for many thousands of years in response to verbal stories and for a century at the movies. Why?

For learning and enjoyment, because fictive stories liberate our imaginations. They enable an audience to participate in the construction of story-artifacts. Attending to a story enables us to exercise intellectual, emotional, and even spiritual energies. And we exercise these psychic energies in a mode of self-reflective awareness. Attending to a story, we are not merely conscious but, because we are participating with the storyteller in the *making* of an artifact, we become conscious of the functioning of our consciousness. Since reflective consciousness is our most distinguishing trait as a species, we are never more thoroughly human than when we are reading a novel or watching a movie. And, to be selfish for a moment, that is why criticism of these activities may be a useful enterprise.

So Kendall Walton's focus on "making believe" is of the utmost importance. Of particular value is his recognition that in enjoying make believe we imagine in highly structured ways. The fundamental structuring form of make believe is narrative. Story has been important in every known culture because it is the primary mode of enabling people to imagine together productively (Nussbaum, 1995, 66). Stories activate subjective imagining so that it can participate in public imagining. This is why psychologists like Bruner have identified a capacity to appreciate stories as central to a child's social maturation.

"Making believe" by adults evolves from what children do in making believe, but adult make believe differs radically from childish make believe, primarily because its rigorous form makes it possible for others to participate in its processes. This imaginative participation animates "believing" that is not the mere application of preexisting beliefs. A story articulates new beliefs, at the least giving renewed vitality to passively held beliefs. To appreciate the importance of adult making believe as deliberate *belief creation*, one needs to recognize that "believing" (like "understanding" and similar terms) refers not merely to mental processes but involves also an orienting of our *behavior*, physical as well as psychic. To believe something, as the philosopher Wittgenstein observed, means to *act* in a certain way, because it is impossible genuinely to hold a belief and not act on it (Turvey, 456).

A novel or movie by enabling us to create belief presents us with an opportunity to entertain possibilities, functioning as a form of thought-experiment, very close to the exploring of a hypothesis. After all, what could be more fantastic than Copernicus's hypothesis that the earth revolves around the sun, when any lunkhead can see the sun every day rising, moving across the sky, and setting? This instance is worth citing if only to disable the weird prejudice that science does not depend on imagination, but more importantly because it reminds us that the value of an excellent hypothesis or excellent make believe is strengthened (not destroyed) by the most severe tests of logic and experience that can be brought against it: make believe "is compatible with all degrees of skepticism" (Ryle, 244).

Even when we are absorbed in a story we retain full consciousness that we are helping to construct the artifact we read or watch. This "doubleness" is "nothing more" than intense exercise of our self-consciousness, becoming aware of how our consciousness is behaving. By willfully "absorbing" ourselves in what we systematically help to fabricate out of our mind, we extend our powers of understanding ourselves and our environment. We make ourselves vulnerable to experiencing unexpected, even unprecedented conceptions and emotions. This illuminates the absolute difference between childish and adult make believe, the absoluteness signaled by the simple fact that no child has ever created an enduring work of art. Children do not possess the intensity of self-awareness of adults. Children may be open to possibilities, but they lack the power of organized self-skepticism about their own fantasy, the self-challenging component in all worthwhile adult make believe, whose most apparent manifestation is irony. Children's make believe is private. Even when it extends beyond a single child to a small group, that group defines itself as against everybody else. Their make believe is not openly accessible to all others—others can participate in it only by joining the self-isolated group. Most of us have had the experience as children of being excluded by the make believe of another child, or a small group of children, whose imagining we perceived as "silly": that armchair is *not* a dragon. Adult make believe, on the contrary, produces a coherent system, a dynamic structure accessible to any imaginative adult, even someone living long after the original make believe was created. We can enter into Austen's or Flaubert's novelistic make believe, not because they are like the reality we know—I at least know very little about the life of the English gentry two centuries ago or about French country life at any time—but because their stories possess a formal order of thought, feeling, and judgment that offers means for organizing one's powers of consciousness. The appeal of adult make believe is to a possibility of enhancing our self-consciousness, especially if the make believe arouses powerful emotions.

Adult make believe is infinitely more durable than children's make believe, which is ephemeral. We outgrow our childhood fantasies. Adult make believe can endure for millennia because at its best it is created against the critical resistance even of its creator, who rigorously tests the coherence of her fantasy against the reality of verifiable facts and the demands of systematic logic. Fine adult make believe does not exclude but welcomes oppositional self-reflection that scrupulously examines its adequacy to psychological and natural truths. Thousands of years of analysis and criticism of *The Odyssey* have increased rather than diminished its value, though we don't even know whether Homer was a man or a woman.

I focus here on verbal make believe because we easily recognize it as originally private; what you imagine I can never share—unless you give it a linguistic form through which I can participate in your fantasy. Such form is not mechanical but developmental, capable of self-transformations. This is why the essential structure of make believe is story, the only form of self-coherent discourse that can be dependent on nothing beyond itself, since the sequence of its sentences, no exterior truth nor falsity, determines what it means (Bruner, 44). Story can accommodate unpredictable contingencies without diminishing their contingentness. The accidental may contribute to the orderliness of a narrative's development without jeopardizing its status as an accident. It is a random shell that mortally wounds Prince Andrew in *War and Peace*. It is purely by chance that Raskolnikov learns when the pawnbroker will be alone in her flat. It is entirely fortuitous that Elizabeth Bennet overhears Darcy's scornful comment on her beauty, and that he returns to Pemberly just as she, through an unpredictable change of plans, is visiting his estate. Charles and Emma Bovary's meeting with Leon at the Opera is a coincidence, and it is purely by chance that in *Great Expectations* Pip goes alone to the house where Orlick nearly murders him. These instances, all from extremely carefully plotted fictions, could be multiplied a thousand-fold. Georg Lukács was correct to identify the central dynamic of the novel as a perpetual tension between patterning of plot built upon unmitigated contingencies. He could have extended his observation to *all* narrative. It is terrible luck that brings murderously rampaging Achilles in *The Iliad* face to face with the young man whose life he had spared for ransom just eleven days earlier.

Narrative discourse is capable of endlessly reconfiguring itself, and that facilitates our engagement in other people's imaginings. This process is most apparent in preliterate cultures, in which the retellings of stories invariably introduce variations, sometimes quite spectacular ones. In societies without writing (which until very recently from an evolutionary point of view were *all* human societies) private make believe continuously flows into the public domain. Dreams, for example, often become matters of public concern and storytelling. Our text-based cultures complicate and obscure the processes of reconstructive feedback between individual and community that give make believe stories social viability through individual reinterpretations. But at least we understand that the meaning of stories is changed by the changing ways they are "received"—that is, reimagined—over time. Homer's *Iliad* for us is not what it was for his original Mycenaean audience. Nor is *Crime and Punishment* for us what it was for its original Russian readers. These are large, sociohistorical manifestations of what each of us knows by personal experience—rereading a novel such as *Madame Bovary* is emotionally to experience the book in a new fashion.

One of the Russian psychologist Vygotsky's major contributions to our understanding of ourselves was his insistence that imagining is an emotional process. The emotional power of adult make believe is increased by the testing of it against practical experience and demands that it satisfy rational minds. But critics have found the quality of the emotions evoked by imaginative literature difficult to specify. Walton identifies them as "quasi-emotions." Certainly the experience of losing one's temper seems different from reading about someone losing their temper. But in what exactly does the difference consist? Vygotsky's answer focused on results. "If at night we mistake an overcoat hanging in our room for a person, our error is obvious. . . . But the feeling of fear experienced at the instant the coat was sighted is very real indeed . . . all our fantastic experiences take place on a completely real emotional basis." We misunderstand the reality of emotions evoked by art because they do not provoke physical behavior—they only intensify imaginative activity. Because of this "internalizing" of emotion and inhibition of "external motor aspects of effect," we "think we are only experiencing illusory feelings" in the work of art. But in fact the feelings are just as real as those we feel in actual life (Vygotsky, 210–215).

To judge definitively whether Vygotsky is right we probably need to have a better understanding of our emotions than yet exists, but his view does find support from the investigations of evolutionary psychologists. They concern themselves with how the development of complex human emotionality may have contributed to the evolutionary success of humans as a species. An obvious survival value of emotions is their blinding speed. They enable us to act without thinking, as many know who have barely escaped automobile accidents. Just how this swiftness is attained, and for many different emotions, remains an intriguing problem, but since all humans appear equally well equipped, this automatic system appears to be a successful evolutionary adaptation. Even more important, the neurological systems that trigger instantaneous actions, "affect programs" as they have been called, are what the distinguished biologist Ernest Mayr defined as "open" programs. Whereas a "closed" program is never affected by experience, an open program "allows for additional input during the life span of its owner" (Mayr, 66), meaning that personal experience can modify one's genetic inheritance. The strong evolutionary advantage to human survival of having an open affect program is obvious.

Paul Ekman, a scientific student of emotion for the past four decades, points out that if emotions enable us to act without thinking in a fashion that may save our life, conscious humans are in the odd position of "being unable to witness or direct processes" of their own behavior of vital importance to them (2003, 19–20). This suggests the possibility that one function of make believe may be to help us understand our emotions and their functioning. This possibility is strengthened by Ekman's discovery in his research that most people are surprisingly eager for opportunities to replay and reexperience a past emotional event, even when it was unpleasant and they are going to be videotaped and have wires attached to all parts of their body. "Give them the chance," he says, to reexperience their emotions, "and it happens almost immediately" (Ekman, 2003, 33).

Ekman observes that whenever we are deeply moved emotionally we "do not seek to challenge why we are feeling a particular emotion, instead, we seek to confirm it. We evaluate what is happening in a way that is consistent with the emotion we are feeling" (2003, 39). When we are furiously angry, for instance, we are incapable of taking in information "that does not fit, maintain, or justify the emotion we are feeling." But at least for very brief periods even such fury may be helpful, because it focuses our attention so intensely. All emotions orient and organize mind and body together. In the grip of powerful feelings we can accomplish things of which we are otherwise incapable. There are, however, other emotions, such as agony at the loss of a loved one that we may not truly experience "unless we are in the presence of others who can and do share our loss." We know what has happened, but its meaning comes home to us only when we tell others about or see their reactions to our loss (Ekman, 2003, 82–88). Both kinds of emotion engage with what is external to us, suggesting that make believe emotions may likewise serve to reveal connections between our subjective being and our social environment.

Ekman offers persuasive evidence for the truth of Charles Darwin's hypothesis that there are universal facial expressions of elemental emotions, that anger, fear, despair, pleasure, are expressed by the same activation of facial muscles and nerves in all human beings, regardless of their race, history, or culture. He identifies complex processes by which particular expressions are created, showing that some of these processes are under our control but that others are involuntary. He has created pictorial evidence of how we may visually decide whether or not someone is lying—these findings are now widely used by law enforcement officers and intelligence agencies.

One of his most interesting discoveries, made possible by motion picture technology, was of "micro-expressions." These are very brief (one-fifth of a second or less) involuntary modifications of facial muscles that are particularly revealing of true feelings. Ekman's evidence may explain the immense attraction of early audiences to movie close-ups. Anyone inclined (as I was) to suspect Balázs was "reading into" Asta Nielson's face nonexistent emotions might doubt his suspicions after looking at Ekman's analyses. His findings might suggest that the emotions evoked by a movie, because aroused by entirely normal process of visual perception, are easier to connect with those of real-life experience than the emotions evoked by a novel. Movies are unusually effective, for example, in presenting the terrifying suddenness of an automobile accident. Few of us, one suspects, would wish to reexperience an actual accident. But the filmed accident offers an opportunity for consciously confronting the experience of the terrifying onset of the unpredictable.

The relation of imagined feelings evoked by a novel to those of actual life appears less direct, yet, following Vygotsky's idea of how emotions are used in art, that appearance may be deceptive—as the form of one of Ekman's recent books suggests. Photographs display faces whose expressions he shows to be revealing of inner feelings, which he then explains by means of little verbal stories, usually invented, but sometimes (as when he uses pictures of U.S. presidents) true historical anecdotes (Ekman, 2001, 299–324). We can interpret (and with training interpret with improved assurance of accuracy) our visual perceptions of human expressions to identify some basic emotions being exhibited—*but that tells us absolutely nothing about the cause of the emotion.* We can learn to interpret expressions so as to make an informed judgment about whether a person is lying, but that tells us nothing about *why* she is lying. Verbal make believe focuses primarily on enhancing understanding of the *causes* of emotion, of the *origin* of inner feelings of which all our gestures and facial movements are rather simplified outward expressions. My face may visually betray that I am afraid, but can't show the qualities and inner effects of my peculiar emotion. These can be revealed by imagining my fright and what provoked it.

We can be "seized" by emotion so quickly that we have the strange sensation of our self-control being usurped—yet usurped by what is our own most personal and essential being. This could explain in part why we do not oppose an emotion but try to make everything conform to it. The reflective consciousness exercised in verbal make believe may help us to understand the dynamics of such processes. When I am furiously angry I am only aware of being angry. In reading of Achilles's furious anger in *The Iliad*, while I to a degree share it (the anger in him I imagine is similar to what I remember having actually felt), I am by Homer's account made conscious of the psychic-physical processes producing and produced by the emotion. I do not feel in reading the full violence I experience when I actually become angry, but in compensation *The Iliad* encourages me to imagine the terrifying and yet fulfilling experiential processes of intense anger, so I am not so separated from the reality of the emotion as I would be by a logical analysis of it. Through *imagining* Achilles's unbridled fury I realize, make real to myself, that however deplorable what I do in anger I can no more reasonably condemn it in itself than a lightning bolt. Through imagining Achilles I am enabled to recognize anger as the discharge, for good or ill, of the highest concentration of emotional energy of which any human being is capable. By imagining anger I can become truly conscious of how dangerous it is.

Feelings are forms of energy that function as organizing forces of our psyche—what we *do* inevitably manifests what we *feel*. We move toward what we desire, away from what we fear. And what we desire or fear is largely determined by our imagining. Neither emotion nor imagination exists without the other. Exercising our imagination orients our emotional life, without, as Vygotsky suggested, dissipating its energy in external activities, while, reciprocally, exercise of our emotions enhances our imaginative capabilities (Moran). This is why the most effective and enduring make believe is as systematically structured emotionally as well as intellectually, and why it is no hyperbole to say that we love it.

Recognition of the coactivity of imagination and emotion helps to explain the old conundrum of why we "enjoy" stories of disaster and terror—whence comes the pleasure we take in tragedies? Tragic stories, such as that of *The Iliad*, reveal how human beings surpass all other creatures in the range, endurance, and unpredictable complexity of their feelings. Any successful human society, therefore, must find means to direct, channel, and exploit these potentially destructive energies. Mature make believe explores the strengths and weaknesses, success and failure, of such means, against specific manifestations of the terrific force of subjective emotion. The pleasure of thus imagining lies less in any resolution attained than in the strenuous exercise of our imagination upon what for every individual and every community is a primary condition of their mutual vitality.

These considerations of *The Iliad* bring us back the issue of rereading. Kendall Walton suggests that when we reread a novel we in effect pretend we do not know the outcome (259–270). This seems to imply that a rereading, or a ninth reading, is essentially a repetition of the first. Experienced rereaders, I think would argue that we reread in order to reassess and we hope improve our earlier reading (Birkerts, 104–105). But how can this be done? Through the exercise called forth by our knowledge of the whole story through what has been termed "configural comprehension" (Mink, 59). This is understanding (when perfected) of how every particular detail of the story is definably contributory to the completeness of the entire story. And it is simultaneous understanding of how the story's completeness, reciprocally, endows with special meaning each detail. Knowing the whole story allows one to recognize a dual function in each of its details — integral in itself and simultaneously an element constituting the total configuration of the entire narrative. Rereading is equivalent to canoeing down a river and simultaneously flying over it in a helicopter, at one time seeing both every detail of local current and bankside and the total form of the river's winding course. Configural comprehension increases the mental activity of readers who already know the story, because that knowledge frees them from the passivity disguised within the pleasures of anticipation. When we know not merely where the river (or plot) leads but more significantly the various twists and turns of its course in getting there, we can appreciate more intensely the adventitiousness of tiny events of our voyage (reading) as well as patterns of their relations to each other and to the grand flow of the entire river (story). This appreciation is further enhanced by our increased alertness to how the stream (narrative) flows in a ways that are not made inevitable by any outside forces and yet "make perfect sense" in terms of its total course. We realize that its course might have turned differently had there been different fortuitous rock slides and fallen trees — that the very certainty of variations in its flowing that we must adapt to as we paddle is founded on principles of uncertainty. Our configurative comprehension itself, therefore, is never static (as differences between this and previous readings/trips testify) but stimulates the exercise of ever-changing processes of our consciousness. I indulge in this extended metaphor because its physicality suggests that true *visual* storytelling is indeed possible, and probably possessed of qualities equivalent to, although not identical with, those we discern in verbal narrative.

CHAPTER 5

SINGLE-HANDED AND COLLECTIVE MAKE BELIEVE

I don't know who first compared the collaboration of filmmaking to medieval cathedral building, but it has been repeated so much, even by practicing filmmakers, it must possess some validity (Bergman, xxii). Jean Cocteau is eloquent on how his work depended on a variety of gifted craftsmen, his accomplishments as director being made possible by cooperative efforts of carpenters, costume-makers, cameramen, electricians, plasterers, and so on (55–57). But medieval cathedrals fulfilled religious aspirations of a feudal society. Movies are capitalistic, profit-making commodities shaped for casual entertainment. Avarice and willingness to accommodate the most vulgar of prejudices commonly distinguish the collaborative creation of movies. There is little similarity between the labors that produced the cathedral at Chartres and *Harold and Maude*.

Movies have from their beginnings been inseparable from mass marketing that panders to (even while manipulating) popular taste. Films, moreover, are easily made to serve propagandistic purposes, and the temptation so to orient them has often been indulged. Of course painters, poets, novelists, composers have been coerced, co-opted, and corrupted by the hope of profitable commercialization, but they can better resist the lure of mass marketeering because their works are created privately and cheaply. Movies are so expensive to fabricate that their financial success must be one of their makers' paramount concerns. And movies are created by complicated mechanical processes requiring contributions from many people whose personal relations to a film's purposes are peripheral. Such originating circumstances go far to explain why movie adaptations of novels by Mary Shelley, Jane Austen, the Brontës, Dickens, and George Eliot (to stay within the English tradition) usually endorse social practices the novels had reviled. All *Frankenstein* films minimize the savagery of Mary Shelley's exposé of social systems that celebrate morally unbalanced scientists who endanger the entire human race. William Wyler's *Wuthering Heights* emasculates Emily Brontë's depiction of the brutality of passion originating in corruptions fostered by class hatreds. David Lean's *Great Expectations* eliminates the novel's most sinister character, Dolge Orlick, thereby destroying Dickens's central point: that the desire to be respectable may be linked to a desire to kill people. And perhaps worst are film adapters' sentimentalized distortion of Jane Austen's subtly devastating critiques of patriarchal tyrannies. The kind of social criticism mounted by nineteenth-century novelists seldom survives the vicissitudes of collaborative film adaptation, because the novelists' critiques (whatever their ideological bias) were an expression of personal opinions. And they wrote their novels all by themselves, with just one hand.

The handwritten manuscript was passed on to a publisher, who saw to the printing and distribution. The novelist, however popular, could maintain privacy. Many readers of George Eliot's novels did not know that the author was a woman. Dickens, who published plenty of polemical journalism, entered vigorously into debates on public issues, and devoted much energy to public readings, retired into absolute isolation when he began to compose his later novels. And the novels' diverse social commentaries all originate in subjective feelings. Dickens's searing attack in *Little Dorrit* on the Circumlocution Office is animated by his personal fury at encounters with bureaucratic systems of "How Not To Do it." Nineteenth-century novelists' judgments remain enduringly relevant because they so effectively express personal biases. Their judgments developed out of deep engagement, pleasurable or painful, with their society. Exemplary are the remarkable women novelists in England (no other nation produced so many) who were so much *inside* their society their position may fairly be compared to that of jailbirds. Their novels consistently express personal antipathy to this invisible imprisonment. After all, social practices are significant only so far as they affect individual behavior and thinking, and the essential purpose of verbal make believe is to make personal imagining publicly efficacious. Verbal make believe is always inflected with some form of personalized social commentary.

Such commentary is less of an inherent characteristic (although always an option) of visual make believe, because movies are built upon an ahistorical foundation. A sight is always something seen now, in the present. We perceive the most ancient building in the world as it appears at this particular moment. Physical monuments' cultural significance is created through some application of language to their sheer perceptual immediacy. Language is a historical phenomenon, inescapably tinged with its past. But today's *sight*, even of the Parthenon, is seen freshly, unscarred by other people's looking at it for centuries. The "innocent eye" is a fictional construct, since our minds determine what and how we see. But there is "innocence" in every sight—an innocence the best moviemakers exploit mercilessly.

Even though what we see (and don't see) is influenced by our cultural training, effectuated principally by language, our visual perceptions are oriented toward novelty because they evolved to deal alertly with a world never empty of unpredictable threats and rewards. Familiarity dulls visual acuity; we don't see the pictures we hung so carefully on our living room wall, because they are the same pictures in the same places. All the artifices by which moviemakers tell their stories, by camera position, lighting, editing the film, and so forth, eliminate the dullness of familiarity to make everything we see in every shot a fresh sight, whether it be exotic dancers in Borneo or Monday's regular freeway traffic jam. This is why a lot of not very good movies offer considerable visual enjoyment.

Each of us, however, sees for himself or herself; visual perception is private. Language, which enters into our mind through auditory systems of perception, is interpersonal, facilitating communication with others (Ekman, 2003, 59–62). Words are communal artifacts. We must *learn* to speak, whereas seeing, however culturally influenced, "comes naturally." There is no visual equivalent for the incomprehensibility of a foreign language. I speak English, you speak Chinese, but we both see human. Yet what we see, we see for and by ourselves. We cannot "share" sights except by using language. So, paradoxically, the privately created novel offers imaginative communion to a lonely reader, whereas collaboratively constructed movie, even in an uncomfortably crowded theater, isolates each spectator. This I believe is why—here I speak from the experience of a long-time conductor of classroom discussions—our subjective opinions about movies (and the emotional commitment to our opinions' validity) tend to be more sharply differentiated and more impassioned than our opinions about verbal narratives. If you want to start an argument in a classroom, show a movie.

Stage drama has often mistakenly been taken as a halfway house between novels and movies (many movie adaptations of novels are in fact adaptations of earlier stage adaptations). But play and movie scripts are entirely different. Dudley Nichols, a distinguished screenwriter who thought carefully about his business, observed that a movie scenario was *intended* to be unfinished. It is only the starting point for the making of a movie (ix–x). A movie scenario does contain dialogue, but more of it consists of directions that will require labor by many people only tangentially concerned with the story that unfolds on the screen. The staging of plays, of course, also demands the collaborative efforts of a variety of people unknown to the audience—although nowhere near the number and variety employed in making a film. The real difference is that the essence of a stage play is speech. A good play can be performed effectively by uncostumed actors on a bare platform. There is no significant silent stage drama, but our archives preserve three decades of films without spoken words.

There are also differences between theater and movie audiences, although many common generalizations about these differences ignore the importance of historical changes. My experience of going to the movies when I was growing up in the 1930s and 1940s differs radically from my experience of going to a movie in a multiplex today. My early experience was close to that described by Vachel Lindsay around 1920. Moviegoing in the 1930s was still very much a casual, sociably open-ended activity. There was always a double feature plus cartoon and "selected" shorts on anything and everything from baking cakes to New Deal propaganda documentaries. People came and went at will. If you liked a movie, you could stay and see it over again. Some people didn't mind coming in at the middle of a film, others hated not seeing a picture from its beginning. As a youngster I went with friends, and we were very noisy on most occasions, making loud witty remarks at the expense of the actors and story and the adults in the theater. We did our best to frighten each other at horror movies when we weren't making jokes about them. I believe such social participativeness comes from attempts to overcome the fundamentally isolating pressure of the visual experience, quite different from the "loneliness" of novel reading, which uses physical isolation for imaginative sharing. Taking a girl to a movie was an enterprise fraught with ambiguities (this was before drive-ins), but (as Dante knew) sharing a book can be a damnably unambivalent experience.

The isolating effect of a movie, however, is an aspect of its power as a singular integral experience. Novels are read over a period of time, days, weeks, even with nineteenth-century serialized fiction, more than a year: *War and Peace* was serialized over half a decade. Novels penetrate, and are penetrated by, their readers' nonnovelistic experiences. Novel-reading becomes part of the texture of an ongoing life larger than any novel, even *War and Peace*. Furthermore, because movies are visual they "Can't Say Ain't" (Worth). The visual, as Freud observed when explaining dreams, possesses no negative. Visual narratives cannot represent what they do not represent, but novels frequently do exactly that. Nor can movies specify out of a field of possibilities one that they *might* represent, as verbal rhetoric so easily does. A movie may vividly expose political corruption, condemn inappropriate social behavior, castigate moral evil—but it must do so without the help of the negations and varieties of paradox that language casually employs for attaining equivalent purposes. As Paul Valery observed, there is no contradiction without diction.

What negation-less movies do best is to intensify normal seeing and productively orient it. They reward and enrich the eye to the benefit of the mind. A good movie forces us to attend to exactly what the moviemaker wishes us to concentrate on exclusively. If an ideological "message" too overtly overrides this relentless visual focusing, the spectators' aroused cognitive powers may threaten the efficacy of the film's vision-enhancing. Good movies may carry strong ideological "messages," but the nature of the medium makes it imperative for moviemakers more carefully than their novel-writing colleagues to disguise their didactic purposes—just as they conceal the deceptions by which they make their shots appear "natural." The highest skill of a movie editor is to cut in a fashion that obscures the cut itself. The ultimate "deceptive concealments" of course are the movie's movements—created by sequences of still pictures.

All movies "propagandize," because they are created by people who have intentions and purposes and who work assiduously to make us see the way they desire. But, beyond the collaborative creating of films, the visual medium denies moviemakers the directness with which a nineteenth-century novelist could go about *her* propagandizing. The novelist possesses, most notably, the weapon of irony, unavailable to visual storyteller, who cannot simultaneously represent and not-represent. But words are polysemic; verbal irony makes some of a word's "hidden," even contradictory meanings simultaneously present. Or, perhaps one should say that irony is statement that includes in itself what it does not state—why irony is often missed by literal-minded readers. Contrarily, a sight is just what we see. Juxtapositions of images, sequences of related perspectives, and other directorial tricks may produce effects equivalent to linguistic irony, but this visual "secondary irony" is not intrinsic to its medium. The difference is made unmistakable by the familiar first sentences of *Pride and Prejudice*, which cannot be rendered visually.

> It is a truth universally acknowledged, that a single man in possession of a good fortune, must be in want of a wife.
> However little known the feelings or views of such a man may be on his first entering a neighborhood, this truth is so well fixed in the minds of the surrounding families, that he is considered as the rightful property of some one or other of their daughters.

The first sentence carries an intonation that provokes readers into regarding its literal meaning with suspicions centering on the validity of the claim to universality. The second sentence confirms such skepticism by concretizing the avariciousness of a neighborhood of "surrounding families" in which the suddenly isolated affluent male is reduced to the "property" of someone's daughter. The process of undercutting and reversal (including that of gender dominance) in the two sentences is enriched by evoking a reader's awareness that the narrator has articulated something fearfully close to a genuinely universal truth about interrelations between sex, love, possession, marriage, and wealth.

The easy, quick-moving, self-reflexive irony at work here is not possible for the moviemaker. One reason is that the words beginning Austen's story come to us from a narrator. Words don't exist until they are articulated by somebody. Sights may simply occur; a good movie tempts us into believing that what it presents is just "naturally" there to be seen—although a crew spent two days setting up the shot. *Pride and Prejudice*'s narrator, moreover, besides saying two different things at once, is in two places simultaneously, "inside" and "outside" the "neighborhood" in which the story begins. This narrator points us toward fiction's "free indirect discourse," discourse that arouses uncertainty as to who speaks, under what conditions, and with what authority, precluding any "claim to truth which lies outside or independent of the text," which "therefore necessarily remains complex, contradictory, diffusive" (Ginsburg, 555–556). Free indirect discourse (used in diverse fashions) is immensely important in nineteenth-century fiction because it so productively complicates clashings of opposed opinions. The mode is peculiarly effective at animating a reader's imagination because it provocatively destabilizes the most elemental condition of verbal discourse, that all words *must* be spoken by some one. Yet free indirect discourse is but one of the verbal (but not the visual) storyteller's repertory of devices of indeterminacy, negation, and contradiction.

Differences in the rhetorical capabilities of verbal and visual make believe appear plainly in the different total structuring of their narratives. Moviemakers, concentrating on controlling our attention, enabling us to see with unusual precision and focus, tend to tell unidirectional, linear stories. It is much more difficult in movies than in novels to develop a continuously recursive, self-reflexive narrative. Such broad differences, however, do not justify the prejudice that movies are a "lesser" form of art than fiction. We should discard preconceptions about make believe that are appropriate only to verbal storytelling. Umberto Eco, for example, used *Casablanca* to proclaim patronizingly that what pleases movie fans is a "hodgepodge" of familiar elements (197). Eco puts the hodgepodge in the wrong place—the finished film instead of the process of producing the film. Like many famous movies, *Casablanca* was created in a way that *should* have resulted in a hodgepodge—but did not. *King Kong*, as iconic a film as *Casablanca*, illustrates this peculiarity of chaotic production conditions resulting in effective finished film even more strikingly, both because economic uncertainties threatened *Kong*'s production and because its collaborations were more intricate than those involved in *Casablanca*. For starters, *King Kong* had two directors. The one who worked the day shift, Merian C. Cooper, was also working as a brand new production manager of the RKO studio. Cooper for many years had wished to make a movie about "a big ape." He shared directorial duties with an old friend, Ernest Schoedsack (both piloted airplanes that we see machine gunning Kong on the top of the Empire State Building). Cooper and Schoedsack had served together as pilots in World War I, and after the war continued aeronautical and cinematic adventuring together. After activities in Eastern Europe that once landed Cooper in a Soviet prison, they collaborated on exotic films, including the justly celebrated documentary *Grass*, and later the popular "ethnographic" movie *Chang!* that dramatized a South Asian peasant family threatened by various wild animals, finally a rampaging herd of elephants. Schoedsack's shots of the elephant stampede were so good they were reused in several later Hollywood movies. Schoedsack's and Cooper's *The Most Dangerous Game* overlapped with the shooting of *Kong*, and the two films shared some sets.

Meanwhile, the chief special effects man on *Kong*, the brilliant Willis O'Brien, was allowed to go much his own way, because he had been improving on filmic representations of dinosaurs and less probable beasts since 1915. As Noël Carroll has pointed out, dinosaurs were appropriate for films because they were "new" creatures, only recently discovered (1998, 120–123). Movies and O'Brien played a major role in popularizing prehistoric reptiles. Despite O'Brien's innovativeness in *King Kong* (which posed some directorial problems), his new extinct beasts seemed to nervous studio lawyers similar enough to those he had created in the earlier *Lost World* that RKO wouldn't proceed with production until it had purchased the film rights to that novel by Conan Doyle, forestalling possible lawsuits but tightening Cooper's budget. Other contemporary films helped to shape how *King Kong* was made—notably, the original *Frankenstein* movie, as well as the burgeoning genre of "jungle romance," of which *Tarzan* is the most notorious. But even movies planned and started but never completed, such as *Creation*, were pillaged in the fabricating of *King Kong* and left distinctive marks on the new story.

Confluences of visual sources for and influences on the movie are easier to identify than who wrote what in the script. Edgar Wallace worked with Cooper on a first version that contained a sketch of the entire film but in detail only one small part of the story. Wallace died suddenly, before officials of RCA (which controlled the RKO Studio) had approved producing the film. Cooper collaborated with at least two other writers, before giving the chief responsibility for the final script to Schoedsack's wife, who had never before written a movie script. In the finished film, Fay Wray screams so much because some scenes were shot before there was any dialogue for her. The economic circumstances of production were as unstable as the writing. RKO (like many studios of the period) had serious financial problems. Cooper and Schoedsack had to economize in many ways, using sets from others films and from other studios that had gone bankrupt. In an irony too fabulous to be fictitious, the great wall and gate King Kong breaks through had been built by DeMille for Jerusalem in his *King of Kings*. The "test reel" made for the company directors to judge whether to approve definitively funds for producing the movie was incorporated unmodified into the finished picture. This reel shows Fay Wray in a tree watching Kong fight a dinosaur. The special effects required her to be photographed in such a way that the actress could not see the events to which she was supposed to be reacting. She had to follow Cooper's off-camera directions when to scream, thus anticipating the brilliant scene devised and filmed later in which we see her take a film test while the director/entrepreneur operating the hand-cranked camera instructs her where to look and when to shriek. This powerfully self-reflexive episode illustrates how accidents in the making of a movie may enhance its formal structure (RCA executives, incidentally, tried to have this scene excised).

The foregoing barely hints at complexities of *King Kong's* production—Max Steiner, imported from Austria, had never written music for a movie and had to be given a crash course by Cooper. All the chaos has been documented in many articles and books, notably those of Erb (1998) and Goldner (1976) and Fay Wray's autobiographical *On the Other Hand*, but even the few items I've noted pose a fundamental question: how the hell does the satisfying formal coherence of a successful movie derive from constructive processes that seem the antithesis of organized creation? *King Kong* and *Casablanca* are not singular. Many movies have been created in a fashion that would seem to make impossible the formal coherence that has endowed them with enduring popularity. My belief is that our ideas of aesthetic creativity are dominated by traditions of literature and the fine arts of painting and sculpture. What in filmmaking looks like hopeless confusion of self-destructive cross-purposes in fact may sometimes be necessary to produce a dynamic of conflictual cooperation. Perhaps a kind of "accidental" achievement of meaningful form may be in some ways essential to a movie's formal vitality. Pudovkin (a generous-spirited and charismatic Russian, to be sure) thought a movie was likely to be better made the larger the number of people involved in its production (164).

Movies are a visual art, and as such they succeed by achieving a total effect of unified simplicity, just as do works by Phidias, Michelangelo, and Picasso. The impact of a successful movie is the impact of an integral experience. But how do the confusions common in movie production result in effective simplicity? I suggest that the processes of meticulous "framing" of individual shots (by preparatory adjustments of camera, lighting, and so forth, and the taking of repeated shots, plus subsequent editing) demand so much scrupulous rationality and precise mechanical control of the context out of which each shot emerges that some inflow of contradictory purposes, collaborative influences, and sheer accident (all characteristic of communal projects) is needed if the final product is to possess imaginative vitality. The history of the making of *King Kong*, at any rate, shows that no individual *could* have exercised the kind of personal control over the making of this visual narrative that Dickens, for example, exercised over the creation of *Great Expectations*.

The attractiveness of the earliest movies derives from their spontaneity, which reflects the degree to which they were improvised. A sense of improvisation is retained even in the most carefully crafted modern films, because the "reality" of visual perception consists principally in continuous unexpectedness. Mack Sennett's ebullient account of how the Keystone Cops came into being captures the spirit of improvisation that seems essential even to the best planned movies.

> We heard our first picture before we saw it . . . A Shriner's parade, stepping to the oom-pah and brass down Main Street.
> "We got us a spectacle, kids," I said. . . ."What's the story, boss?" Pathe asked. "Got no story. We'll make it up as we go along . . . run over to the department store and buy a baby doll."
> Mabel Norman could throw herself into any part instantly, even a part that didn't exist. "Who am I?" was all she asked . . . "A mother," I said. "I would be the last to know."
> "Now take this doll."
> " — I'm a poor lorn working girl, betrayed in the big city, searching for the father of me chee-ild," Mabel finished the sentence.
> Mabel put on the comicalest act you ever clapped eyes on, pleading, stumbling, holding out her baby — and the reactions she got from those good and pious gentlemen in the parade you couldn't have caught on film after six days of D. W. Griffith rehearsals. . . . One kind soul dropped out and tried to help Mabel. Sterling Ford leaped in and started a screaming argument with the innocent Shriner. . . . The police moved in on Ford and Mabel. Ford fled, leaping, insulting the police, and they — God bless the police! — they chased him. . . . I never got their names, but if there are any retired gentlemen of the Los Angeles Police Department who remember taking part in that incident, let them bask in fame: they were the original Keystone Cops. (Sennett, 86–88)

The mysteries of movie production may be illuminated, ironically, by the reception history of iconic films such as *Casablanca* and *King Kong*. The bibliography of criticism on *King Kong*, for example, is not only very large but is currently expanding — although one would think the film would by now seem quaint. Yet the visual immediacy of the killing of Kong seventy years later remains effective when everything we see (especially the airplanes) is out of date, and the scene itself has been reduced to a visual stereotype by hundreds of reproductions, many of them campy jokes. Kitschy it may be, but it remains effective — like the Statue of Liberty. Young children frequently cry at Kong's death. And I notice in showing the film to hyper-cynical, sophisticated

Columbia students, when we come to the final scenes the room becomes very, very quiet. The formal symmetries that are concretized by Kong on the Empire State Building (where RCA executives might well have been meeting a few floors below to decide whether to fund *King Kong*) allow circumstances (now forgotten) that affected the movie's production to penetrate the movie's form (McGurl). Partly this comes about through intentions of its makers, but those intentions were shaped by unforeseen accidents in the realizing of them. When bullet-riddled Kong, like the stock market, crashes to the dark New York street, we are visually reminded of the beginning of the movie, when Carl Denham the entrepreneur, after passing a soup-kitchen line of despairing women, discovers the heroine he wants when, trying to steal an apple, she faints from hunger. The echoing here was deliberately plotted, but at the time of its creation it was infiltrated by features of the Depression era more indirect and diffuse, starting with the strongly impinging but narratively irrelevant fact that RKO was struggling to avoid bankruptcy. *Kong*'s enduring appeal is that it is a make believe *of*, not a commentary on, the Depression. That helps the most cynical viewer to find something very "real" about this absurd fantasy of a big ape on top of the Empire State Building.

Fantasies originate only in individual psyches. But an adult fantasy that is tightly enough structured through testing by a skeptical intelligence and practical knowledge becomes publicly accessible, inviting participation by others. What we see in the production of movies are processes wherein the elaborate technological and sociological and financial mechanisms needed to realize one person's make believe allow early entry, so to speak, of others' imaginings into processes of public realizing of the private fantasy. The systematic rational planning (beginning with how to raise the money) required to make a movie, and consequent need of contributions from intensely specialized professionals, permits a variety of individuals to enter into highly localized areas of the make believe *as it is taking shape*. Anyone who studies film productions must be struck by how profoundly they are historical processes, determined by an interplaying of different people in which *when* things happen may be crucial, when somebody has a bright idea, or an accident occurs to an actor, or when natural or political events interfere with a planned shooting schedule. At such times many people's energies become focused in unexpected ways on the realization of the make believe. In these "collaborative moments" unanticipatable features may affect the production process, sometimes to the finished product's detriment but sometimes to its benefit.

The movie-producing process has an interesting analogue in the development of human embryos. Every human face is unique because, beyond genetic differentiation, although all humans undergo the same processes of embryonic development, how the processes develop varies in every case. Particularities of the mature organism are often determined by the chance of *when* in embryonic development certain molecules connected—or did not connect—with others. These minute variations in the interplay of thousands of molecules of diverse kinds *in the beginning of the history* of a person's life produce decisive variations in the structure and appearance of the "finished" adult (Edelman, 1989, 209–212).

A different kind of insight into how collaborative make believe achieves its unique effects is offered by *King Kong*'s famous final words, said over the body of the fallen Kong. "It was beauty killed the beast" self-consciously identifies the movie as a modern version of the old fairy tale. But that concept of the movie emerged only in the midst of the vicissitudes of constructing a film about a big ape. In the messy collaborative actualizing of the movie's make believe, unexpected connections and implications emerged to endow specific shots and scenes with possibilities of unanticipated echoes and overtones Kurosqwa's, "kiln changes" (Goodwin, 64), thereby altering the affect of the whole. This kind of shaping cannot be attained through more rationally ordered creation. To start with a firm plan to make a modern version of "Beauty and the Beast" in fact precludes the kind of dynamic multiparticipation in a communal make believe that is the source of the continuing vitality of *King Kong*. Evidence for this view is provided by Jean Cocteau's pleasantly entertaining *Beauty and the Beast*, which through rigorously conscious control transfers the literary fairy tale into a visual form far less interesting than *King Kong*—to judge by the amount of commentary on each. I like Cocteau's film and value his insights into the art of movie-making, but I find that his *Beauty and the Beast*, despite some superficial visual experimentalism, (connected to his subverting of the story's heterosexuality) remains imprisoned within a conventional literary conception of narrative. Because *King Kong* is thorough-going visual make believe it succeeds in evoking, as Cocteau's film does not, the peculiar continuing relevance of the fairy story to fundamental issues of contemporary life, including some very nasty issues of sexuality and racism. *King Kong*'s iconic status (like that of several other celebrated films) derives less from its rather modest success at its original release than from its popularity in rereleases ten and twenty years after its original showing. This seems evidence that this retelling of the fable tapped into historical undercurrents that, however unarticulated explicitly, were shaping feelings about beauty and bestiality in the twentieth-century world. The messiness of the movie's collaborative production left openings for the infiltrating of potent but as yet undefined (and sometimes contradictory) subterraneous tendencies in modern culture that a more orderly creation process would have aborted. These tendencies in fact are lost in the carefully constructed and sentimentalized politically correct remakes of 1976 and 2005.

CHAPTER 6

MOVIES AND HYPER-VISUAL CULTURE

The difference between verbal and visual make believe is ultimately rooted in physiology, distinctions between hearing and seeing, but historical processes have also affected both modes (Carroll, 1980, 145). We can all see that "contemporary culture is a visual culture." (Baetens, 45) The long historical development of Western Culture toward hyper-visuality has cogently been described by Walter J. Ong (1967, 1977), with the result, as W. J. T. Mitchell (16) astutely observed, that "spectatorship . . . and visual pleasures may be as deep a problem as various forms of reading . . . and that [now] visual experience might not be fully explicable on the model of textuality." Motion pictures validate that insight. The invention of printing in the Renaissance, to cite perhaps the most obvious example, shifted the primary basis of literary imagining from sounds heard to sights read on the page. Since then, however, there has been no equally significant transformation in the nature of the texts that stimulate verbal make believe: we read *Don Quixote* in the same way we read the most recent novel. The cultural context within which we read *Don Quixote*, of course, is radically different from that of its original readers, and for my purposes the primary difference is the hyper-visuality of modern society.

Usefully to define the effect on verbal make believe of a social existence saturated with visual stimulations of every kind, although desirable, is beyond the scope this study. But I can point to one concretely discernable effect in children's literature. Teaching this material to undergraduates today, I have to recognize that virtually all the classics that I (like everyone else from the origins of such literature in the mid-eighteenth century) read as a child my current students may or may not have read but have all seen in movie or animated versions. For them to read Hans Christian Anderson's "Little Mermaid" after having seen Disney's "Little Mermaid," to cite a simple instance, is a startling different experience. And of course the effects of this phenomenon ramify, to the nadir where a National Merit Scholarship student can believe that *Winnie the Pooh* and *Wind in the Willows* were invented by Disney.

Subtler changes are more significant. Jonathan Crary (1–79) has traced effects of nineteenth-century conceptions of the nature and value of concentrated attention affecting how people trained themselves to use their eyes. His work reminds us that all cultures train people to use their perceptions in particular ways. Such training is illustrated by South Seas aboriginal swimmers demonstrating superiority to Europeans at perceiving features in underwater coral reefs, and the classic but unverified claim that Eskimos distinguish many more kinds of snow than do Texans. The accelerating tendency in Western culture to emphasize vision is intimately connected with the increasing industrialization of society since it is helpful in mechanizing and standardizing human behavior, the kind of behavior that is required for many of the processes essential to the collaborative creating of motion pictures. Novels, however, are still mostly created in the same way Cervantes created his, with a little facilitation from Bill Gates. Movies are the more modern form of make believe, not only because invented more recently and because primarily visual, but also because a movie today is produced, distributed, and exhibited differently from the way it was created and made public a century ago. Yet the old movies, and the newest DVD, appeal to physiologically unchanged features of our visual perception.

The tendency toward emphasis on the visual in Western culture may explain the persistence of the myth (there is no authenticated account of such an event) of preliterate peoples being unable to see that a still photograph depicts anything—until enlightened by the camera-carrying Westerner. It is significant that this patronizing legend seems never to have been promulgated about motion pictures. There is, in fact, abundant evidence that technologically unsophisticated people immediately understand what motion pictures are and do. Often, however, their attention focuses on aspects of a film quite different from what Westerners expect. Years ago some European engineers showed native Africans a film about keeping water pure. Comment by the audience afterward was lethargic until one African started an animated discussion by saying he'd been surprised at the behavior of the chicken. There isn't any chicken in the film, objected the Europeans. But when the film was reshown, sure enough, in the background of a crucial scene focused on well-construction there appeared a chicken behaving peculiarly—one suspects because harassed by the film crew.

The importance of the anecdote is less cultural than physiological: it draws attention to the extraordinary *selective* potency of our perceptual system, that perception may be controlled by active choice, that, as William Blake put it, we see *through* not *with* the eye. A recent experiment conducted on presumably technologically sophisticated people in New York drives home the point that humans possess formidable powers of willfully oriented attention. Participants in the experiment were asked to watch a film showing a group of men dressed in black and white uniforms passing a basketball about and to report on how many times the ball was thrown. Midway in the film, a young woman dressed in gorilla suit walks in front of the men and gesticulates before lumbering off. Fully half of the participants when asked what they thought of the girl in the gorilla suit replied, "What girl? What gorilla?"

Our current hyper-visual society is epitomized by a lone individual staring at a computer screen (what I am doing as I "write" this) with cognitive and emotional energies concentrated by perceptual focus *away* from sensory contact with any other living being. Today, everywhere one encounters individuals watching technologically produced images on computer and television screens that encourage one's separation from other people, and even from the full panoply of one's own bodily processes, simultaneously diminishing auditory, tactile, and kinesthetic awareness both of the external world and one's own internal being (Ong, 1977, 125). And visual perception is essentially analytical. Herbert Read, one of the earliest and most acute philosophic critics of film, identified *analysis* as the primary characteristic of motion picture art (8). A string of leading directors have supported his observation in their descriptions of filmmaking. Illustrative is Alfred Hitchcock's account of how the scene from *Sabotage* in which Verloc is stabbed by his wife was "made up entirely of short pieces of film, separately photographed." Hitchcock summarizes the process:

> You gradually build up the psychological situation, piece by piece, using the camera to emphasize first one detail, then another. The point is to draw the audience right inside the situation instead of leaving them to watch it from outside. . . . And you can do this only by breaking the action up into details and cutting from one to the other, so that each detail is forced in turn on the attention of the audience. (9–10)

Hitchcock contends that effective movies give a viewer the sense that "you are watching something that has been conceived and brought to birth directly in visual terms" (8). The analytical processes he mentions are enhanced by artifices that diminish the complicating confusions of phenomena we see in the natural world, artifices producing what I call "visual stylizing." Our culture increasingly encourages us to exercise our eyes on technologically produced artifacts (as opposed to natural phenomena) to the benefit of an analytical understanding that downgrades more synthetic and dynamically fluid qualities of consciousness—precisely the qualities that are appealed to and strengthened by novel reading.

The novel reader, to be sure, seeks privacy—but for the purpose of imaginatively entering into the consciousness of the novelist and the characters he has created (Birkerts, 82–94). Language, we say, "communicates," but that ponderous term obscures the exciting interactivity it contains, beginning with the Latin origin of "to make common," to move from the private to the public. Dictionary definitions of "communication" emphasize interchange and mutuality of endeavor: "to give to another as a partaker," "to impart, inform, bestow," "to share in; to use or enjoy in common with," "to open into each other." We know of no human culture that does not depend on language, because language is the foundation of human socialization, the give and take, including productive disagreement, which enables private imaginations of every kind to be realized by other people through competitive/cooperative activities. The supreme paradox of language is that it enables us to share what is most profoundly private and idiosyncratic, to "make common" what is purely subjective. Verbal make believe alone permits mutual sharing of subjective individualities. I am persuaded that a cause for the efflorescence of superb novels in the nineteenth century was the imperiling of this power of verbal make believe. Beyond the threat of "scientific" history, there was the ominous pressure against their imaginativeness posed by depersonalized urban life styles dominated by bureaucratization that increasingly privileged representations of reality dependent on the superficial accuracy of the visually verisimilar.

Symptomatic of the hyper-visualism of our own era is the extensive intellectual commentary on language that is negative—a litany of how language falsifies, betrays itself, conceals rather than reveals. Much of this is true. But this negativism misleads when it obscures the bonding and unifying powers of language, above all its unique capability to evoke imagining in its addressees. The very qualities that make language deceptive arise from its efficacy in arousing consciousness rather than limiting and imposing upon it. Language can at once stimulate diverse, even contradictory ideas, feelings, fantasies; at its best it encourages reciprocal interaction rather than enforcing uniformity. Of course language has again and again been misused, especially to compel conformity. This is what Bakhtin called mono-logic discourse, the discourse of dictators and self-righteous absolutists who hate differences of opinion, which always find expression in different uses of language. The finest nineteenth-century novels Bakhtin perceived as deploying linguistic resources in exactly the opposite fashion, dialogically and polyphonically (1981, 324–355; 1984, 5–46). Fiction in the nineteenth century was the main form of story-telling, and verbal storytelling's essential function is to preserve and develop willing interchange among members of a community. Storytelling embodies the unique power of language to enable people who differ significantly to work and live together productively. If language relationships are restricted or crippled, relationships become mechanical, determined by physical force. Language alone allows me of my own volition to reject your idea and tell you why, or of my own free will to adopt your idea, opinion, or feeling, to take it *into* myself, modify it, and offer it back for you to accept or reject of your free will. The polysemism of language, which makes it so slippery and frightening (especially to philosophers), alone makes possible open and dynamically productive social negotiations. Without freedom of speech other human freedoms are unlikely to appear or to endure.

Although the novel reader and movie spectator each respond from an isolated situation, the nature of their responses are antithetical. In a movie theater, carefully structured organization of displays of technologically generated images *impose* themselves on the audience's perceptual systems, making imaginative responses secondary. Exactly the opposite process is fundamental to novel reading. The words, whether read by the eye from the printed page or heard from someone reading aloud, instantaneously evoke private fantasizing. The distinction has been obscured by modern criticism's tendency to reduce imagining produced by language to mere image-making, a falsification representative of how we more and more think in visual terms. J. R. R. Tolkien countered this misconception by contrasting visual art's necessary imposition of a single "visible form" of representation with the verbal storyteller's presenting his audience with the indeterminacy of "*bread* or *wine* or *stone* or *tree*," each of which words "appeals to the whole of these things," as the visual representation cannot, because it shows *a* glass of wine, *a* particular rock or *a* specific tree. Tolkien observes that a writer's language enters directly into a reader's mind where it evokes what I call associative imagining, in part to capture Tolkien's point that the imagined "whole" of the thing is *not predetermined for the reader:* the bread, wine, stone, or tree the writer imagines will *not* be exactly the bread, wine, stone or tree that each individual reader imagines (95–96). Tolkien's distinction supports Gilbert Ryle's observation already noted on the verbalized "image" of a mountain that it misses "just what one would be due to get, if one were seeing the mountain." Wolfgang Iser reinforces the distinction by demonstrating how in writing, " 'imagining' depends upon the absence of that which appears in the image" (137) inadvertently echoing the classic formulation of John Ruskin that:

> imagination is a voluntary summoning of the conception of things absent or impossible; and the pleasure and nobility of the imagination . . . consist . . . in the knowledge of their actual absence or impossibility at the moment of their apparent presence. (8, 58)

Entirely different is the visual embodiment in the painter's static or filmmaker's mobile picture of a fluted glass of wine or crusty loaf of bread or mossy stone or sycamore tree, each of which is exactly and only what the viewer *must* see, a determinate sight. This restricts the spectator's personal associative imagining. Viewers are at first confined to responding to a singular image outside themselves, although what you and I see will differ, if for no other reason that we see from slightly different perspectives. A conventional illustration of this is the color-blind person who does not see the same traffic light a normally sighted person does. Yet both do see the same physical object, whereas *readers* encountering "traffic light" may imagine quite different objects, since traffic lights are manufactured in diverse shapes.

The sequence of images in a good movie, however, secondarily evokes imagining, what I call, following many commentators' emphasis on the role of inference in movie viewing and in contrast to the associative imagining excited by verbal make believe, "conjectural imagining." In teaching us how to use our eyes better, good movies activate a focused mode of imagining that enriches the meaningfulness of perceptions—sometimes, however, in the paradoxical fashion of creating doubt about our understanding of what we see so plainly and so precisely. *La Strada* in this fashion provokes appreciation of the enigmaticness in each of its major characters. Zampano, Gelsomina, and The Fool are surprising and alien to us in a peculiarly modern way: we recognize what they do, something of how they live, and we can "place" them in the circumstances of twentieth-century life. But the more we watch, the more we recognize that our categorizings depend upon our ignoring their true individuality, how our judgments depend on not looking closely at such people, the way we don't look at street beggars. The movie, however, compels us to examine them intensely, and that quickly leads to imaginative conjecturing. But this imagining tends to baffle rather than to produce understanding: we realize that concentrated clear sightedness here does not result in better comprehension but confrontation with an enigmatic humanity. Watching the movie, we become deeply interested in these people because we come to recognize that by not looking at them (our practice in real life, mostly by living where they don't) we have cut ourselves off from an impressive portion of the reality of our world. But the longer we look, the more we have difficulty in confidently judging the exact meaning of what we see. In empowering us to see more and to see better a movie such as *La Strada* forces us to admit the limits of what we can understand solely through visual inspection. This paradoxical process is the cause for so many excellent movies leaving us not feeling emotionally and intellectual clarified, but, to the contrary, frustrated, conflicted, uncertain about what to do with the emotions that have been aroused in us. This disturbing quality Italian moviemakers seem especially adept at evoking—one remembers with peculiar pain *Paisan, The Bicycle Thief, A Special Day*, and *Umberto D.* But uncertainty, not satisfaction, is the final effect of many superior movies, an uncertainty peculiarly agitating because deriving from spectacular stimulation of our visual perceptions.

What we learn, even in our bafflement, about the characters of *La Strada*, however, is salutary, because so many of our human relations are now made superficial by technological distancing. The desperate need of our painting, movies, and fiction to foreground sexual touching, "the general pornification of society" in Francine Du Plessix Gray's words (86) reflects many peoples' isolation from kinesthetic realities, encouraged hyper-visual culture. *La Strada*, of course, is another structure of mechanically displayed images seen at a distance, but, as with all fine movies, its make believe enables us to imagine the inadequacy of our ordinary awareness of the fierce complexity of diverse human lives in all their physical and psychic dimensions, thereby heightening our consciousness of fearful complexity of realities the conditions of our lives encourage us to ignore.

Movies are produced by technological processes most of which have been spin-offs from developments in unrelated industrial enterprises, warfare being a primary source (Wollen, 16). This reveals the linkages between industrialized and visually oriented culture that have increasingly pervaded Western culture since the Renaissance fostering of print and perspectival "realism," supported by those critical scientific devices, the microscope and telescope—not to forget the camera obscura, which led to the first popularization of what we now call virtual reality. It is only toward the latter part of the eighteenth century, however, that this tendency began to take on its characteristically modern form, as is described in a recent book by Gillen Wood, *The Shock of the Real*. Wood demonstrates how then a spectrum of visual forms, everything from engravings and prints to spectacular dioramas and panoramas, began to challenge the traditional dominance of literacy in shaping the orientation of cultural life. New ideals of visual verisimilitude appealed to the taste of nonelite members of society, who were becoming empowered, both economically and politically, by the expanding industrialization and democratization of society. When Wordsworth in his preface to *Lyrical Ballads* described his poetry as an antidote to the "savage torpor" of the general mind brought on by a "thirst for outrageous sensation," he was responding to that challenge. In its more sensational forms, such as Belzoni's "Egyptian Tomb," the ideal of visual verisimilitude spectacularly prefigures the blockbuster summer movies of our day, such as the Indiana Jones series. This shifting in fundamental assumptions about art and its social functions away from commitments to the literary imaginative would seem to make the invention of photography and then motion pictures predictable, if not downright inevitable. And from this perspective the career of David Garrick looks exemplary. He revolutionized Shakespearian acting by concentrating less on the language of the plays than on silent, pantomimic representations of characters and actions. Garrick thrilled audiences by his visual style that relied on expressive bodily postures and striking changes of his mobile features. His elevation of the visual toward parity with the verbal accompanied and encouraged decisive transformations in the physical character of theaters—his era marking the rise to prominence of opera, the emergence of pantomime as a major popular form, and the substitution for small, intimate theaters of large auditoria, in which for the first time plays were performed within elaborately realistic sets.

Garrick, furthermore, worked as assiduously as a contemporary movie star to assure the successful marketing of his image. There were more representations of Garrick in the later eighteenth century than any other Englishman except King George the Third (who had the advantage of all those coins). Garrick has a good claim to be the first "celebrity" in the modern sense (Braudy, 1986). He established a taste for going to the theater as much to see Garrick as a specific play—starting the trend toward the star performer—the visible virtuoso—eclipsing the invisible writer. Garrick's example made possible Sarah Siddons's career as "the greatest actress of the last quarter of the eighteenth century," her most famous role being that of Lady Macbeth, in which the woman's

> suffering is not merely declaimed in blank verse but readable on her body. In fact the body is often more important as a signifier than the broken words which constitute the words given to the character . . . "attitudes," gestures, facial expressions, and gazes are commented on much more frequently . . . [than] at any other period of dramatic criticism. (Gay Penny, 33, 35)

Garrick and Siddons would have been spectacular silent movie actors. And the popularity of visually oriented dramatizations continued to flourish throughout the nineteenth century, with increasing emphasis on spectacle. Martin Meisel has shown, for example, a characteristic feature of Victorian staging was the "realization," in which the actors fell into positions in relation to one another that was recognized by the audience as reproducing some well-known painting (1983, 38–51). Meisel has also demonstrated the importance to the nineteenth-century theater of the genre of melodrama, which historians of motion pictures identify as the primary source for both the subject and the style of early cinema (Vardac).

Although nineteenth-century novels also reflect these tendencies, admitting "pictorialism" in a variety of ways, most strikingly in their admitting of literal illustrations within their texts, novelists deployed language so as to enhance appeals to their readers' participative imaginations. From a twentieth-century vantage point, the language of nineteenth-century novels does appear eminently "readable," as suggested by Roland Barthes, who also astutely called attention to the importance of their self-descriptions as "works" rather than "texts" (Barthes, 90). The "readable" writing of these "works" is neither syntactically nor semantically "difficult," seldom experimentally innovative, and not intensely self-reflective, because it adheres to rhetorical, dictional, and syntactic traditions (precise in use of sequence of tenses, for example), and is consistently oriented toward welcoming ordinary readers' entry into the world of literary make believe as respected participants. Even such a generalized summary suggests reasons why film adaptations of nineteenth-century fiction are seldom successful. In contrast to the more "visual" literary style of most contemporary fiction (whose authors have seen many films and customarily hope their books will become movies), the earlier novelists appealed to (thereby contributing to the creation of) an audience conceived of as engaged in an historically based—although quite contemporaneously vital—linguistic commonalty. Motion pictures both for financial reasons and as visual form can and do aim to please larger and more diverse audiences. Movies, furthermore, developed under conditions of rapid and radical changes in the fundamental technology and economics that sustain the medium. The film adaptation of, say, *Wuthering Heights* in 1940 had in every conceivable way to be a different enterprise from the movie adaptation of the novel in 1920. In the past hundred years, while the nature of verbal storytelling in fiction has changed very little except in its aesthetic form, visual storytelling has also undergone a series of drastic physical revolutions originating in technical and socioeconomic innovations. There is, for instance, no twentieth-century literary equivalent for the invention of "talkies"—unless it is the impact of motion pictures upon all imaginative writing.

Again, the topic is too vast to be precisely articulated, even summarily, but it would be irresponsible in developing the basic contrast I concentrate upon not to at least mention the profound and almost continuous transformations in how visual make believe has been fabricated and displayed—transformations with no real parallel in twentieth-century history of publishing and book distribution. Among the best of the commentators on the movies' technological history is Peter Wollens, who has offered intelligent analyses of the interrelation between the economics of exhibition and distribution as well as of detailed technical changes in the physical making of films. He points out that the most important technical innovations in the film industry came from chemistry, which affected film stock, above all in the production of faster and more sensitive emulsions. Sound movies had an extraordinary impact on all aspects of filmmaking, since they demanded synchronizing of visual image with sound track (not perfected until the invention of the photo-electric cell, which permitted synchronization through a component in the projector), and required the introduction of amplifying systems into movie theaters. Sound, in fact, introduced what Wollen calls

a chain of bizarre secondary problems and solutions. The carbon lights hummed and the hum came through on the sound-track. The tungsten lights which replaced them were at the red end of the spectrum and so the old orthochromatic film, which was blind to red, had to go. . . . This change brought changes in make-up; the fortunes of Max Factor date from this period. Studios replaced locations; multiple camera set-ups were introduced; the craft of script-writing was transformed . . . timing had to be standardized . . . the camera was no longer hand-cranked. . . . Every aspect of the laboratory was automated and there were standardized development and printing procedures . . . the laboratory became completely divorced from the work of the director and cinematographer. (17)

Equivalent changes in production and marketing came with introduction of color—and with equivalently ramifying secondary and tertiary effects. Among these, to my mind the most significant, is that indicated in Wollens's last sentence—the divorce between laboratory technicians and those working with the cameras. To that division can be traced much of the depressingly mechanistic quality of many recent movies. Through an evolution generated by its very success, moviemaking, by reducing itself toward little more than a digitalized commodity, may be endangering the source of its unique strength as collaborative make believe. That there appears to be no analogous threat to verbal make believe may be cause for a subtler concern. It is possible at least to conceive of the supersession of fiction by movies as the most successful form of popular entertainment as symptomatic of deep shifts in the kinds of sensibility that can flourish in contemporary societies. A plausible case could be made that since World War II there have been more movies produced than novels written that possess the enduring qualities of superior art. Be that as it may, there are qualities of consciousness that verbal make believe alone can excite which plainly are to the advantage of our species. This enhancement of self-consciousness and its spread to ever larger portions of the world's population has been the most important benefit of increases in literacy over the past few centuries. Even the shadow of a threat to that advance by visual technologizing of culture must be cause for concern.

CHAPTER 7

LA STRADA AND THE CONJECTURING IMAGINATION

Moviemakers create their films by moving cameras about, changing the lighting and lenses, taking numberless shots, and editing them in a variety of ways. I will subsume reference to all these manipulations under a term borrowed from the Socrates of film critics Noël Carroll, "variable framing" (1980, 201–207). The umbrella concept frees me from entanglement in the myriad of technical details of filmmaking, which most movie critics can only pretend fully to understand. I certainly do not—as will be confirmed by the kindly faculty of the film division of Columbia University's School of the Arts with whom I have consulted. "Variable framing" also serves as a reminder that visual narratives can be constructed only through complicated processes of deception. (Carroll, 2003, 10–58) These processes are easily forgotten because the dominant thrust of visual narratives creates clarity and intelligibility—whereas the controlling thrust of novelistic narrative is toward self-reflexive ambiguities.

Film critics have fretted about how spectators adapt to special camera positions, especially to sudden switches in perspective. Many bizarre psychological explanations have been proposed to account for phenomena better explained by normal use of our eyes. Seeing is a dynamic process of continuous physiological/psychological adjusting and readjusting, including, as J. J. Gibson has shown, the power of conceiving sight from a position different from the one we happen at the moment to occupy (75, 197). Seeing is a temporal process, a scanning that never stops, and one that enables us to adjust instantly to changes in viewing circumstances. It is the never-ceasing continuity of this self-reordering flexibility of visual perception that variable framing orients, focuses, intensifies. In normal vision the most "natural" connection between sights (in movies called "shots") is sequentiality, a foundation of narrative. If we ask more specifically what is the particular method by which a moviemaker links up his successive frames, the Russian director Pudovkin replies, by a sequence of scenes that pose questions that are answered by subsequent scenes (77–78). In a drawer behind the bar in Deadwood we see a loaded revolver: Will Jack McCall use it to shoot Wild Bill from behind as he plays poker? In movies more subtle than DeMille's *Plainsman*, narrative form is created by a more intricate interlacing of questions-to-answers (Carroll, 1998, 170–179), becoming sequences of possibility-realization, what Carroll terms "erotetic narrative." Toward the conclusion of Fellini's *La Strada*, for example, the possibilities an audience entertains differ in number and quality from those it conceived at the movie's beginning. Progress of the movie story accompanies an evolution in *how* the audience anticipates.

At the opening of *La Strada* spectators know nothing about Zampano, Gelsomina, or her family, even where the action is taking place, except that it is on a seashore. The condition in which we begin watching the movie, however, is something more than mere ignorance—otherwise we would never enjoy seeing a film more than once. We come to the film *innocently*, alert for possibilities, eager see what the movie has to offer, disposed toward active discovery. That is why we paid money to get into the theater. The opening scene interests us because there are so many open possibilities presented to our eyes. Zampano is visually impressive, but sinister, and we wonder how to assess him. Rosa is dead—but who is Rosa? We see contradictoriness in Gelsomina's mother's attitude toward accepting Zampano's chintzy offer, but we cannot be sure of what her ambivalence implies. Nor can we fully understand what Gelsomina herself thinks of the proposition to go with Zampano. As the movie progresses, our power to understand what the characters are and why they feel and think as they do improves. But with that improvement goes a developing sense for the limited ways in which their desires and fears can be fulfilled. As possibilities for these people narrow, they also provoke in the audience more intense but probably more ambivalent feelings along with increasing uncertainty of how to judge what we see. We come to recognize, for example, that Gelsomina is not simply childlike: she has internalized some conventionalized conceptions, dramatized by her readiness to imitate, a readiness that cuts across her charming spontaneity, and displayed by her readiness to "show off." As we understand her better we find her ever stranger. Her Harry Langdon face appears simultaneously revealing and misleading, and the intricacy of *her* innocence is epitomized by the "inappropriateness" of her male clothing. These features, along with the actions of the plot, compel us to realize that we cannot predict or even be sure we understand Gelsomina's behavior. In the episode with the hydrocephalic boy, for example, the expectations of the children, that the clown may make the boy laugh, and of the nun who chases them away, are clear enough, but what Gelsomina makes of the boy, whether in fact the event has any significance for her, remains obscure for spectators. Perhaps a scene so impressive to us, the audience, is much less meaningful to her, because the conditions of her life make it impossible for her to be "sensitive" in the way we are toward her, although we have come to recognize her as a creature of unusual sensibilities.

La Strada illustrates the paradox that the more clearly we see the characters in an excellent movie, the more enigmatic they are likely to become. Visual perception may sharpen our awareness that we cannot fully know what goes on in their minds. We become ever more conscious that we can only conjecture from appearances we recognize are often misleading. Because we see Zampano's face so precisely and perceive his bodily movements so exactly, we feel we should understand him, and, in fact, in some respects we do come to comprehend why he behaves as he does. Yet simultaneously we become alert to a baffling quality in this overtly repulsive person (as we are equivalently provoked in a different way by sympathetic Gelsomina). When in the movie's final scene I see Zampano clutching the sand in anguish, my appreciation of his despair accompanies a realization that I do not know precisely how this man suffers, that I can never suffer as he is suffering. Because I have come to *perceive* Zampano vividly, thanks to Fellini's skillful manipulations of variable framing, I cannot escape an underawareness of my separation from him that opens a fissure of doubt about the meaning of what I perceive. This uncertainty is peculiarly disturbing because I respond intensely to the anguish of this despicable, stupid, destructive man.

The same paradoxical response is evoked in another fashion by Gelsomina. In the progress of the movie's story, the strength of our visual familiarity with her grows (to the point that we feel certain we would recognize Gelsomina anywhere) simultaneously with a sharpening awareness that the very distinctiveness of this unusual person makes her ever more mysterious. We are made to see Zampano and Gelsomina as what they really are—profound puzzles. This is not because they are "complex" characters but because they force us to recognize how even "simple" human beings are not to be explained by mere visual inspection. The clarity with which this insight into our blindness is dramatized by the film contributes to its power to leave us not emotionally satisfied but troubled. This frustratingly fascinating opacity of movie characters may be highlighted by a contrast with novelistic ones. Heathcliff in *Wuthering Heights* surely is for most readers a mysterious figure. Yet readers of *Wuthering Heights* have had the experience of "imagining into" Heathcliff in a fashion denied us by the visual art of *La Strada*. Our experience of the film is of concentratedly *watching* Zampano; we never enter into the kind of imaginative "sharing" provided by Emily Brontë's depiction of Heathcliff, although she never directly represents his inner feelings and thoughts. We spend the two hours of *La Strada* with growing awareness that even though we see Zampano so distinctly from so many angles, we can only speculate about his inner being. Despite Heathcliff's mysterious parentage, the obscurity of the devices by which he gains wealth, and the fact that other characters in the novel are consistently baffled by him (his wife even wondering if he is truly a human being), we readers feel that we have participated in his strangeness, which has become a part of us. He becomes for us "familiar" in a way that Zampano never does, even though we possess a far more distinct visual image of Zampano. We have no more need for a precise visual image of Heathcliff than we do of ourselves.

Illustrative of the difference between characterization through verbal and visual make believe is the haunting scene in which Zampano deserts Gelsomina, leaving her sleeping by a broken wall in a desolately beautiful winter landscape. By this late stage in the story the audience can with assurance infer from his expressions and movement the intolerable pain she induces in him after The Fool's death—that pain in some measure rising from his unadmittable dependence upon her dependence. We observe signs of the simultaneous fear and guilt and shame he experiences (especially when he sees her little trumpet and lays it beside her) as he sneaks away. Yet the deepest poignancy of the scene (our last view of Gelsomina) derives from an underawareness evoked by the very clarity of our perception of Zampano's action that complete appreciation of his motivation is impossible. We feel simultaneously the necessity for him to desert her, and that the desertion is a destructive self-evasion, a deserting of himself. Watching his actions, moreover, we recognize how he closes down his future possibilities, without knowing what these may be. When we first see the movie we do not know that Gelsomina will die, but her death does not surprise us. Zampano's breaking off the relation stringently limits what *can* happen—in contrast to the opening of the movie, when almost anything seemed possible. In fact, we as viewers have ourselves undergone an emotional evolution in watching the interaction of the characters. Not only have the characters changed, but we who watch have been changed by watching them. We know more, which includes knowing that we also know less than we had thought we could, and this process carries us harrowingly close to something terrible intrinsic to all human experience.

Understanding producing bafflement, feeling separated from what we come to sympathize with against our prejudices, these and analogous conflicts are aroused in different ways by excellent movies. The key to these effects lies in the activity of spectatorship provoked by moviemakers' variable framing to create sequences of events with increasing affective power. We may sit quietly in our seat at a good movie, but psychically we are not at all passive, because seeing is not passive reception—it is proactive scanning. And our cognitive and emotional systems ratchet themselves up to gain the most meaning possible from our physiological probing into the visual environment offered by a movie. Looking at paintings in an art gallery demands a notable expenditure of energy—the better the paintings the more energy expended. Motion pictures are even more arousing, because they display motion, and our perceptual system is oriented toward seeking out what moves so as to activate elemental impulses of fear and desire.

The importance of spectator proactiveness and of the context of motion as determining the emotional effects of what we see was perhaps proved by what has been called the "Kuleshov Experiment," an experiment that in fact may never have taken place. The experiment Pudovkin claimed he conducted with his colleague-mentor Kuleshov:

> [We took] several close-ups of the well-known Russian actor Mosjukhin. We chose close-ups which were static and which did not express any feeling at all—quiet close-ups. We joined these close-ups which were all similar, with other bits of film in three different combinations. In the first combination the close-up of Mosjukhin was immediately followed by a shot of a plate of soup standing on a table. It was obvious and certain that Mosjukhin was looking at the soup. In the second combination the face of Mosjukhin was joined to a shot showing a coffin in which lay a dead woman. In the third the close-up was followed by a shot of a little girl playing with a funny toy bear. When we showed the three combinations to an audience which had not been let into the secret the result

was terrific. The public raved about the acting of the artist. They pointed out the heavy pensiveness of his mood over the forgotten soup, were touched and moved by the deep sorrow with which he looked at the dead woman, and admired the light, happy smile with which he surveyed the girl at play. But we knew that in all three cases the face was exactly the same. (168)

There are very good reasons for doubting this account, or that if the experiment was ever carried out it was not conducted in the manner Pudovkin describes. The reasons for such skepticism have been admirably laid out in a essay by Norman Holland, who rightly observes that the facts scarcely matter, because virtually every critic of film has discussed the experiment as if it had really taken place (79). This is not just a sign of bad scholarship but also evidence that, whether fact or fantasy, Pudovkin's story dramatizes with singular cogency the creativity with which audiences respond to movies (Bordwell, 1985). The effectiveness of the "experiment" according to Pudovkin's account lies in the use of "static" close-ups, essentially still photographs of the actor's face, that were interpreted so variously. The truth of movie viewing being revealed here originates in what I have called the "enigmaticness" of visual sights, which imperiously demand "interpretation." An unpleasant example of how we understand human expressions less in themselves than by interpreting them through the context in which we see them was a widely published photograph of relatives of astronauts who died in the malfunctioning of the Challenger spacecraft. The photograph was captioned as displaying their horror as they saw the rocket explode. In fact, the photograph recorded their pleasure at the rocket's apparently successful lift-off moments before the disaster.

A professional New York newspaper photographer once told me that every newspaper photograph (including his own) was a lie (unconsciously echoing Richard Avedon's judgment, "A photograph is always accurate; it never tells the truth" (Okrent). The newsman's point was not that many pictures were staged, but that a still photograph represents only a single instant, the full meaning of which is only determinable from what immediately precedes and succeeds that instant. That context is excluded from every still photograph, but is very much present in every motion picture—and as Pudovkin claimed, that local context determines audience response. This is why Paul Ekman's research on "reading" expressions has been so dependent on motion pictures: only through the study of facial changes was he able to identify the processes by which expressions come into being, that is, to understand facial configurations in their most immediate and significant contexts.

The principal feature of such contexts is the mobility of expression, or the potential for mobility, as is apparent in double-takes, and in close-ups such as that of Asta Nielsen Balàzs admired. But even a close-up of a thoroughly impassive face (for older moviegoers the inscrutable Alan Ladd may come to mind) is radically different from a still photograph or a painted portrait. In the movie one perceives if not actual motion the *possibility* for change, or, what is actually rather unusual in real-life expressions—that there is no change. With a still photograph or painting there is of course no possibility of transformation, nor can we see that an expression is unchanging. One of the most justly famous closeups in movie history is that of Chaplin at the very end of *Modern Times*, and anyone who takes the trouble to compare the shot in the movie with a still reproduction will be impressed by the vitality of the former, most powerfully embodied in its manifestation of transience, its being about to change—into to what we can never know.

Movies dramatize that seeing may not correlate with understanding— indeed, clear sight may be a cause for uncertainty. Many of the best movies utilize the perspicuousness and intelligibility of the visual story (produced by meticulous variable framing) to compel spectators to recognize the opacity of what has been so plainly exhibited. The foundation of this effect is that all that we ever see are surfaces, opacities. We literally cannot see something transparent. Seeing a movie is the perceiving of surfaces of ever-changing visual events that provoke imaginative conjecturing and reconjecturing. We learn to make ever more illuminating judgments about successive sights which in themselves are lucidly unrevealing. To watch a good movie is to engage in an active learning process, about ourselves, what we are able to make of what we see, as well as about what we observe in itself. In following the unfolding of the story we change ourselves. It is not easy to find an analogy with which to illuminate this process because, in fact, there is no experience quite like it. My best effort is to adapt the psychologist's Ulric Neisser's (180–181) analogy with playing chess, assuming the game has an ethical dimension. One begins with all possibilities of the game open, and with the first move the possibilities begin to narrow, and continuously narrow further as the game progresses. This increases the overt significance of each move until the final "checkmate." Yet the best movies avoid that simple finality: as Fellini said, there should be no end to a movie. The game may indeed suggest something about movie watching as a process of learning, not a rote lesson that is the same for every student, but a lesson different for each viewer. Here the simple analogy can be expanded to suggest how good movies appeal to a wide spectrum of sophistication—virtually a necessity for art aiming at mass audiences. Such differentiation of response Neisser compares with stages of maturation. To an infant, the chess board and pieces seem mere things, whereas an older child sees the pieces as distinctive objects like toys. A still older child can appreciate that pieces and board make a specific game possible. Without tracing out all the ages of man, one recognizes how increased knowledge transforms understanding of how the pieces on the board are perceived. Someone who has played a bit may notice the arrangement of pieces as constituting an end-game. A chess expert may identify that end-game as one concluding a famous match between grand masters. The analogy does at least suggest how the experiences of variously sophisticated movie spectators will differ while they undergo the same process of having their original innocent openness evolve into a sharpening comprehension of ever narrowing possibilities. This progress is congruent with the fundamental paradox that the better we see the characters and appreciate the importance of what happens to them, the more clearly we may apprehend that our improved vision evokes an ultimate uncertainty of feeling and under-standing. Catharsis, the state of mind Aristotle described as produced by the completion of stage tragedy—in John Milton's famous phrasing, "in calm of mind, all passion spent"—is *not* the psychic condition produced in us by most excellent movies. To the contrary, we leave such movies in a state of some emotional turmoil, to a degree frustrated by feelings wrought up but not entirely worked through or resolved. This is one reason why happy endings are so important for run-of-the mill films: it is all too easy for a visual narrative to create frustration—generally regarded as poor box office.

The experience of a movie is constituted of actual visual sensa-tions. We literally see the figure of Zampano embodied by the image on the screen of Anthony Quinn. The visual sensation is as real as seeing the nose on your spouse's face, even though it is a sensation of something pictured. To speak, therefore, of "image" is to open the door to almost as much confusion as using the term "illusion." But some bewilderment may be avoided if we admit that the figure we really see on the screen is "incomplete," is an "unnatural" object of perception. The figure is unnatural not because we see it imaged on a screen, but because it is incapable of reciprocation. We see Zampano, but Zampano does not see us. The strangeness of the movie experience is that we see so distinctly "people" who never have any possibility of seeing us—something that seldom happens in real life. We never look at people without the awareness that they at least *might* look at us. At a movie we don't worry about eye contact. The movie image is of a human figure who cannot even respond to being seen by us. What is true of the character is equally true of every element in a film. In actual life, seeing is intensely interactive, engaging viewers with the living dynamism of their environment. The environment of the movie screen in which we immerse ourselves is not only flat but also nonresponsive. Normal seeing in real life is dynamic discovering in a live environment, one capable of exposing us, even of revealing ourselves to ourselves. And within this vitality of life one encounters the particularized vitality of living creatures, above all people, who respond to being seen. Movie characters are never affected by our seeing them, whereas in real life people are constantly being affected (however subtly) by our looking at them. The physicists' celebrated idea that an observer has an effect on what he observes is one of the commonest experiences of everybody's daily life. Here the obvious contrast between movie and stage drama again become illuminating. Stage actors are keenly aware of being seen, and we in the audience respond to their awareness, even as we know they *might*—but don't—return our looks. At a movie we see (thanks especially to careful lighting arrangements, one of the most important features of variable framing) with unusual clarity and incomparable detail human figures with whom no reciprocity is possible.

The lack of reciprocity, however, enables us to focus our attention on characters and behavioral traits unfamiliar to us in real life or that we would normally avoid. Zampano is not a good man; "Gummy," the Fool's name for him, is apt, for he is a confused person whose accomplishments and ideas are horribly limited. He is not a man of any importance or attractiveness; it is difficult to have any sympathy for him even as a victim of some kind. In no way do the two hours of *La Strada* make us see virtues or attractive qualities in him, but watching him intently compels us to respect simply what he is, his sheer existential being. We see him in such detail and with such lucidness that we come to appreciate his individuality even in his brutal coarseness. The fundamental nature of the movie story assures that we come to know Zampano with a visual intimacy we rarely attain with anyone in real life. The same, of course, happens in a more complex fashion with Gelsomina, but I use Zampano for illustration to highlight the movie's success in establishing so powerfully the visual actuality of so ungifted and so unappetizing a person. Without derogating Anthony Quinn's fine performance, I suggest that the affect of Zampano's existential being is only partly due to skillful acting. It is difficult, of course, to assess movie acting, because so much of each performance is a matter of the actor or actress simply being seen, and that is often the result not merely of the actor's skill but also of the director's, the cameraman's, or a lighting technician's expertise. Much of Quinn's success in *La Strada* lies simply in his appearance, focusing our attention on what may really drive this man so transparently brutish. The strength of Quinn's Zampano is that he appears so vividly to be what he simply is. In real life we seldom look carefully at people (especially unattractive persons). We seldom even have the opportunity to examine in such detail the possible relation of appearance to being as we are compelled to do by this ugly man.

La Strada, in fact, is exemplary of movies' amazing capacity to represent people as visual objects without diminishing their humanness. This capacity (which inevitably reminds us of sculpture) helps to explain why social critique is a tricky business for filmmakers. Had Fellini, for example, emphasized Zampano as a victim of social circumstances (what left-wing critics condemned him for *not* doing), or employed him as a vehicle for *any* programmatic ideology, he would have weakened the baffling idiosyncrasy of his visible being, and thereby the deepest interestingness of a crude, commonplace, conventionally vicious person. This understanding reveals in turn why visual narrative is not hospitable to fantasy. What we regard as "real," of course, is to a major degree conventionally determined. But whatever our particular standard of "reality," we prefer visual storytelling congruent with that standard. We may learn from a movie that to see is not necessarily to understand, but we always want very much to believe that what we see is truly there, even when we recognize "there" as make believe. We very much, and very rightly, wish to trust our eyes. That, paradoxical as it may at first seem, is why we are so untroubled by the knowledge that the movie on the screen is "make believe." We know we are not directly seeing "reality" because we are seeing super-intensely—if only a fabricated narrative artifice. We are enabled by the movie to witness events and interrelations of events we could never in actual life possibly see so precisely in all their unique detail. But to enjoy this experience we must trust our eyes. With that trust (however unsoundly based), our payoff may be tremendous. The *visual* intimacies we attain in seeing the story of

Gelsomina and Zampano is available nowhere except in a movie. We surely do not like Zampano, indeed, in actual life we would probably go to some lengths to avoid him. But there are in fact plenty of Zampanos in the world, who will not disappear just because we don't like encountering them. One reason *La Strada* is a motion picture of enduring power is that, without preaching, it teaches us what the world really looks like if we use our eyes to perceive how much is concealed by our pious clichés about "common humanity."

The final shot of Zampano on the beach is evocatively enigmatic because it is not a still picture. There are movements in the scene; more important, we see not the end of Zampano but a terrible yet passing moment in his life. He will get up and go back on the road. As Fellini wished, his movie never stops moving, even as "Fina" comes on to the screen. The key to the enduring effect of the film (and in this it is exemplary of visual storytelling) is its ongoingness—therefore its title. *La Strada* would falsify itself if it attempted definitive closure. But closure, both local and partial and conclusive of the whole, is always possible for verbal storytelling. Its forward-moving sequences never leave its past entirely behind. That, paradoxically, means that a verbal story can make the pastness of the past definitive. The very evoking in our mind of possibilities concurrently with the representation of what did in fact happen can enforce ultimate recognition that those possibilities will never be realized. And the end of a verbal narrative—however elaborately it may suggest the future—is conclusive of the story told. A verbal story may be retold, but, unlike a movie, it *should* end. This difference in the form of the two kinds of make believe may be illustrated by a contrast of the conclusion of *La Strada* with the almost paradigmatic ending of Tolstoy's last novel, *Hadji Murad*. Hadji falls mortally wounded by Russian bullets.

> He did not move, but still he felt. When Hadji-Aha, who was the first to reach him, struck him on the head with a large dagger, it seemed to Hadji Murad that some one was striking him with a hammer, and he couldn't understand who was doing it, or why. That was his last consciousness of any connection with his body. (Tolstoy, 1912, 288–289)

After Hadji Murad's head is cut off and carried away by the Russians, just before the novel's final sentence, we are told that the nightingales, which had been singing in the brushy covert where Hadji had taken cover and was killed, once more began to sing. This carries the reader's mind back to the moment when Hadji made his fateful decision to escape from the Russians and rejoin his own people. He heard one of his followers singing a ballad of how an earlier Chechen warrior had been killed in a grove where birds sang, and that, in turn, reminded Hadji of a song about himself composed by his mother just after he was born. Later when he was a child at his request she would sing this song to him.

> Thy sword of Damascus-steel tore my white bosom; / But close on it I laid my own little boy; / In my hot-streaming blood him I laved; and the wound / Without herbs or specifics it was soon fully healed. / As I, facing death, remained fearless, so he, / My boy, my *dzhigit*, from all fear shall be free! (Tolstoy, 1912, 260)

The words of this song were directed at Hadji Murad's father. When Hadji Murad was born the wife of his clan leader also gave birth to a son, and she sent for Hadji Murad's mother to be his wet-nurse. When she refused to leave her son, Hadji Murad's father stabbed her with his dagger and would have killed her if she not been taken away from him. Hadji Murad

> remembered how his mother put him to sleep beside her under a cloak, on the roof of their *sáklya*, and how he asked her to let him see the place on her side where the wound had left a scar. Hadji Murad seemed to see his mother before him — not wrinkled, grey-haired, with gaps between her teeth, as he had lately left her, but young, handsome and so strong that she carried him in a basket on her back across the mountains to her father's when he was a heavy five-year-old boy. (Tolstoy, 1912, 260–261)

The evocation of this memory-within-memory from earlier in the novel accentuates Hadji's death as the last act of a long life, which also embodies the "primitive" mode of life the Russians are destroying. Then in his final sentence — "It was of this death that I was reminded by the crushed thistle in the ploughed field." (290) — Tolstoy literally forces our memory back to the paragraph at the novel's beginning in which he introduced Hadji's story by telling of the incident with the thistle which recalled that history to his mind. Effective verbal story-telling may define itself by its intrinsic recursiveness as a "finished" linguistic artifact — even when, as with Tolstoy's story, it emphasizes the eternal continuity of natural life as equally indifferent to humankind's special sufferings and heroic endeavors.

CHAPTER 8

MADAME BOVARY: LINGUISTIC FIGURINGS OF IMAGINATIVE CORRUPTION

The inner life of *La Strada*'s heroine eludes us. The inner life of Emma Bovary is displayed with unmatched completeness, even though that life is constituted largely of mental confusions and inauthentic desires. Readers of Flaubert's novel *share* in Emma's consciousness (as we do not in Gelsomina's), so we too undergo psychic confusions and self-deceptions. We enter into Emma's mental processes not just at special moments but also during the chronic dreariness of her daily life. We even participate in the gradual devolution of her consciousness as she slides into courses leading to ghastly self-destruction. We are appalled by the black liquid that pours from dying Emma's mouth because we have imaginatively been a party to her self-poisoning.

Emma's is not the only consciousness that Flaubert empowers us to share—most notably beyond his narrator's, of course, that of Charles. The reader experiences how the Bovarys' inner lives relate, both by interconnecting and by failing to mesh. This is one reason reading the novel is so totally different an experience from seeing *La Strada*, even though formally both stories adhere to a chronologically linear order of biography. But we respond to Gelsomina's life as a unitary, integral experience, even though a considerable period of time is covered in the film. We register Emma's biography in the rather confused manner in which we understand our own lives, progressing from childhood to full maturity in a continuous-discontinuous fashion, intensities interspersed among routines and diverse patterns intersecting inconsistently, coherent only in an indefinably definite way. Emma's life history extends beyond its literal temporal duration and spatial limitations through her dreams, memories, and fantasies of the future in all their confused convolutions. That history is also entangled with many other lives in *their* different continuities and unpredictabilities. We see Gelsomina's life almost entirely in relation to Zampano's—and briefly The Fool's; all her other relations are transient episodes. We are made to imagine Emma's life as a continuous intersecting of diverse histories.

Flaubert's narrator also tells of Emma's life by means of suggestions of how it appears to others within the novel. We imagine her through others' imaginings of her. Thus we are enabled to conceive of Emma's experience as something more than our or her own perception of it. Because we as readers share her limitations of perception (even while recognizing them as limitations), we are continuously positioned simultaneously to sympathize with her and to pass detached judgments upon her. We neither entirely sympathize with Gelsomina, who always remains "strange," nor feel able adequately to judge her, although we see her with extraordinary vividness and watch her with passionate fascination.

This contrast illustrates the essential historicity of all verbal make believe. Emma's particular difficulties arise from her specific historical in-between-ness. Primary of course is her social position. Coming from peasant stock, she has been educated beyond her original station; in marrying an officer of health (not quite a doctor in our sense), she edges toward the bourgeoisie. Her movement is perhaps most sharply articulated in the scenes of the ball at Vaubyessard, and these scenes in consequence have presented movie adapters with interesting choices. Jacques Chabrol's early 1990s French version (which one disgruntled critic described as produced by a descendant of Monsieur Homais), as much as possible diminishes Emma's role, making her disappear into the encompassing sensual splendor of the aristocratic gathering—a tactic well suited to the film's emphasis on static, painterly scenes foregrounding sumptuous colors and antique-show sets. The 1940s Hollywood adaptation produced by David Selznick to the contrary makes Vaubyessard central to its narrative structure, giving it much screen time and overtly contrasting it with the later "dance of death" at Rouen. This involves some deliberate distortions, especially of Charles' behavior (would any Frenchman ever cry out, "I want to dance with my wife"?) But it takes advantage of the dancing to give visual embodiment to Emma's illusionary self-enchantment. In thus focusing upon her physical experience, however, the film must eliminate (except for the breaking of the windows) the most important moment of her inner experience in the chateau (a moment also deleted by Chabrol).

> The air in the ball room grew heavy; . . . A servant clambering on a chair broke two windowpanes; at the noise of shattering glass, Madame Bovary looked around and saw some peasants with their faces pressed to the window staring in at her from the garden. Memories of Les Bertaux came back to her. She saw the farmhouse, the muddy pond, her father in a smock under the apple trees, and herself in the dairy skimming the cream from the milk cans with her fingers. But among the splendors of the present moment, her past life, so clear in her mind until now, was vanishing, and she was almost unsure that she had lived it. She was here, at the ball; outside the ballroom everything was merely shadowy darkness. (1:8)

There is no way for any moviemaker to capture this fleeting moment of memory that epitomizes Emma's social position as she perceives it, because for the reader her remembered sensations are just as "real" as those of the physical breaking of the glass against which the peasant faces are pressed. We remember with Emma, but we simultaneously recognize the fragility of the artifice that separates her from, but cannot render her invisible to, what she believes (both rightly and wrongly) she has transcended. And this doubleness of our response sets up a possibility for reflexive verbal resonances. Thus at the end of the chapter we are told that the memory of the ball became a preoccupation for Emma.

> Every Wednesday she would say to herself when she awoke, "Ah, A week ago today—two weeks ago—three weeks ago I was there." Little by little the faces blurred in her memory; she forgot the quadrille tunes; she could no longer see the livery and the rooms so clearly; gradually all of the details faded away, but the regret remained. (1:9)

Emma's forgetting is indelibly impressed on the reader's memory by these fading echoes. Exemplary are "the faces blurred" in Emma's memory, because two especially memorable earlier passages focus on faces. The first is the old man eating alone among the women, who bends "over his full platter with a bib knotted in back like a child, gobs of gravy dribbling from his mouth." This is the Duke of Laverdière, "once a favorite of the Count d'Artois" and said to have been a lover of Marie-Antoinette. Now a

> servant behind his chair was shouting into his ear the names of the dishes; the old man, mumbling, would point to one with a trembling

finger. Emma could not help staring at the slack-mouthed old man as someone remarkable, celebrated. He had lived at Court and slept in the bed of queens! (1:8)

Here the distinction between how we and Emma perceive pitilessly exposes her illusionary vision. Shortly after, the male members of the aristocratic family are described through qualities to which we recognize Emma, lacking the narrator's experience, is simply blind.

They had the complexion of wealth, a whiteness skin like the pallor of porcelain, or the glimmer of watered satin, the varnish of fine furniture, flesh that is nourished by exquisitely prepared food. . . . Those who were beginning to age looked youthful and a strange maturity tinged the faces of the young men. The coolness of daily satisfied passions appeared in the indifference of their glances, but their quiet demeanor did not mask an essential brutality arising from easy conquests, handling of thoroughbred horses, and familiarity with fallen women, which exercises the muscles and sates vanity. (1:8)

These comments by the narrator permit us to imagine what we understand Emma does not, a failure of perception for which she pays later with Rodolphe. Illustrated in these passages is how readers are drawn into a make believe consisting of a temporally complicated web of tenuous implications and associations surrounding, paralleling, intersecting with, even contradicting the evolving processes of Emma's mental life in which we share. The "inner life" here portrayed—which is so difficult for visual make believe to display—is not merely that of the novel's characters but also calls upon that of its readers.

The most celebrated and overt form of self-reflexive make believe in *Madame Bovary* is the use of novels within the novel as a key destabilizing force in Emma's life (Peter Gay, 73–109). Novels encourage her commitment to the possibility of an existence totally different, both physically and emotionally, from that into which she was born. Everyone, starting with Flaubert, has condemned Emma's foolish way of choosing and reading novels, yet we continue to read *her* novel with fascination, for, in truth, she reads for some of the same reasons we do. Emma is not the only person who has sought in fiction relief from an unsatisfactory life. But for us as well as her more important than escape is the encouragement of aspirations and wish formulations, however unlikely to be realized. The enduring power of *Madame Bovary* derives in part from its success in stimulating readers through sharing Emma's poor taste and superficial reading habits to improve their capacity for psychologically more profitable novel reading. Aside from escape and aspiration, *Madame Bovary*'s self-reflexivity about reading fiction illuminates the appeal of the distinctive technique we noticed in *Crime and Punishment* called side shadowing (Morson, 1994, 117–174). The first identifier of this rhetorical device was Mikhail Bakhtin, who observed that language is capable of simultaneously evoking, along with imagining of something that actually happened, what *might* have happened but in fact did not. A formalized set piece that suggests why side shadowing is useful to novelists appears in George Eliot's *The Mill on the Floss* when the narrator tells of how Maggie Tulliver's native town of St. Ogg *would* have reacted to her return there as a married woman after she had been carried off by Stephen Guest. In fact, however, she has refused to become Guest's wife out of respect for his commitment to his fiancée Lucy Deane, and the trust in her of the crippled Philip Wakem. She comes back to the town unmarried and morally compromised, and is savagely condemned by the townspeople. But

> if Miss Tulliver, after a month of well-chosen travel, had returned as Mrs. Stephen Guest with a post-marital trousseau . . . public opinion (in these cases always of the feminine gender) . . . would have judged in strict consistency with those results . . . would have seen that two handsome young people . . . having found themselves in a false position, had been led into a course . . . which was highly injudicious, and productive of sad pain and disappointment, especially to that sweet young thing, Miss Deane. Mr. Stephen Guest had certainly not behaved well; but, then, young men were liable to those sudden infatuated attachments; and bad as it might seem in Mrs. Stephen Guest to admit the faintest advances from her cousin's lover (indeed, it *had* been said that she was actually engaged to young Wakem . . .). Still, she was very young—and a deformed young man, you know!—and young Guest so very fascinating; and they say, he positively worships her (to be sure, that can't last!). And he ran away with her in the boat quite against her will—and what could she do? She couldn't have come back then: no one would have spoken to her. And how well that maize-colored satinette suits her complexion. . . . Poor Miss Deane! . . . but, then, there was no positive engagement . . . if young Guest felt no more for her than *that*, it was better for her not to marry him. What a wonderful marriage for a girl like Miss Tulliver—quite romantic—(Eliot, 7:2)

Eliot's elaborate evocation of social attitudes is all in the subjunctive mode, which carries exactly as much imaginative "reality" as her following narration of what "actually" occurred. The passage includes side shadowing within side shadowing ("She couldn't have come back then"), illustrating language's extraordinary ease at involuted configurings. Most fictional side shadowing, however, is woven more unobtrusively into the texture of ongoing narrative, as is always the case in *Madame Bovary*. But in both novels the difference between what happens and what might have happened invariably focuses on ethical judgment. If "might have" is put alongside "was," "should" or "should not" becomes inevitable.

Madame Bovary exemplifies the most common use of side shadowing by nineteenth-century novelists: to dramatize the moral significance of commonplace events of ordinary life. In fact, it is difficult without some form of this technique to narrate interestingly unspectacular events and behavior, especially if habitual. Side shadowing, as Bernstein says, can do justice "to the richness, both humanly and philosophically, of the claims of the ordinary, because it recognizes how various the strands of that ordinariness really are." When made attentive to the intersecting pressures of routine and randomness, as well as to the psychological intricacies in even the least dramatic of our experiences, side shadowing becomes "an indispensable foundation of moral judgment" in the representation of commonplace behavior (Bernstein, 89, 93).

Visual narrative can directly depict only a present moment and only what is visible; it lacks a subjunctive mode and cannot display what might have happened simultaneously with what in fact does happen. Verbal narratives can do all these things, utilizing diverse tenses, modes, and syntactic constructions to facilitate imagining what might but didn't happen. The range of language's "figurative" capabilities has often—ironically—been obscured by critical concentration on metaphor, metonymy, and analogous formal tropes. These are important but specialized features of a fundamental purpose of human language (regularly employed by all speakers in the most everyday, casual discourse): to entertain possibilities. We live always in an environment full of uncertainties in which only a small fraction of what could happen does happen. Our visual perceptive system is splendid for helping us to survive from moment to moment in a Darwinian world. But human language is more useful in foreseeing potential contingencies and in facilitating assessments of past experiences so that we can prepare new means for meeting the exigencies of a dynamic environment—and practice in such mental exercises is one of the pleasures offered by verbal make believe.

Few fictional narratives are as continuously and complexly and provocatively side shadowed as *Madame Bovary*, because the novel treats not only of these processes in their normal functioning but also as becoming exaggerated and distorted. There is scarcely a page that does not present events as occurring amidst possibilities not realized. All it takes is a simple "would have."

> She would have liked to confide all these things to someone. But how do you describe an intangible uneasiness that shifts its shape like a cloud and blows erratically as the wind. Words failed her—as well as opportunities and her courage. If Charles had only suspected, if his eyes had only once penetrated into her mind, it seemed to her that a sudden abundance would have fallen from her heart, as ripe fruit falls from a tree when a hand touches it. (1:7)

Here through a characteristic manipulation of free indirect discourse (is the simile of the tree the narrator's or Emma's?), readers are enabled to enter into Emma's estimate of possibilities and simultaneously to recognize their dubiety. Emma may well be wrong about Charles. What really might have happened had he suspected what is in her mind?

Frequently we are allowed to share more than one consciousness when the awarenesses differ radically, as happens repeatedly with Emma and Rodolphe, later with Emma and Leon, and often with Emma and Charles. A striking instance occurs with the Bovarys' response to the failure of Charles' operation on Hippolyte's club-foot, but equally telling are passages representing chronic behavior, where events fall into a repeated pattern, as in a celebrated passage:

> Meal time was hardest for her to endure in that tiny room on the ground floor, with the smoking stove, the creaking door, the damp walls, and the moist flagstones; all the bitterness of her life seemed served up to her on her plate, and the steam from the boiled beef brought up pulsations of nausea from the depths of her soul. Charles always ate slowly. She would nibble at hazelnuts, or, leaning on her elbow, would entertain herself by tracing lines on the oilcloth with the tip of her knife. (1:9)

The representation of Charles's lack of sensitivity and Emma's repression of her disgust as contrasting negatives appear not as unique events but as recurring discomforts, persistent conditions of repulsion, boredom, frustration. The passage illustrates Flaubert's skill at giving dramatic embodiment to such continuities of ordinary life in which what is terrible is that "nothing happens"—one of the primary foci of nineteenth-century fiction. Side shadowing makes it possible for particularized specific acts—nibbling hazel nuts, drawing with a knife point on oilcloth—to manifest the significance of a behavioral patterning of attitudes, perceptions, and emotions. Entirely distinct and individualized events are presented so they can be imagined *both* in themselves and as constituents of consistency of behavior.

Madame Bovary's concentration on the continuities of ordinary life is characteristic of much nineteenth-century fiction, but runs counter to a strong tendency in contemporary novels, which, influenced by motion pictures, favor singular and more ostentatiously violent actions. Much present-day fiction and criticism assumes that epiphanic events reveal as nothing else can the profoundest truths about human thought and behavior. This conviction that the apocalyptic moment is the prime bearer of the deep truth is connected (as Bernstein has observed) to current faith in the supreme value of personal testimony, a faith reflected in the modern preference for novels given first-person narrative form. Like many novelists of his time, Flaubert was suspicious of the ultimate value of personal testimony and was cautious about depending on first-person narration in verbal make believe. Nineteenth-century novelists by no means avoided the first-person form. But the "autobiographical" mode was uncongenial to free indirect discourse, side shadowing, and the direct sharing with the reader of multiple consciousnesses. It also discouraged the activity of imagination Wolfgang Iser linked to the "wandering viewpoint" as an essential feature of storytelling. Nineteenth-century novelists were not hesitant to build their fictions around subjective accounts of narrators reliable and unreliable—besides *Great Expectations, Jane Eyre*, and *Notes from Underground* may immediately come to mind. But these novelists did not share our contemporary "pervasive myth" of the "absolute authority given to first-person testimony," which implies imagination is incapable of giving meaningful shape "to experiences not autobiographically grounded" (Bernstein, 47). And nineteenth-century novelists were centrally concerned, as today's writers of fiction seldom are, with the significance of transformations in the foundations of ethical behavior from a faith in religion to a faith in "historical" truth.

Although extreme in the unsparingness of its revelations, *Madame Bovary* is exemplary of Flaubert's century in exposing the inaccuracy of most people's judgments about their personal experience, because their evaluations arise from socially nurtured preconceptions in various degrees invalidated by processes of historical change. Charles and Emma are characteristic of their era's fiction in exhibiting how the internalizing of conventional prejudices jeopardizes any attainment of authentic individuality. The vividness of Flaubert's presentation is rarely matched by his contemporaries, but his fundamental theme is familiar in his era: how daily life has become pervaded by prefabricated, one-size-fits-all ideas and aspirations. Emma's private fantasies are appalling because they are not merely clichés but commodified clichés. She projects on Rodolphe and Leon emotions romanticized advertising has persuaded her she should possess, but which she is incapable of feeling. Like many people today, Emma cannot understand "things that didn't manifest themselves in conventional forms" (1:7). This is why Flaubert needed devices such as free indirect discourse and side shadowing. Emma has so thoroughly internalized "approved" (often what now are called "politically correct") modes of thinking and feeling that she is unable to modify herself or her relationships on the basis of the specific realities of her individual being. She is as incapable of genuinely personal experience as Dostoyevsky's Underground Man, but less aware of her incapacity. So, like many of her novelistic peers, she is incapable of learning about herself—as we would now say, she cannot reinvent herself. Like current TV watchers, therefore, she is both bored and boring to others. Most strikingly, she cannot put conventions to use for her personal benefit, as Elizabeth Bennet does, shaping her individuality to accommodate evolving social situations with increased efficacy. Elizabeth is admirable not because she is unconventional, but because she is persistently sensitive to the shifting pressure of convention upon her but equally persistent in attempting to make those forces strengthen her integrity as an individual.

Emma's helplessness against the subversions of true individuality by the mechanisms of industrialized advertising arouses our sympathy: we recognize hers to be an extreme example of a condition threatening us. Flaubert forces us to imagine how Emma's social circumstances make her peculiarly vulnerable. This entrapment within the history of her time and place could scarcely be so disturbing if we heard only Emma telling her own fantasized story. Flaubert's narrator continually provokes in us both dismay and compassion for Emma as a figure victimized as well as self-victimizing, and even exulting in being a victim. We hesitate to condemn this woman from a peasant background offered tantalizing glimpses of a luxurious urbanized life style and of the possibilities of dazzling new kinds of emotional experience, who nonetheless gratuitously destroys not only herself but also her husband and child. Emma's career at every stage is horribly wasteful, yet I think most of us in our hearts wonder: in her circumstances, would I do any better?

This play on readers' likeness to/difference from the heroine (entering into her life even while judging it with self-concerned detachment) to create ethical uncertainties is ever-present in the novel. A typical passage is that in which Emma's early relation to Leon is described.

> The women admired her thriftiness, the patients her courtesy, the poor her charity, but inside she felt a turmoil of envy, rage, and hatred. . . . She was in love with Leon and she longed for solitude to dream about him undisturbed. Even the sight of him upset the voluptuousness of her meditation. . . . the more Emma grew aware of her love, the more she repressed it. She wished Leon would suspect it, and she dreamed of risks, even catastrophes, that would reveal her emotion. What held her back was laziness and fear and also modesty. She thought that she had spurned him too strongly, she had missed her time, lost all opportunity. But pride and the rapture of telling herself, "I am virtuous" and of looking at herself in attitudes of resignation to some degree consoled her for the sacrifice she believed herself to be making. . . . But then fleshly appetites, yearning for money, and the melancholy of unrealized passion combined into pure agony. . . . She was exasperated that Charles was unsuspecting of her suffering. His confidence that he had made her happy seemed a stupid insult to her sensitivities, and his self-satisfaction boorish ingratitude. For whom was she being virtuous? (2:5)

While few readers today have difficulty understanding Emma's psychological turmoil, her concern about virtue may seem old-fashioned, not merely because our verbal make believe is seldom concerned with ethical issues. "Virtue" scarcely appears in present-day make believe about sexual relations. It is, as the first President Bush might say, not a twentieth-century thing. Especially significant is Emma's final question to herself — since traditionally virtue was not for anyone else because it referred to an integrity of self. Emma dramatizes how "virtue" is devolving into present-day "values," the final stage in the amazing transformation from "virtue" as manliness in the Latin *virtú* into the nineteenth-century restriction of the word to female chastity. With the break-up of that narrowly patriarchal limitation, "virtue" has ceased to function as a significant term of practical ethics. How and why virtue was to be replaced by the attenuated and less personally confining terms such as "values" *Madame Bovary* dramatizes with incisive prescience.

Such forecasting has been an attribute (appreciated only in retrospect) of Western European fiction since *Don Quixote*, because verbal make believe, as we've observed with Jane Austen, inevitably entangles itself with ethical standards as historical phenomena. *Madame Bovary* is the first major novel to engage its protagonist in the moral difficulties of a society becoming shaped principally by an advertising mentality. When Leon's presence disturbs Emma's voluptuous meditations about him, we have started down the wintry road toward *Fargo*, where real murders are bothersome because they interrupt TV programs. Most interesting in the passage is the connection it draws between the blurring of Emma's morality and her perception of herself as victimized, a perception that intensifies as the novel progresses and culminates in her suicide. Emma *is* a victim of her sociohistorical situation, which is most destructive in encouraging her through the stimulation of unrealizable fantasies to revel in victimhood. Like anyone exposed to the seductive falsehoods of a society founded on advertising, Emma is handicapped for learning about herself, and in acting for herself, because her conception of herself is largely a commercialized fabrication. Most disastrously, of course, she dramatizes the effects of commodified temptations to indulgence in sensual gratifications for their own sake.

Flaubert's novel demonstrates how commercially fostered daydreams are the opposite of genuine make believe, because they encourage an insidiously antisocial subjectivity. The novel displays not merely the historical circumstances of Emma's life, but the grim historicity of her inauthentic subjectivity. In part this is achieved by the narrative's persistent focusing on the inadequacy of words to articulate the psychological realities they seem to define and describe. It is the concealing of this duplicity that enables advertising's falsifications to evade exposure as outright lying. The most explicit statement of this phenomenon in *Madame Bovary* appears in two celebrated sentences:

> No one can ever express exactly his desires, or conceptions, or sorrows. Human language is like a cracked kettle on which we bang out a tune for a dancing bear, while hoping with our music to move the stars. (2:12)

Characteristically, these apparently objective words are a piece of indirect discourse, for what can be read as the narrator's self-condemnation is delivered through a metaphor implying a critique of its source, Rodolphe's judgment of the falsity of what Emma says. The sentences illustrate the complexities that can be articulated lucidly through free indirect discourse and why it was in various forms central to most nineteenth-century fiction, which, albeit less overtly than *Madame Bovary*, took account of existences permeated by many kinds of commercialized discourse. Figurative language is a prime means for resisting such stultification. A simile or metaphor, for example, in calling attention to the likeness of unlike things necessarily reminds us of its medium, language—which of course does not literally represent what it enables us to imagine. The word "pine" is without cones. Metaphor stimulates us to fill in the gap it makes explicit between an "actuality" told of and a linguistic artifice of the telling. And a novel such as *Madame Bovary* works as a kind of vast metaphor by continually reminding us (here the narrator contributes importantly) that all we read is make believe, that Emma is as much a product of imagining as her wildest flights of fancy.

Excellent novels do not, in Coleridge's misused phrase, provoke mere "suspension of disbelief." Good novel readers are far too actively imaginative for that. Flaubert has "nothing" but words ("mouthfuls of air," as Yeats said) to create his make believe. But by exploiting the potency of words' evocative indeterminateness, he offers readers the opportunity to exercise fully their powers of making believe. In that exercise the forming of judgments becomes inevitable, because all languages (since they are a medium of sociality) possess an intrinsic evaluative valence (Nussbaum, 1990, 5–22). And the success of a novel such as *Madame Bovary* lies in its continuous evocation in its readers of judgmental imagining *not* dependent on any extra-novelistic moral system. Good verbal make believe always exposes its evaluations to imaginative assessments that bring into question their basis, our creation of them. Verbal make believe, instead of merely asserting preexistent and abstract moral patterns, arouses, refines, and deepens our power of evaluating the *systems* by which we have learned to formulate our judgments (Booth, 1988, 7).

One is tempted to regard *Madame Bovary* as a kind of overarching metaphor because Flaubert's novel is so dense with specific judgmental metaphors and similes. Exemplary is the account of Emma's response when she and Charles sit silently, each contemplating the failed operation on the club-foot, and he suddenly exclaims, "Perhaps it was a *valgus.* . . . Emma started as the shock of the statement crashed into her thoughts like a lead bullet into a silver dish" (2:11). The stark violence of the simile intensifies our judgment of its appropriateness, or inappropriateness—the question that every metaphoric formation provokes. Verbal make believe is constituted by such provocations of simultaneous awareness of action told of and the action of telling, dual awareness that demands questioning of the validity of assessments into which we are thus made imaginatively to enter. An equivalent but differently structured and more complicated conceit appears earlier:

> She believed that love should appear abruptly with thunder and lightning—a tornado from the skies throwing life into turmoil, twisting unpredictably, tearing moral resolutions away like leaves, and plunging the heart into an abyss. She never considered that rain forms lakes on house terraces when the gutters are choked up, and she remained ignorantly confident until there suddenly appeared a wet crack in the plaster wall. (2:4)

This is a mini drama of verbalization—a dream of love as meteorological storm collapsing into a homeowner's nightmare—that accentuates the conventionality of Emma's metaphor by contrasting it with the narrator's stunningly original comparison of love to a leaky roof. So violent an exposé of sublime fantasizing forces our attention to the verbal troping itself, which, in turn, sharpens our awareness of how we, not just Emma, tend to think and speak in terms falsified by convention. A subtler instance of this technique appears later when Emma has been more thoroughly corrupted by her indulgences in sensuality.

> The memory of Rodolphe she had buried it at the very bottom of her heart, where it remained more still and solemn than a royal mummy in a subterranean tomb. A fragrance emanated from this profound embalmed love, suffusing with tenderness the atmosphere of immaculate purity in which she thought she lived. (3:14)

Once more the complexity of the comparisons forces readers' awareness out of simple attention to the story into increased consciousness of how the story is being told—what *visual* make believe normally conceals. This awareness, intrinsic to *verbal* storytelling, opens up ironies revealing how Emma's self-misunderstandings are nurtured by her society's celebration of commodified glamour. The "fragrance" emanating from the corpse of a faithless love does indeed define—but as false—the "tenderness" and "purity" of her desires. Flaubert's make believe thus heightens our awareness of how language serves to socialize subjectivity—for good or ill. Specifically, his make believe empowers each of his readers to imagine how so narcissistically antisocial a person as Emma Bovary is a predictable creation in a society purporting to extend to everyone purchasable means for total self-expression. Madame Bovary, c'est moi?

CHAPTER 9

RASHOMON AND WUTHERING HEIGHTS

Madame Bovary exhibits techniques of storytelling inaccessible to creators of movies. A contrast of Akiro Kurosawa's *Rashomon* and Emily Brontë's *Wuthering Heights* will highlight features of visual storytelling beyond the reach of any fiction writer. *Rashomon* and *Wuthering Heights* are narratively opposite. The movie tells the same story over and over; the novel repeats no events, and almost never gives us different perspectives on the same incident. The multiple narrators (sometimes narrating others' narratives) always focus on "new" happenings. The novel, furthermore, treats of decades, although these are recounted within Lockwood's single year of tenancy, a year defined by careful indicators of seasonal change from wintry beginning to autumnal closing. Longer-term familial and social transformations are manifested by both direct comment and seemingly casual references, for example, the gradual physical deterioration of the Gimmerton chapel. *Rashomon* offers us multiple perspectives on a single incident, the whole affair covering only a few days, and the central action taking little more than an hour. The contrast is exemplary: movies normally present a singular, integral experience, whereas novels, frequently treat long periods of time, even generations.

Rashomon, despite critical esteem, and its historical importance in the popularizing of Japanese movies in the West, takes an unusual form that has seldom been imitated. Kurosawa works against the grain of common movie practice by telling his story through semi-repetitive flashbacks and repeatedly forcing viewers to become aware of the positioning of his camera. On this matter of the spectator's "consciousness" of the camera and its angles a Black Sea of ink has been wasted. But analyses of make believe, especially that by David Bordwell and Kendall Walton, have cut through the fuzziness of earlier speculations. And the philosophical studies of Noël Carroll and

Gregory Currie, although they disagree with Walton on some matters, have cleared the way for more sensible evaluations, such as Jerrold Levinson's:

> In experiencing much normal narrative film one standardly and appropriately imagines (a) that one is seeing the events depicted as if from the implied perspective of a given shot, but without necessarily imagining that one is *physically occupying* that position, and also, (b) that *some unspecified means* makes this possible, when physical presence in the scene would be problematic. (73–74)

Levinson's view is supported by the fact that seeing is a mobile activity that adapts swiftly to changes of position (Anderson, 101, 113). Because in using one's eyes one moves along a path of observation, normal vision is a commitment to *no* single point of view. Ordinary seeing is keyed to the probability that what we see now we will see differently as we take the next step, duck our head, blink our eyes—even as the environment within which we see is changing every instant.

These facts account in part for our discomfort watching parts of *Rashomon*. We see well by not paying attention to how we see, as we walk well by not thinking about how we walk. A skillfully manipulated camera (followed by adroit editing) can shift rapidly through a next-to-impossible sequence of viewpoints that doesn't bother us at all. But this easy acceptance prevails only so long as the camera is not "self-consciously" made to draw attention to some peculiarity of its position. As soon as attention is drawn to *how* the camera is being used, interactive reinforcements between sight and cognition are likely to be interrupted. As *Rashomon* itself illustrates, such interruptions may be exploited for impressive effects, but the value of the conventional mode is implied by the paucity of imitations of Kurosawa's venture.

Yet by concentrating our attention, in part through ingenious camera manipulations, on limited and repeated actions, *Rashomon* does succeed as a historical film. Few other movies portraying events from centuries ago make us forget their ancientness. Kurosawa's film absorbs us into the presentness of events long past. Illustrative of this absorption is our ready acceptance of the testimony by the husband's ghost. By the time the medium appears we have become so curious about what happened in the glade that we accept as unhesitatingly as do the people in the film the validity (if not the accuracy) of the medium's articulation of the dead husband's account.

Rashomon presents a series of elaborately staged flashbacks constructed by a multitude of very brief shots. These flashbacks contrast absolutely with scenes in the prison courtyard in which the camera tends to hold to a fixed position, forcing viewers to see longer shots from a single perspective—that of an unseen official. So rigorous is this structuring that when we first watch the film we miss the importance of the *order* of the different accounts of what happened in the glade—not least because the versions are so incompatible. The dramatic contradictions in behavior evoke intense concentration on each flashback in itself. It is only in retrospect that we become aware how different the effects of the stories would be if, for example, the bandit's account came last.

All this careful structuring has contributed to near universal disappointment with the movie's concluding scenes, which have seemed to many simplistic, both formally and morally. After the vagabond steals the abandoned infant's clothes, the woodcutter volunteers to take the child into his overcrowded household, and the priest says that this generous act has restored his faith in human goodness. This conclusion, in fact, sustains the movie's formal structure, which consistently superimposes an evaluative narrative upon a story of violent and uncontrolled impulses—the husband trapped by his greed, the wife and bandit driven by pride and lust. This superimposition is accomplished by contrasts among three radically different visual settings: the Rashomon Gate where the rain continually crashes down in floods, the prison courtyard in which a magistrate examines those involved in the case, a brightly sunlit, bare piece of ground virtually without shadows that appears always from the same angle, and, finally, the forest, especially the glade in which the murder/rape occurs, a tranquil woodland opening of speckled light and shade, rich foliage, loamy earth, a gently flowing stream, silently beautiful (Kaufman, 316–324). The visual force of these absolutely contrasting settings is increased by the limitedness of what happens in each. In the courtyard, participants in the murder/rape are each questioned separately in the same fashion by an always unseen authority within whose position movie spectators are confined. Each witness carries us back into the forest and the interactions of the same three people, while after each of these episodes we return to the other threesome (woodcutter, vagabond, priest) sheltering from the rain at the ruined gate who offer questions about and judgments on the action we have witnessed. It is the visual distinctness and rigid orderliness of this reiterative structure that creates *our* difficulties in arriving at a satisfactory interpretation of events and the judgments on them. *Rashomon*'s form compels us to seek a rational meaning beyond the relativism of differing interpretations—but the meaning offered by the "resolution" of the final scene has seemed woefully inadequate to most critics.

It is notable that the different "versions" of what happened in the glade are only to a minor degree confined within the subjectivity of each teller. In the bandit Tajamuro's account, for example, we do not see solely from his point of view, and in the first report of the woodcutter we see, as he himself could not, for example, the sunlight flashing off the blade of his axe through the tree tops. Each flashback is presented in the conventional manner of movie narrative—so each contrasts most starkly with scenes in the courtyard. Here the camera *is* rigidly confined to the view and position of the invisible examining magistrate. Here spectators are constrained within a single subjective viewpoint. The ironic importance of this disconcerting inflexibility appears in the Kafkaesque result of these "official" courtyard examinations—absolute inconclusiveness, no judgment whatsoever. From the public, official point of view, which the audience has been forced to assume, the events in the glade are not comprehensible nor of any significance. But these are views nobody watching *Rashomon* will accept. The utter meaninglessness of the authoritative position we have been compelled to share is made more painful by the fact that wife, bandit, husband, and woodcutter have each told with the persuasiveness of clear visualizations what each desires to be understood as a "true" account. Each of the contradictory versions seems as possible as the others. From these incommensurate stories we cannot attain any absolutely certain understanding of what happened. That seems to block any decisive moral judgment upon events that cannot, however, be observed with ethical indifference. We the movie spectators have no doubt that something very bad happened in the glade.

This is why the characters at the Rashomon Gate (two of whom are absent from the film's literary sources) with which the movie begins and ends, and whose setting is the only one that changes (the torrential rain at the end clears off as the sun emerges), are essential to the film's ethical purposes. Their *verbal* comments, like the accounts of the participants, offer no definitive interpretive solution to the puzzles of the killing and rape. But the *behavior* of the three at the gate *visually embodies* definite moral responses. The vagabond, who throughout shows a shrewd, practical and hedonistic cynicism (he tears wood from the sheltering gate for a fire to warm himself), responds to the tellings by stealing the clothing of an abandoned infant. The woodcutter, who has been identified as both a thief and liar, picks up the naked infant to shelter it in his overpopulated family. The priest who has throughout been paralytically bewildered and depressed responds to the woodcutter's act by asserting that it has restored his faith in the goodness of human beings. The movie thus concludes with acts of moral behavior from which the audience may derive meanings that have nothing directly to do with the question of which of protagonists of the glade drama, if any, told the full truth. But that the woodcutter has been shown to be a thief and liar may remind us that many humane and decent acts, such as saving a baby, are performed by unattractive, even repulsive, people. On the opposite side, without condoning what the brutal vagabond does, we may find his actions understandable, and certainly in no way—alas—uncommon. One doesn't like him, but he does seem more intelligent than either priest or woodcutter. It is he, after all, who exposes the woodcutter's lie, and even his fire-building suggests a not entirely despicable activeness that contrasts favorably against the paralysis of priest and woodcutter—a paralysis broken only by the vagabond tearing the clothes from the abandoned infant, rather as he tore wood from the gate. The distinction is emphasized by the others' exaggeratedly passive and despairing attitudes when they first appear; the woodcutter may be feeling guilt, but the priest seems little better than a pious fool who is the spiritual equivalent to the silent, invisible secular magistrate. This is, indeed, why his final remark is troubling; we don't want this "official" to speak for us, yet after seeing the violations of elemental morality in the glade we want very much to be able to believe in human goodness.

Any honest person must have doubts about so believing in the light of how people often act, egregious instances of which *Rashomon* displays sensationally, so it is unnerving to be reminded that selfish and deceitful people do sometimes act generously. But the behavior of the priest and woodcutter echoes earlier ambivalences: we may be repelled by the bandit, the wife, and the husband, but each has exhibited qualities that are not unadmirable. Virtually every event in the movie blocks both easy sympathy and easy condemnation. All of this has made us literally see how often we desperately seek to justify what we ourselves regard as bad motives and bad behavior, our desperation suggesting that we may not be so despicable as our actions make us appear. Perhaps what the priest finally learns—not from what people say but from what they do—is that the strangest of human hypocrisies is how effectively we conceal our better selves—even from ourselves.

What we learn from *Rashomon* is not what any official doctrine can teach us, and the lesson is taught by its absolute lucidity—even of definitively uninterpretable events. The continuous movements on every plane from the moral to the physical are never blurry. In none of his films does Kurosawa exhibit more consistently his innovative skill in rapidly changing camera movement, lighting, and editing in so many diversely subtle ways (technical achievements that have rightly attracted the detailed admiration of critics (Ritchie, Goodwin)) to reveal unmistakably the difficulties in comprehending human behavior. All our interpreting evoked by the uncertainties of what happened in the forest glade, the diverse evaluations at the ruined, rain-drenched gate, and through the fruitless interrogations in barren but brilliantly lighted prison courtyard result from our intense scrutiny evoked by the film's limpid visual inventiveness. We never identify with any of the characters, because we are made to witness their behaviors with the exactness of almost scientific objectivity. The one "identification" that is enforced, our confinement to the magistrate's position, we resist. And everything we need to see to interpret could not be more distinctly delineated. It is difficult visually to represent an ambiguity directly, but *Rashomon* beautifully displays how effective a movie may be in revealing an intrinsic ambiguousness of human actions because they are human. The repeated returns to identical scenes appeal to (while in fact frustrating) our instinctive desire to *see* correctly and so to look again and again until we see accurately. The dubiousness not merely of intention but of actual behavior of our fellow creatures has never been visually embodied more unmistakably.

Rashomon exhibits another fundamental power of visual story-telling: its capacity to depict the minutest of actions contextualized within the totality of a natural environment. A characteristic instance occurs at the beginning of the bandit's testimony, when the officer next to the bandit volubly describes his capture of this Tajamuro, who has not yet spoken and whom we are seeing for the first time (bound like the samurai he captured). As the officer speaks with eager egoism to the invisible magistrate, there is a quick close-up shot, as if the magistrate had glanced his way, of the bandit squinting silently up at the sky across which high-massed storm clouds are moving (carrying the rain we see at the Gate?). For the moment he seems indifferent to the officer's voice we continue to hear. The intriguing doubtfulness of this minute action is provoked by its presentation beneath the vastness of the sky. It is no accident that there are no interior scenes in Kurosawa's *Rashomon*, even though the most powerful segment of his source story takes place in a dark room inside the Rashomon Gate. The film, however, shows us only the tattered outside of the gate, even as the magistrate's interrogations take place outside the prison. Movies can effectively show interiors, even very dark ones. But movies possess the unique capability of displaying even the most inconsequential behavior amid the boundless surrounding ambience of natural light, the fundamental condition of all visual experience. In doing this they may endow trivial acts with a significance that can be bestowed by no other art form.

All of *Rashomon* takes place out of doors, but almost all of the action of *Wuthering Heights* occurs inside houses. The contrast is neatly if ironically dramatized by the movie adaptation of 1940 directed by William Wyler, which did much to establish Laurence Olivier as a star: on its first release it was seen by over 200 million people. Much of this movie emphasizes the moors—showing far more of them (and Catherine and Heathcliff on them) than the novel tells us. This "infidelity" is entirely appropriate for a translation of novel into movie, and much of the film's effectiveness derives from the transposition into the spectacularly visible of what is sparingly described in the novel. The movie also shows much of Heathcliff and Catherine as children. It softens the novel's violence and brutality (we don't see Hareton hanging puppies), and it cleans up both Joseph's appearance and his Yorkshire dialect, part of the denaturing of Emily Brontë's Dostoyevskian religious critique of her society. It reduces the complexities of Catherine and Heathcliff's love to an unambiguous romance. But the extended depiction of the protagonists as children, while it subverts the novel's challenge to accepted conventions of gender, and even fears of incest, is not an unreasonable decision, if one grants the moviemakers' right to create a movie with mass popular appeal.

The key to the adaptation is Pennistone Crag, the scene of a famous promotional still of Olivier together with Merle Oberon. In the book, the crag is trivial. But the central movie scene of the childhood of Catherine and Heathcliff focuses on this outdoor site, where Catherine urges Heathcliff to play the part of a noble knight slaying a dangerous enemy to save her, casting herself in the role of a conventionally helpless princess (Stoneman, 1996, 132–133). The movie thus affirms the most traditional social gendering, whereas much of the fascination of the novel arises from its revelations of frightening ambiguities at the heart of such conventions—as in Catherine's "betraying" Heathcliff by marrying Linton. This rather selfish woman wants to have both men. She rejects the idea that marrying Linton needs to shut her off from Heathcliff. That is why she accuses *both* men of killing her. The movie's utter conventionality sets into bold relief how Brontë attacked fundamental social attitudes toward gender without reducing Catherine to a mere victim of a stereotypical oppressive masculinity. The question in the novel of why in fact Catherine marries Linton is not easily answered. When Heathcliff asks, "Why did you betray your own heart, Cathy?" (Chapter 15), he implies that she has truly loved only him, that no essential part of her could have been attracted to Linton. But Catherine is not that simple: she loves Heathcliff, but is also attracted to Linton. Heathcliff later accuses her of killing herself, and it is true that her death is in a significant fashion suicide. Yet she is not unjustified in accusing both Heathcliff and Linton of driving her to self-destruction. Like Lamia in Keats's poem (which Brontë knew), Catherine is destroyed by two men who insist on treating her protean dualities of feeling as stereotypical "female duplicity."

The movie weakens Catherine's poignant emotional uncertainty by portraying the foundation of Catherine and Heathcliff's passion in their unambiguously joyous experience as children on the moor. The movie displays explicitly and unambiguously what the novel carefully keeps obscure and doubtful. The novel forces us to speculate on their doings through hints and tangential references, as when Catherine recalls Heathcliff building a cage over a nest of young birds so their parents cannot feed them and they will starve. Had the film shown this pretty piece of playfulness, it would have destroyed its representation of Heathcliff and Catherine's love as conventionally pure. Yet unless the movie is radically to transform the novel by eliminating the protagonists' early experiences together, it must *display* Catherine and Heathcliff's childhood, for much the same reason that a movie of *Pride and Prejudice* must show the wallpaper in the room where Darcy first proposes to Elizabeth. Buñels' adaptation of Brontë's novel, *Abyss of Passion*, does eliminate the childhood experiences, one result being a film more melodramatically romantic than Wyler's picture. But Wyler in *showing* inevitably falsifies the childhood experiences, because the novel makes them obscure, offering only tantalizing hints evocative of the mysteriousness of the children's relations and thereby endowing them with an aura of strange dangerousness.

When Heathcliff tells Nelly about his race with Catherine to Thrushcross Grange, he reports Catherine was beaten because she lost one of her shoes. Beyond its implication of how they behaved on the moors, the detail also suggests that Heathcliff regarded Catherine as nearly his equal as a runner. More than posing a challenge to conventional gender distinctions, the casual reference supports the blunt diagnosis of Dr. Keith later in the novel that only some psychological trauma can explain the physical decline of such a "stout, hearty lass" as Catherine. This arouses readers' suspicions that her early relationship to Heathcliff was in some way "unhealthy." Any moviemaker might reasonably decide such subtle allusiveness to be inappropriate for his medium and aim for an adaptation at the least true to the novel's impassioned love story. *Honi y soit qui mal y pense.*

More problematic is Wyler's evasion of Brontë's honest presentation of savage physical and emotional brutalities as a commonplace features of domestic life. Brontë, to be sure, is truthful in a way few moviemakers are—as Peter Ranier observed, "for all their smoking shotguns and crimson-drenched samurai swords, Quentin Tarantino's epics of mayhem tell us nothing about real violence" (64–65). There are no exotic, romantic adventures in Brontë's *Wuthering Heights*; the beatings and bloodlettings, the emotional torturings, humiliations, and unmitigated sadism usually take place in bedrooms, parlors, and kitchens. This is the foundation for the novel's fearful invitation to imagine how the most wonderful experience a human being can have, passionately loving another, may be inseparable from hatred and destructiveness as commonplaces of domestic life. Catherine's assertion, "Nelly, I *am* Heathcliff" (with its complementary, "he's more myself than I am") is famous because it articulates what many who have been deeply in love have felt, yet it is also pathological. Catherine's and Heathcliff's "great" love may be most exemplary in that it destroys them (and others) to no positive result whatsoever. Their love may be sterile exactly because it truly is love. Heathcliff digging up Catherine's decomposing corpse so as to be sure his dead body in disintegrating will mingle with hers deliberately indulges in sensationalistic Gothic spookery to dramatize the possibility that genuine love may also be genuinely morbid. Sex, after all, is Mother Nature's way of assuring a continuous supply of decomposing bodies.

Our fascination with Catherine and Heathcliff is empowered by fear. They reveal a truth we'd prefer not to face up to, that emotions are always dangerously contradictory, and the stronger the more dangerous. This is the kind of truth that language can precisely articulate, both intellectually and emotionally, because of its self-reflexive power. Language can undermine itself, mystify even while enlightening, but it can also disperse its mystifications to uncover clear understanding of what we shrink from admitting. This self-subverting/self-reconstituting potency of language is fundamental to "ironic intensifications of parody that are designed to discredit a literary . . . genre" (Morson, 1989, 69). Morson's concept of intensified parody derives from Bakhtin's definition of the parody of "hidden polemic." In this mode

> every statement about the [referential] object is constructed in such a way that . . . a polemical blow is struck at the [parodied] other's discourse on the same theme. . . . The [parodied] other's discourse is not reproduced, it is merely implied. (Bakhtin, 1984, 195)

In Brontë's novel, familiar features of Gothic fiction are deployed so that their conventionalized strangeness, violence, and fearfulness highlight by contrast the real savageries of commonplace life in a civilization that has lost its ethical coherence (Sedgewick, MacAndrew). Gothic novels, beginning with Horace Walpole's *Castle of Otranto* and continuing to this day in works by such best-selling writers as Stephen King, exploit the shadowy space of unreality that appears with the waning of authentic belief in the distinction between the natural and the supernatural fundamental to the Judeo-Christian religious tradition. What had been supernatural blurs into superstitiousness, vague feelings of pseudo-belief lacking both accepted theological-philosophical foundation and the support of accepted social practices. Without these bases the hyped-up preternatural events characteristic of Gothic fiction (and Gothic films), such as the return of the dead, haunting by spirits, vampirism, and the like, are morally meaningless. Brontë utilizes such Gothic elements parodically to sharpen her polemic against the deterioration of genuine religiosity in her probable readers. "Spirituality" in *Wuthering Heights* consists in self-indulgent fantasies of superstition (this spectrum extending from Nelly's debased folk beliefs to Lockwood's fashionable *faux* orthodoxy) or the self-righteous fundamentalism of Joseph. The novel in effect demonstrates that a society in which Gothic fiction flourishes lacks the moral strength to resist raw economic aggressiveness manifest in Heathcliff, and implicit in Lockwood, who is "a product and beneficiary of the social structure that justifies the oppression and abuse at the Heights" (Jacobs, 80). "Gothicized" society is simultaneously ineffective at silencing the fanatical fundamentalist pseudo-religiosity expressed by Joseph.

Wuthering Heights thus exemplifies verbal storytelling's power to use ironic/parodic modes to critique the very forms of its own creativity (which is why so many novelists, from Cervantes to Hemingway, have begun their careers with satire). This productive deconstructiveness is possible because language (unlike other semi-otic systems) is an internally open system (DePryck, 97–103): its structures are defined by no external constraints (save the capabili-ties of the larynx)—one reason there have been so many human lan-guages, all equally effective. One of language's major functions is to *create* contradictions, thereby forming a basis for reconstituting its own systems of articulation, definition, and representation. The paradox of the Cretan who tells you "All Cretans are liars," for exam-ple, can be productively transformed by putting the last word in quotation marks. Language may present us with irreconcilable incon-sistencies revealing a deficiency in its own explanatory effectiveness, which it then "repairs" by constructing out of the defect an improved capability. *Verbal make believe is a primary tool by which humans self-reconstruct mental processes that are proving inadequate to emotional, intellectual, or practical needs and aspirations.*

Nowhere is the mind's self-reconstructive power more subtly exer-cised than in imaginative storytelling. Consider, for example, the tiny but revealing way language facilitates self-mystification in *Wuthering Heights* when Edgar Linton addresses his daughter as Cathy, because he called her mother Catherine—since his enemy Heathcliff addressed the older Catherine as Cathy. A more significant exemplifi-cation of language simultaneously concealing and revealing the inter-play of conscious and unconscious purposes occurs in Lockwood's account of his terrible dream near the novel's beginning (Shannon; Jacobs, 63). He tells of the familiar experience in which one simulta-neously dreams and is conscious of dreaming. Aware, because of his former dream, that the sound now troubling him in his current dream is that of an actual fir branch striking the window, Lockwood dreams that he breaks the glass of the window to stop the branch's banging, and when he thrusts his arm through the opening, his hand is seized by the tiny cold hand of "Catherine Linton." This deftly evokes our imagining of the systematic illogicality of dreaming—from the breaking of the glass to reach a fir branch to the paradoxical identifi-cation of the spirit as "Catherine Linton" the mother who never was "Linton" as a child and the daughter who is now the widow Catherine Heathcliff. By stimulating our imagination into conceiving how our consciousness engages with contradictions, language encourages us to enter into make believe of self-conflicting psychic processes, even into feelings that in real life would horrify us. Lockwood tells us, for example, that unable to persuade the weird child to release his hand, he dragged its wrist back and forth over the broken glass until its blood soaked his bedclothes. Actual sight of this hideous act would prompt us to distance ourselves from it: we would perceive the brutality as Lockwood's, not ours. Language, however, invites us imaginatively to join in Lockwood's unconscious-consciousness; in imagining ourselves as Lockwood dreaming of committing the terrible act we encounter the brutality concealed within our civilized intelligence.

A verbal account of a dream, moreover, enables us to imagine the physical *unreality* of its images. Language alone, as Freud so well understood, permits the most private subjective experience to enter into the public domain, to be communicated, to be entered into by another. Freud could claim special efficacy for his "talking cure" because human language depends on reciprocity between community and individual. As Saussure insisted, only the former assures the existence of a linguistic system as a continuing competence available to every individual and making possible collaborative thought and action. But language is only realized through specific utterances by individuals. And of course these subjective articulations possess a potential for modifying the common language. These features of language explain the radical difference between linguistic and visual "imagery." The representation we see in a photograph, a painting, or a movie is truly an image, something literally seen, what psychologists call a percept. When we read a novel the only percepts we encounter are the black marks of endlessly repeated letters and often repeated words. The word "pine" is not sixty feet tall, and can mean very different things, some having nothing to do with needles or cones. The visual image, to the contrary, is constrained by its particularity. The more sharply distinct a visual image, the less it is like any other percept. Contrarily, the uniqueness of any verbal utterance inescapably carries within it traces of previous, even quite different, uses of the same sound/script percepts: when we read of a lover who "pines" connotations of the irrelevant tree may slide into our mind, and the genius of a superior writer appears most distinctly in her ability productively to manipulate these inevitable "contaminations."

Every sight we see, contrarily, is a new sight, and one sight is always immediately superseded by another. Audial perception is blurrier, because our ears pick up sound waves that are radiating in every direction. We do not focus our hearing as we focus our sight

(Carpenter, 67). Verbal narrative, written or spoken, makes use of the "overlapping" qualities of language-sounds to create meaningful structures of "self-allusiveness," the persistence in the present word of traces of its previous contexts. A good analogy is the way that music organizes remembrances of note patternings of what we *have* heard while introducing new arrangements. Although we certainly do remember vivid sights, these are memorable for their singularity. One of language's prime values is the power of continuous self-allusion that establishes a coherence of associations and connections (some of these conflictual) between what may be utterly unlike. Language most persistently evokes imagining of the current relevance of what we recognize as past. Nineteenth-century novelists were especially concerned with this special capability of language, as is broadly illustrated by their fondness for "historical novels." Their focus is most significantly displayed by their attention to the historicity of subjective experience, as is apparent in *Wuthering Heights*. That such concentration upon the historical dimensions of subjectivity is contrary to a basic orientation of visual narrative is suggested by its absence from so brilliant a historical reconstruction as *Rashomon*.

Emphasis upon the historicity of subjective experience in *Wuthering Heights* explains our mistaken remembrance that the novel lavishly describes the natural world, particularly its stormier aspects. In fact there are no extended descriptions of natural phenomena (like those in the fiction of Thomas Hardy or D. H. Lawrence), and as many of the passing references to natural phenomena allude to calm, bright, lovely conditions as to those that are "wuthering." That a novel consisting chiefly of talk between people inside houses could produce such mistaken memories of itself illustrates Brontë's success at enabling readers to enter into the subjective histories of violently emotional characters whose psyches have been shaped by life in a harsh environment. Her achievement is, *mutatis mutandis*, representative of most successful novelistic narrative—even Hardy and Lawrence don't provide their readers with literally sensory images—as any second-rate movie can.

Wuthering Heights's evocations of subjective continuities is intensified by the artifice of different people telling different parts of the story. We do not *see* from different people's perspectives so much as we *hear* Lockwood, Nellie, Catherine, and the rest tell us about specific feelings or events that we hear about from no one else. Most frequently we imagine these characters addressing other characters. As there is no author in the novel, there can be no directly addressed reader. Emily, unlike her sister Charlotte, never speaks *to* her audience: she cannot because she does not exist "in" her novel. As with Shakespeare, we hear only her imagined characters speaking to other characters (or Lockwood writing). Brontë's elimination of both the third- and first-person narrator is not idiosyncratic (novels in letters, such as Richardson's operate in the same fashion) but it highlights the single most distinctive feature of all novelistic "dialogue." We do not in reading a novel, as we would at a play or movie, literally hear the characters speak (or *watch* others listening). Reading a novel we imagine characters speaking and listening. The very obviousness of the difference I have already discussed may conceal its profound significance, so I repeat. When a character in a novel "speaks," readers share imaginatively in the speaking. Readers do not simply listen to what the character says, as spectators at a play or movie do. Reading a novel, we imagine a character's speech both as that of another individual and also as an utterance in which we somehow participate in articulating. This imagining ourselves both uttering and hearing explains why so often conversation in novels that appears to be dramatically effective falls flat when transferred verbatim to a stage or film adaptation. Because *Wuthering Heights* is entirely "dialogic," including long accounts (especially by Nelly and Lockwood) that contain reports of extended tellings by others, it illustrates with especial clarity this distinguishing feature of verbal storytelling. When in Chapter 17, for example, Isabella shortly after Catherine's funeral bursts in upon Nelly (with a casual Brontëan reference to blood pouring from her ear slashed open by Heathcliff's knife), as soon as she begins to tell of the events at Wuthering Heights, we as readers not only imaginatively hear Isabella as she speaks to Nelly but we also begin to imagine her speaking—we enter into her vocalization. This participation in speaking is a cause for our ability to distinguish subtle changes in tonality and vocabulary used by the characters (with the important exception of Joseph) to different addressees, as when Heathcliff, for an obvious instance, speaks to Nelly rather than to Catherine.

Even Lockwood's ruminative self-misinterpretations, thinking he desires a solitary life and is possessed of unusual insight into human feelings, tend to make us silent partners in his pretentious misunderstandings. In this case there is a special edge to the imagining Brontë evokes, the cause of many of her first readers' distaste for the novel: the conventionally skeptical Lockwood "suffers from the inanity his author attributes to the average London reader into whose hands her book will fall" (Woodring, 303). The confusions confronting Lockwood and readers beginning the novel, of course, are daunting, since he and we suddenly encounter, along with snarling dogs, a pile of dead rabbits and a Hareton Earnshaw two centuries after his name was inscribed over the door, a "second" Catherine before we are told about a first, a woman with the unusual name of Mrs. Heathcliff who is not married to the only living Mr. Heathcliff. These "confusions" offer a wonderful illustration of why a second reading may be more rewarding than a first. When we begin to reread *Wuthering Heights*, because we now understand the full implications of Lockwood's blunders and who Cathy is, we can appreciate, as we are unlikely to on first reading, the significance of the "failed" repetitions represented by the baffling nomenclature. And now we register the full significance of Heathcliff's first speech, responding to Lockwood's babbling apology, " 'Thrushcross Grange is my own, sir,' he interrupted, wincing." Not only does the claim call up for the *re*reader memory of the painful and morally unsavory fashion in which Heathcliff gained possession of the Grange, but the word "wincing" carries a considerable load of ambiguous connotation. Perhaps Heathcliff is only offended by Lockwood's pomposity, but he may also wince at the memory of a deeper pain—a sense of guilt for how he acquired the Grange, or for the loss of Catherine that made the acquisition possible. On rereadings we adapt our original acts of discovery to a deepened and more nuanced evaluating of the words we reencounter—for example, in what the second Catherine says in this opening scene. We understand more clearly the terrible position from which she speaks at Wuthering Heights when Lockwood arrives: there is literally no one for her to address meaningfully. This awareness complicates our understanding of the significance of the first Catherine writing from an analogous yet different isolation, one mitigated solely by Heathcliff, the subsequent silencer of her daughter. Catherine must write to herself or an unknown reader because there is no one around her to whom she can address her feelings about and experiences of Heathcliff. That *he* cannot be her addressee helps to define the strangeness of their emotional partnership, which a rereader recognizes as inversely refracted through bizarre relations between him and the second Catherine. These understandings, of course, are facilitated by the rereader's intensified recognition of Lockwood's dubiousness as a reporter. His unreliability becomes more intriguing because we understand more completely the implications of his obtuseness. His blindness on second reading seem less personal deficiency than necessary features of his social circumstances (idle urban buyer of titillating fiction) and his economic position, beneficiary of an economic system that sustains the power of brutal oppressions exercised more overtly by both Hindley and Heathcliff at Wuthering Heights (Eagleton, 99–109). Like all superior verbal make believe, Brontë's story is shaped by the densest possible self-reflexive referencing that assures increased effectiveness with each return of a reader to the unchanged text.

This enhancement of returning to the novel at another time reflects how verbal make believe facilitates our experiencing of different modes of time's passage. Not all verbal narratives encompass such long spans of time and such intricacies of "historical" accounts as *Wuthering Heights*, yet all evoke imagining of temporal processes, if only by telling of events put into the past by the telling. The variety of narrators in Brontë's fiction and the extension of the story across two generations permit continuous cross-cuttings of natural and cultural temporality. Despite Catherine's hyperbolic contrast of her love for Linton as an oak in a flower pot to her affection for Heathcliff as eternal as rocks beneath the turf, her relations with Heathcliff alter almost as radically as her relations with Linton. In her first encounter with Heathcliff she spits on him. There is nothing static in all of *Wuthering Heights*, which demands that we imagine every kind of experience, personal and social, as constituted of transitional processes.

And by continuing her story into a second generation Brontë adds depth to the interplay of subjective and social transformations to make the love-hate relation of Heathcliff and Catherine meaningful beyond the Hollywood version's "timeless" romance. Catherine dies, but Heathcliff lives on developing revengeful feelings nurtured by her loss, forcing young Catherine into a marriage with his physically feeble and morally debased son, all the while trying to brutalize Hareton. But gradually Heathcliff loses not his desire for revenge but the capacity to act on his desire. Representation of this change is one of Brontë's impressive accomplishments, for it is (to my knowledge) a unique dramatization of an intrinsic self-destructiveness in revengeful feelings. As Heathcliff's power over Hareton and Catherine weakens, they fall in love, and the novel ends with them apparently destined for a happy marriage. There have been, and perhaps there must be, two antithetical responses to this second love story. Some readers regard it as exposing the feebleness of conventional romance, which by its triteness and sentimental character makes more vivid the "true" power of the Heathcliff-Catherine love. Others see it as a recovery from the pathological extremism of the older couple, a reestablishing of social stability that permits a productive exercise of affections. Both responses possess validity. Cathy's forced marriage to the wretched Linton Heathcliff is in some respects the most vicious portion of the novel, including as it does the first explicit representation in fiction of a man physically beating a young girl. Yet in a sense Cathy defeats Heathcliff by yielding to his demands, because she makes a relatively unselfish moral choice. Her partner Hareton's moral strength emerges in his refusal to condemn Heathcliff who would brutalize him. Hareton resists sinking to the self-destructive revengefulness that was Heathcliff's response to identical treatment. Young Cathy and Hareton thus seem morally superior to their elders. Yet indubitably they are less compelling figures—every reader's imagination is seized more powerfully by Heathcliff and Catherine. The younger pair embody a generational dimension of the continuous processes of change of all kinds that characterize every aspect of the world portrayed in *Wuthering Heights*—and make it seem compellingly true to normal experience, despite the extremism of many actions and emotions in it.

Its doubled romances magnify to the macrolevel of plot the recollective quality by which words, phrases, sentences and finally episodes in the novel continuously suggest complex relationships to what we have read before. Brontë's artful naming I have already pointed to, and it is further exemplified in the contradictory connotations of Linton Heathcliff. All her naming reminiscences contain within themselves differences. The "Hareton Earnshaw" written over the door to Wuthering Heights is ironic until the living Hareton Earnshaw finally learns to read that name. That the latter *learns* to read illustrates how so often characters, despite psychological fixations and persistent sociological oppressions, change significantly— Heathcliff perhaps most obviously, but also Catherines, Hareton, Hindley, Isabella, and even Nelly. The contrastive exception is Joseph, present from the very beginning to the very end, incapable of tempering his Yorkshire dialect or the self-righteousness with which he criticizes and complains about everything and everyone. His atrocious dialect perfectly embodies the sterile aggressiveness of a rigid fundamentalism unwittingly nurtured by a society that has lost the capacity for genuine spiritual experience. Dialect which, starting with Sir Walter Scott's novels, played a major role in nineteenth-century fiction progressively diminishes in twentieth-century fiction. The diminishment reflects the homogenizing of verbal intercourse characteristic of modern life. For the nineteenth-century novelist, dialect was useful as simultaneously giving imaginative form to a character's personal idiosyncrasy and to his regional, class, or occupational and social circumstances. And of course dialect imperiously called readers' attention to the peculiarities of the very language evoking their imaginings. Beyond the obviousness by which dialect may differentiate one character from others, dialect's awkwardness in written form forces us to think about the "artifice" of our reading what is spoken, bringing to consciousness the strange way in which we imaginatively "hear" words not sounded but printed.

It would be interesting, but beyond the scope of this study, to pursue the contrast offered by movies in their treatment of dialect, starting with the observation that, perhaps even more than modern novels, films have usually avoided heavy use of dialect. Silent movies, of course, had little choice, and people making movies with sound tracks don't wish to diminish the size of potential audiences by introducing incomprehensible speech—dialect usually seeming not eligible for subtitles. But formal issues should not obscure how in *Wuthering Heights* Joseph and his dialect force upon readers' attention to the significance of his religious fanaticism, for virtually all his speeches are fundamentalist tirades. Finally, a definitive analysis of make believe—verbal or visual—ought to confront the relation of the beliefs created by imagining, whether associative or conjectural, to the imaginative beliefs which we call spiritual. I suspect that any venture into this uncharted territory will find Brontë's *Wuthering Heights* and the novels of Dostoyevsky equally rewarding, for these are the two great novelists most concerned with the relations between religious experience and make believe.

Chapter 10

Form in Visual Storytelling: Buster Keaton's *The General*

otion pictures instantaneously seize our attention—even stupid films possess something of this tyrannical power. It is more difficult *not* to look at a movie than at still photographs or paintings. The compulsion exercised by seeing movement irresistibly attracts us into watching a visual story. Usually it takes longer for us to be drawn into a verbal narrative. Oral storytellers tend to begin with leisurely introductions, gradually securing our interest. Even stories by skillful writers of thrillers employing a dramatic "hook"—*The threatening letter came Monday; on Wednesday the bomb itself arrived*—soon slide into slower exposition. The difference reveals visual make believe to be less personally threatening. The visual catches our attention, yet allows us to remain essentially "objective" viewers. Verbal make believe by entering into our imagination is likely to arouse, along with interest and curiosity, some anxiety. If this is inadequately allayed, a reader will be hesitant to enter into the story (Lesser, 46–48). Verbal storytelling tends to begin cautiously, because it may so hugely magnify the psychic tension-building Freud identified as the essence of verbal jokes. A visual joke, especially slapstick, carries less personal threat—we see it happening to somebody else.

The most popular form of silent films was slapstick comedy. Slapstick requires no speech, which made it perfect for film audiences everywhere in the world—thus habituating movie producers to immense profits. But effective slapstick demands careful planning, precise timing, and total bodily control—in all of which Chaplin and Keaton excelled. They knew we don't laugh when granny slips on a grapefruit rind in the kitchen and shatters her hip. We do laugh when in *The General* Johnny Gray (Keaton) grandiosely directs an artillery crew's cannonading by flourishing a sword whose blade keeps flying off its hilt, while a hidden enemy sharpshooter methodically shoots dead three of Johnny's artillerymen, then is himself killed when Gray's flying sword fortuitously skewers him. We laugh merrily seeing four people murdered, because we care nothing about the three anonymous Confederates and the Union sniper.

We also laugh because Johnny Gray is *not* killed, and we have come to care about him. We are sympathetic to him, we root for him. But *about, to, for* reveal how far we are from "identifying" with him. Because we do not see ourselves *as* Johnny we can laugh at his bewilderment as his artillerymen drop dead, and we can wholeheartedly cheer *for* him, following his adventures with an unrestrained emotional bias in his favor, rather as we invest our feelings in the fortunes of our favorite football team. This highly emotionalized nonidentification reinforces the unique potency of movies to make story line and line-of-visual-action coincide, for plot to *be* the sequentiality of activities of the characters we watch—although few films attain the near perfect fit of plot to action as *The General*. The coincidence is achieved in good measure by exploiting the limitations imposed by a train chase, in which the course of evasion and pursuit are confined to fixed tracks, and so are physically formalized. Almost every event in *The General* is constituted of counteractive movements, from the overarching *mise-en-scène* of the Civil War, through the fundamental story, pursuit of the stolen locomotive north, escape in the restolen locomotive south, down to the minutest details, such as putting on or taking off the "correct" uniforms. Continual backward and forward movements of the trains are persistently complicated by counteractions on them, such as someone running toward the back of a train that is racing forward or scrambling toward the front of train traveling backwards, these reversals reflecting the reversals and rereversals of intertwined plots of love and war.

Keaton's genius as a filmmaker was founded on his fascination with the technology of motion pictures. His *Play House*, in which he plays forty different characters, *The Cameraman*, which shows *auteur* theory to be mere monkey business years before it was promulgated, and *Sherlock, Jr.* with its movie-within-a-movie remain after nearly a century unsurpassed as explorations of movie technology in the service of fitting the attention-seizing power of visual phenomena to the unfolding of a story. *Sherlock, Jr.* fools us into recognizing how illusion may lead us out of the blindness of our preconceptions, a key scene being that in which we see Keaton adjusting his tie and coat and primping before what appears to be a mirror. When he steps through what we thought was a mirror we realize that he was standing between two rooms identically furnished but arranged in reverse. We perceived mistakenly because of a natural preconception, since mirrors are commoner than such rooms. But the gag is not random, since the entire movie is constructed out of trick-shot dramatizations of how preconceptions prevent us from seeing correctly. This structure is thematized by the "real" projectionist's romance being derailed by a false accusation overturned during the projectionist's dream of being Sherlock, Jr. in the movie-within-a-movie. The reversal of the superimposed stories climaxes morally at the conclusion when the projectionist confirms the girl's love by directly imitating the actions of the projected movie's hero—until that film's final shot reveals the awful truth of where all real-life romances end.

Keaton was unusually systematic in making his gags contribute to the evolution of his movie's total plot (Trahair). Illustrative of this fusing of stunt-into-story (possible because every slapstick gag is itself a mini-story) is the adventure of the nonexploding pool ball in *Sherlock, Jr.* The episode is built upon the viewers' having seen that ball number 13 on the pool table is filled with an explosive that will blow Sherlock, Jr. to smithereens when touched by another ball. After we have tensely watched a series of excruciating near misses, we finally see Keaton smack ball number 13 with another ball—without any explosion. The startlingly funny nonevent bewilders us, until we remember that we saw Sherlock, Jr., before taking up his cue, adjusting his tie by looking into a mirror (this time a real one) which enabled him to see the villains behind his back substitute the explosive-laden ball for the normal one, so that he knew to reverse the switch as they left the room to avoid the catastrophe. We have time to figure out how Sherlock, Jr. pulled off his stunt because it is not left behind as the plot unfolds. When Sherlock, Jr. leaves the house after outwitting the villains, he gleefully pulls the "true" exploding ball from his pocket and tosses it high in the air—and almost doesn't catch it. Then near the end of the movie, when he and his girl are almost caught by the pursuing villains, he eliminates them by throwing the deadly ball into their automobile to demolish it.

This use of visual deception to reveal the truth beneath false preconceptions is the obverse of Keaton's physical stunting in *The General*, which depends more on the hero's improvisations to contend with the unpredictable. Long camera shots allow us to appreciate that Keaton truly does all those inventive things (even to his way of waking his captured girl friend so she won't make a sound at the surprise)—with amazing grace. And the literal truth of what we see Keaton do reinforces (as it is reinforced by) the overarching historical/ moral truths of the story. In Georgia today one can still see the actual "General," because Keaton's movie is based on true events, reported by a Union newspaperman who participated in the train-stealing. After the war, he improved his story by discussing the affair with Southerners who had been involved in the adventure, including William Fuller, the engineer whose dogged pursuit of his locomotive upset the Union plan (Pittenger).

The General was produced not long after World War I, in which Keaton (unlike most of his actor-contemporaries) had served in France. Memories of the Civil War, from which there were still surviving veterans, had not entirely vanished—after all we are now farther from the making of Keaton's film than he was then from the Battle of Gettysburg. These immediate and more distant echoes of war fitted neatly into Keaton's long-time fascination with railroads (which of course played a major role in American history). The loco- motive determines *The General*'s structure and informs its deepest meaning. The movie scarcely pretends to documentary accuracy, yet the hijacking of the locomotive at Big Shanty, and the beginning of the chase are astonishingly faithful to historical facts. Even Keaton's running after the train on foot reenacts what William Fuller actually did. He assumed (as does Johnny in the movie) that the hijacking was committed by disgruntled Confederate draftees (conscription having just been introduced in the South) who could be expected quickly to abandon the train and scatter. Even in finding a hand-car to continue his pursuit, Johnny is true to Fuller's experience—although Fuller was more fortunate than Johnny in picking up eight men to help him. At this point Keaton's moral purpose supersedes historical literalism. Johnny runs down the tracks chasing his locomotive, finally stopping and looking back to observe that the soldiers who at first had run with him have given up and turned back. Though disappointed, Johnny doggedly continues his pursuit alone: the civilian sticks to his patriotic task, while the soldiers quickly give up.

In the actual stealing of the train in the early years of the Civil War, this issue of civilian versus soldier was of the utmost importance, because the train hijacking required disguise of military personnel in civilian clothes and the putting on of Confederate uniforms by Union men. These disguises enabled the Confederates to claim the perpetrators of the train theft acted as spies, not soldiers. This justified executing some of them, including the expedition's leader, Captain Andrews. Outrage against the executions on the Union side led to Andrews and others in the party being awarded some of the first Congressional Medals of Honor in our history, Congress having instituted that award just before the sensational train hijacking attempt. Through the classic comic techniques of reversal and doubling (besides the Union hijackers putting on Confederate uniforms, Johnny disguises himself as a Union soldier to steal back his locomotive) Keaton slides in the question of how much patriotism is only a difference in dress.

Johnny's lonely pursuit of his locomotive without support of the soldiers develops the irony of the movie's opening scenes. There we see Johnny's heroic efforts to volunteer himself into the army rejected because he is more valuable as a civilian engineer (the reason that the actual engineer Fuller was not drafted). But Johnny's girl won't have anything to do with him unless he proves his patriotism by becoming a uniformed soldier. The dubiety of such socially approved patriotism is exacerbated by all the soldiers in the film appearing to be fools or worse. The only intelligent people we see are civilians with practical, technological training. Nor do any of the men in uniform display commitment to their cause equal to that of Johnny. *The General*, in fact, is a brilliant antiwar movie, with its critique concealed in plain view by the continuous excitement of its nonstop hilarious actions.

This "disguising" of ideological purpose by embedding it within a plot essentially identical with a sequence of visible actions is exemplary of fundamental processes of "deception" that endow visual storytelling with unique power. The best description I know of these processes is that of V. I. Pudovkin. This Soviet filmmaker was committed to Stalinist ideology. Illustrative is his *Storm over Asia*, which contains my favorite dying speech by a noble hero: "Wait for instructions from Moscow." But when Pudovkin analyzes details of filmmaking, his ideology disappears in his passion for his art. The following description was provoked by his friend Eisenstein's botched representation of men scything—men waving sticks, Pudovkin complained. Carefully watching a man, bared to the waist, working with a scythe while rain was falling, Pudovkin noticed the following:

> The muscles of his back contracted and expanded with the even sweep of the scythe. Its damp blade, flying upwards, caught the sunlight and

burst for a moment in a sharp, blinding flame. . . . The scythe buried itself in the wet, rank grass, which, as it was cut away beneath, slowly gave down on to the ground in a supple movement . . . Gleaming in the slanting sunrays, the raindrops trembled on the tips of the pointed, drooping grass-blades, tumbled, and fell. . . . For the first time I was seeing how its stalks fall as they yield to the sweep of the scythe! (175)

Trying to determine how he could convey to his audience this sharpened vision in a film, Pudovkin imagined a scenario for shooting the scene, in the central portion of which one would see the following:

> The blade of the scythe slowly turning at the culmination of its sweep. A gleam of the sun flares up and dies out. (Shot in "slow motion."). . . . The blade flies downward. (Normal speed.). . . . The whole figure of the man brings back the scythe over the grass at normal speed. A sweep—back. A sweep—back. A sweep. . . . And at the moment when the blade of the scythe touches the grass—slowly (in "slow motion") the cut grass sways, topples, bending and scattering glittering drops. (177)

Pudovkin refers to the foregoing as "a very approximate sketch." For the actual shooting he would have to edit the scene more complexly, using shots taken at a variety of more finely graduated speeds, attaining in the final film what he believed a "new rhythm, independent of the real, deriving from the combination of shots at a variety of speeds" that resulted in an "enriched sense of the process portrayed" (178). He insists, therefore, that deliberately "arbitrary" variation in speed of projection "is not a *distortion* of an actual process." To the contrary, it "is a portrayal more profound and precise, a *conscious guidance* of the attention of the spectator." Processes represented in this fashion "seem endowed with a rhythm peculiar to themselves, a sort of breath of life of their own." And concludes Pudovkin:

> They are alive, for they have received the vital spark of an appraising, selecting, and all-comprehending concept. They do not slip by like landscape past the window of a railway carriage beneath the indifferent glance of a passenger familiar with the route. They unfold and grow, like the narrative of a gifted observer who has perceived the thing or process more clearly than anyone else has ever done before. (181)

Especially noteworthy in this impassioned account (which surely expresses the aspiration of every serious moviemaker) is Pudovkin's emphasis upon the need to make visually perceptible *sequences* in the scything action, because clear perception of any action must include its temporal form. To enable us to see this rhythm with a clarity we have never before attained, Pudovkin "falsifies" the actual unfolding of the grass-cutting process, creating an artificial "film sequence" which, though different from the process of the physical scything, permits spectators to perceive in the representation the truest rhythm of the "real" action. Pudovkin here captures in miniature the essential process of all movie art. In so doing he reveals why successful visual make believe usually conceals its artistry. Were one to become aware of the artifices Pudovkin describes they would interfere with perceptions of the "true" scything *rhythm*, the meaningful *sequence* of actions. What is true of the visual detail is equivalently true of the macro-rhythm of the movie as whole, why "propagandistic" purposes, Stalinist or otherwise, are most effective if adroitly embedded in processes of visual action. Thus the antimilitary critique of *The General* is successful because one's first impression is that the movie doesn't have any "message" at all.

Good visual storytellers recognize, furthermore, what Pudovkin's analysis of scything demonstrates, that all actions are the result of immediate, or as philosophers say, proximate, causes. Orange juice is spilled because the sleeve of my wife's gown catches the edge of the glass. One of the principal strengths of movies is their ability to represent convincingly proximate causes without blurring their particularity and purely local, and usually fortuitous, character. For a novelist, on the contrary, it is difficult to spill orange juice without endowing the mundane event with meaning beyond its sheer phenomenal immediacy. A movie's strength is its special power to present convincingly the casual and the accidental as vividly casual and accidental. That very power, however, tends to obscure the particular action's role in larger patterns of meaning of an entire movie story. Contrarily, if that larger role is made too conspicuous, the specific little event will seem staged, "unrealistic." Movies are cursed as well as blessed by being the only visual art that can be faithful to the unbroken continuity of "normal" phenomenal experience. Movies surpass every other art in their capacity to represent with minute fidelity the "spontaneity" of physical actions, that is, their coming into being from the apparent random play of proximate causes. A moviemaker's skill consists principally in deliberately creating what falsely seems to be spontaneous happenings. He is careful to keep his shots free of anything that suggests they have been purposefully arranged, as all of them have been—very painstakingly.

One fashion of concealing is to make apparent to the movie audience the structure of the situation in which an action occurs, the configuration of a particular set of circumstances that makes the event appear "spontaneous." Noël Carroll in explicating this process observed how many actions in *The General* are funny because they are intelligible (1996, 154; 1998, 64–79). Thus the audience is shown a curve in the railroad tracks that enables it to understand why, when the big cannon pointing directly at Johnny and his engine fires, its shell misses him and hits the train he is pursuing. In contrast to the nonexploding pool ball, this event would not be so funny if we were not shown the exact physical relationships that "explain" the unexpected happening. A different kind of "intelligible" act occurs when Johnny is on the cowcatcher of his locomotive and, having just lifted from the track a timber that would have derailed his engine, escapes that disaster posed by a second railway tie lying across the tracks. He succeeds by striking its end with the end of the timber he has just lifted from the rails, somersaulting both the new and old menaces away. Few if any viewers foresee how Johnny will save his locomotive, but as soon as he acts, the brilliantly simple logic of what his does becomes spectacularly apparent. Our relief at his escape is reinforced by admiration for his thinking more quickly than we have.

This latter event illustrates why the reseeing of a good movie can be more enjoyable than a first viewing—and that, in turn, illuminates the kind of logical patterning (the mega-form of Carroll's "intelligibility") by which visual storytelling creates its deepest meanings. Seeing *The General* a second time, we know beforehand what Johnny is going to do, and can anticipate his ingenuity with delight, as well as enjoying his quick-wittedness and physical skill. It is true that in a second viewing we cannot experience the surprise of an unexpected action. But in losing one pleasure we gain another more valuable, because we are able now fully to appreciate this as an instance of Johnny's combining of mental and physical dexterity in surmounting unpredictable threats, the capacity that distinguishes him favorably from the mental and physical rigidities of the other characters, above all, the uniformed patriots on both sides. Seeing the film more than once enables us to recognize how *The General*'s exuberant humor celebrates human capacities for improvisation in a society dangerously hostile to individuality and spontaneity of behavior. Yet, simultaneously, this patterning produces a paradox, because Johnny the wonderful improviser loves a machine. A resolution of the paradox is best achieved by recognizing Keaton's love for moviemaking as a technological art—not least because it empowered him to expose through gifts of his bodily grace the dangers of modern life ever more dependent on mechanisms, physical and social.

We probably ought to attend more carefully to children's voracity for seeing again and again films that they enjoy. The repetition is not boring for them because it permits them to derive more meaning from each experience, especially better to interconnect what at first were only separately exciting events. The same is true of adults in a more complicated fashion, because the sensory impact of a first viewing of details in a good movie is so intense that it is difficult to respond adequately to the film's larger patternings. Indeed, the value of reseeing movies may be greater than the value of rereading fiction. Of course the reward of rereading a fine novel may be tremendous, but a first reading is likely to carry one deeper into its total form than may the first seeing of a fine movie. Novel reading normally is not, like seeing a movie, a single, unified experience. A novel enters into our life as we enter into its extent and complexity over a significant span of time. And verbal narrative's recursive structure, its constant activation of memory of itself, tends to make us conscious of the patterns developing through the representation of spontaneous actions and unique events. The gripping sensory immediacy of a good movie virtually requires a later return to it if we are to reap the full rewards of the careful planning that made it *seem* as unpredictable as actual life. A first-rate comic film is probably the best illustration of this paradox, for the laughing it provokes interferes with the appreciation of its subtler meanings, because laughter manifests a disruption of conventionalized ideas and emotional attitudes.

In *The General* we should see Johnny Gray's improvising skills as complementary to the care he lavishes on his locomotive. No one else in the film attends to anything or anybody as he does to his engine— and his girl, when she'll let him. *The General's* continuously involuting patterns of physical countermovements embody the personal-political contradictions intrinsic to Johnny's dual loves. The concluding scene, with Johnny propped against the motionless engine kissing Annabelle while saluting the endless horde of assembling soldiers, visually reverses in a morally problematic fashion the end of the opening "prologue," with its famous shot of Johnny forlornly perched on the driving rods of the moving engine vanishing into the black emptiness of a tunnel. The reversal can carry us beyond the "happy" ending into questions the film has from its opening subterraneously provoked about connections between sentimental love and sentimental patriotism.

Oscar Wilde, arguing that sitting in a café reading Baudelaire is as "natural" an act as chopping wood, observed that "to chop wood with any advantage to oneself, or profit to others, one should not be able to describe the process" (G. Wood, 51). I have myself taken much pleasure in swinging an ax, even with some profit to others, and I believe Wilde is absolutely correct—about verbal description. A motion picture, however, does not describe but *enacts*, as with Pudovkin's man with a scythe, or Keaton with *his* ax. In one scene of *The General* we see Keaton chopping wood atop the tender of his train racing north, while behind him his military compatriots retreat helter-skelter southwards. These countermovements, including contrasts between machine and horses, demoralized soldiers and a hardworking civilian, are given firm visual embodiment by the physical realism with which Keaton swings his ax. I know of no other movie scene in which an actor conveys so convincingly the combination of total bodily coordination with mental concentration that wood-chopping requires. The significance of the contrast between graceful movements by an individual civilian and the army's retreat with every man out to save himself enacts the movie's most potent "concealed" theme. When Johnny's ax handle breaks, he desperately and foolishly tries for a moment to cut with the blade alone. The ridiculous act dramatizes the intensity of his frustration deriving from the intensity of his commitment—contrasting with "patriotic" soldiers galloping away from nothing more than a vague threat.

This splendidly funny/troubling scene epitomizes the paradox of planned spontaneity central to the success of all good movies. And it illustrates how essential meaning of a film may be embedded within its sequence of events verisimilar in their contingent immediacy yet exhibiting the clarity of formal structure essential to any visual art. *The General*'s train chases differ radically from the innumerable automobile chases that have entertained moviegoers for nearly a century. Car chases lack inherent form. The freedom of an automobile to drive almost anywhere (especially in movies) makes it difficult to formalize car movements so that they exhibit coincidence of action and theme. In automobile chases, moreover, actors can do little but lean to the side and move their hands over a steering wheel (and on occasion shoot wildly). Drivers have no intimate relation to their vehicles, which are often stolen and as often easily abandoned or replaced, and that require no servicing during a chase. Johnny Gray's pursuits and escapes are restricted to the tracks on which the trains must run, and he has constantly to attend to his engine's welfare, stoking its fire, oiling and watering it. His girl, Annabelle, no passive passenger like most females in car chases, even sweeps the locomotive with a broom while they are being pursued.

The "spontaneity" with which most actual events in our lives seem to occur makes us think of them as just happening to happen. Much of power of movies' "realism" derives from their representation of the unexpected as unexpected. This is much more difficult to do in verbal narrative, because the very naming of a thing or event tends to endow it with symbolic significance while linking it into the verbal network created by the storytelling. Yet enormous efforts of planning and organizing make it *seem* to movie spectators of continuous physical actions that the curve just happens to come at the right time for the shell from the cannon to miss Johnny. It must appear that he luckily has just enough time to get one piece of lumber balanced so that he can upend another off the track ahead. Johnny's sword must appear to fly off its handle entirely by chance to kill the enemy sniper. But all these "accidents" create meaning by contributing to underlying patterns of symmetry, inversion, and parallelism only fully realized in the completion simultaneously of visual action and plot of the movie. Superior visual make believe must create its deepest significance while beguiling us into responding to each particular event as if it were as spontaneous as events in actual life. Only in this way can a movie narrative develop the rhythmic coherence of a totally integrated visual experience that is *worth* reseeing.

This experience is almost the exact reverse of reading a verbal narrative. Memory is continuously active in novel reading. And memory of what we have read enables us to read a novel coherently despite many interruptions—dramatically illustrated by the serial publication of nineteenth-century fiction. The words the novelist employs always resonate with her earlier use of them, are freighted with their own history. Sights are essentially "original" and in themselves lack connotations. Visual narrative therefore must concentrate on the forward pointing immediacy of actions in and of themselves. Thus when in *The General* the satirically named heroine Annabelle Lee irritates Johnny by rejecting a piece of wood with a knothole as not fit for firing the locomotive's engine, we see him first pretend to strangle her and then kiss her. We are amused by this action in the midst of their desperate efforts to escape (the critic Walter Kerr thought this shot superior to anything in Chaplin's films), and we don't at once connect the funny little moment to earlier incidents. But in retrospect we realize that the alternative Johnny faces from the beginning is whether he should kiss Annabelle or strangle her. She certainly deserves strangling. Although Johnny is obviously of more value to the Confederacy as an engineer than as a soldier, she, on the grounds of mindless patriotism, refuses even to speak to him until he has enlisted—and this despite his heroic efforts to be the first in their town to join the Confederate army. Annabelle's foolishness gives personal depth to *The General*'s condemnation of patriotism blind to all but the spurious nobility of war: before the final battle she has to help Johnny dress the Southern general as if he were a child.

Annabelle's appalling conventionality (even to her narcissistic assumption that Johnny has penetrated Union lines to rescue her, when he is after a locomotive the South needs) is impressive because (like most of Keaton's heroines) she is an energetic, gutsy, independent young woman, and if not Keaton's equal as an acrobat (who is?), she undergoes physical battering with grace and resilient goodwill. Despite Johnny's contempt for her innovative method of delaying their pursuers, her idea of roping together two trees is partially successful. She comes out of the bag in which she has been imprisoned and trampled on triumphantly clutching the pin she stole from the train-coupling to release the locomotive, even though it happens the pin is now useless. She displays imagination and quick intelligence, even a sharp sense of humor, as in an opening scene when she follows Johnny and *his* young followers into her own house. She learns how to run the locomotive and put it in reverse, even if at exactly the wrong moment. When Johnny links his hands so she can step on them to get up into the locomotive, she bounds past him. What provokes the strangle-kiss is that as they flee in the locomotive Johnny is driving, she finds herself for a moment with nothing to do. Not being the kind of passive heroine Chaplin preferred, Annabelle sets to work within the conventions she has been taught, and industriously starts sweeping the engine. When Johnny suggests that in their special circumstances she would do better to fuel the engine, she takes up this task readily, making fine housewifely discrimination between what seem to her good and bad materials.

Johnny loves Annabelle, and we are happy he finally wins her, for she is in many ways an admirable young woman. At the same time, *The General* may have injected us with a nagging doubt as to whether the conventional love story might not be symptomatic of social values askew. Annabelle's rejection of Johnny overtly raises the issue of volunteerism and conscription, which had had peculiarly strong effects in the Civil War—such a war, of course, explicitly making problematic the very concept of patriotism. *The General* continuously ridicules militarism in every conceivable fashion. The most famous instance is produced by the Union General's decisive assertion, "that bridge is not burned through." The consequence is one of the most expensive shots in Hollywood silent films—the train falling into the river through the burned out bridge. This is followed by the deadliest representation of military intelligence in movie history—the shot of the general's vacuous face. Smaller devastations of military glory abound—such as Johnny's pistol going off just at the moment of the Union officer's ceremonious surrender of his anachronistic sword to his dim-witted Southern counterpart. The wild humor of *The General* is necessary because the film so unsparingly satirizes the mindlessness that underlies modern patriotism celebrating mass killing—especially of civilians. Keaton's movie allows us to apperceive a sinister connection between our most innocent-seeming romantic fantasies and the murdering of our fellows. But this powerful "lesson" comes to us disguised in laughter—which illustrates necessities imposed on moviemakers both by their medium and by its sociological functions in twentieth-century civilization. A nineteenth-century novelist, George Eliot, let us say (but Manzoni, Tolstoy, Zola, and many others would do as well), tells a story so as to offer her readers the opportunity to share in her consciousness and in that of her characters. The commonest means for such sharing are *opinions*, what a dictionary defines as "beliefs or conclusions to which one adheres without ruling out the possibility of debate." Such opinions constitute the substance of all major fiction since *Don Quixote*. These opinions enter into readers' consciousnesses, where for a time we may imaginatively entertain them as if they were our own—but without necessarily giving up other, even contradictory, opinions which guide our actions in real life. This entertaining of opinions (an additive not a substitutional process) is the essence of the make believe of novel reading.

This process of entertaining opinions in verbal make believe could not occur, of course, except under particular historical conditions. Even the most popular nineteenth-century novelists, Dickens, for example, wrote for audiences that were—in contrast to twentieth-century movie audiences—sociologically, ideologically, economically, and educationally very much of a piece. Even *Uncle Tom's Cabin* with massive sales, ten times greater than Dickens', appealed to a readership far less heterogeneous than that of current moviegoers. In order to read a nineteenth-century novel you must be highly literate. For such readers (and only such readers) make believe built upon the entertaining of sharply conflicting opinions can evoke powerful imaginative experiences. Even the finest motion pictures are not aimed at so exclusive an audience. That does not mean they are, in consequence, inferior works of art. Throughout human history the visual arts have usually addressed much broader audiences than has literary art. Movies are the first visual art capable of effectively addressing virtually every citizen of every culture. It is a "mass audience" in this sense that validates the profundity of Bela Balzás' observation that the machine is the muse of the movies. Not only did he mean that movies are shot with a camera, but also that every aspect of the creation of a motion picture and its distribution and exhibition and its enjoyment by audiences is made possible solely by civilizations dependent upon machine technologies. *The General's* historical accuracy, for instance, is made possible by photographic techniques, many deceptive—for instance, the uniforms which have been praised for the authenticity of their appearance were of course not originals. The movie's skillfully misleading title sets the pattern for the film, because Johnny Gray's *The General* is more useful and impressive than any army officer we see in the film (although the literal meaning of locomotive applies to all the human generals we are shown). But the big, powerful protagonist machine requires constant attention—the machine only functions well if people work intelligently with it and for it. And in *The General* only trained civilians do this—as is illustrated when a host of army men can't figure out how to free the switch Johnny has tied shut, until a trainman severs the chain with a single contemptuous ax blow. Throughout the film, military people are associated with horses, and old-fashioned prejudices, civilians with railroads and telegraph, and intelligent thinking for themselves.

Johnny is successful because he is a brilliant improviser. But machines can't improvise—why the trains' confinement to prepared tracks is stressed throughout the movie. This opposition between human ingenuity and rigid mechanisms produced by human ingenuity reinforces the social critiques hidden within the film's funny accidents—as when the explosion of Johnny's pistol spoils the absurd formality of the sword-surrender. The final battle scene includes Tolstoyan features, if one can imagine Tolstoy in a slapstick mode. The final Confederate success is due to Johnny's cannon flipping out of control and fortuitously sending a shell into an upriver dam, which bursts to release a flood of water that washes away the Union troops. So much for strategic planning. This machine-made movie does not simple-mindedly celebrate mechanization. It is not merely that the locomotive depends on Johnny's loving care, but that Keaton's physical gracefulness continuously offers a counterforce to the efficacies of the technology he loves. The elegance of Keaton's movements, which in this film are invariably expressive of his quick-wittedness, persistently remind us of how threatened is the very physical basis of our humanity by a civilization that not merely relies on machines but has itself become a machine—as appears most clearly with the advent of war. We leave *The General* smiling and delighted, and we remember the movie with pleasure. Yet it sticks in our mind as something with a value beyond laughter—its humor nags at our memory—until the next war breaks out and we recognize Keaton's cleverest stunt.

CHAPTER 11

GENRE AND THE TRANSFORMING OF SOURCES: *HIGH NOON*

Forenoon

High Noon has aroused more controversy than any other Western movie. Its plot and unusual musical score influenced a number of subsequent Western films, and, besides launching Grace Kelly's career, it was the first Hollywood Western to present a Mexican actress (Katy Jurado) in a major role. This ethnic innovation is symptomatic of the movie's subversion of the traditional sexism of Westerns, suggesting that John Wayne's Montana-militia hostility to *High Noon* was partly fueled by the violation of a convention he appears to have cherished. Wayne became almost pathological in his attacks on the film and especially its scriptwriter, Carl Foreman, boasting of having driven Foreman out of the country, and even after twenty years was still vilifying the writer and his script. In fact, however, few Hollywood studio films more fully exemplified the collaborative process of moviemaking than *High Noon*. Foreman and the director Fred Zinneman were of course important, but everyone from the producer Stanley Kramer to the final editor John Edwards participated in almost every aspect of the shaping the picture—even Dimitri Tiompkin, the Russian Hollywood veteran composer whose fake Western ballad contributed much to the movie's success, had some input in fashioning the movie's plot (Drummond; Zinneman, 1992).

High Noon also illustrates spectacularly how a fine visual story may be derived from a feeble verbal narrative. The film was adapted from a crude tale by J. W. Cunningham, "The Tin Star," which, as published in *Colliers*, even confused the names of two of the villains, making the narrative of the final shoot-out incoherent. But who was J. W. Cunningham? He seems never to have published anything else.

Was this a pseudonym? If so, for whom? How did Foreman happen on the story? These questions draw attention to the frequent difficulty one encounters in identifying authorship of movie scripts, even when there is no deliberate concealment, as with blacklisted writers. Movie scripts, in fact, more often than not are "authored" in a confusingly collaborative fashion (exactly how novels are *not* written)—in part, as film writer Dudley Nichols pointed out, because a written scenario is only a launching pad for visual storytelling.

"The Tin Star" is a short story, and many of the best film adaptations are of short fiction, verbal brevity offering freedom to moviemakers' invention and at the same time encouraging a simplicity of structure helpful in visual narrating. Sometimes, as with *Babette's Feast* or John Huston's *The Dead*, the brevity of the original permits moviemakers to be meticulously faithful in translating minuscule verbal details into visual ones. But more frequently it is a badly written short story that encourages a movie adapter's visual imagining. This appears with even so elementary a feature of adaptation as naming. "The Tin Star's" Sheriff Doane becomes *High Noon*'s Will Kane, resonating of course with Abel's killer. Cunningham's nameless town is named to recall Mark Twain's story *The Man Who Corrupted Hadleysburg* to extend the movie's irony. The story's passing reference to a "Mexican section" of town is enlarged and focused in the new character of Mrs. Ramirez, the silent partner of a store and owner of the town saloon, and, as a spectacular addition, the lover of Kane, Miller, and young Harvey.

The character of Harvey emerges through radical transformation (influenced by the young killer in *The Gunfighter*, released the year before *High Noon*) and of Toby, Doane's deputy in "The Tin Star," who plans to quit law-enforcing until inspired by Doane's heroic death. Toby then determines, despite being himself badly wounded, to carry on the unappreciated and underpaid job of honest law-enforcer. Had the movie followed the story, John Wayne would have loved it. By turning loyal Toby into Kane's unsuccessful young rival, both for Mrs. Ramirez and for his job, the movie simultaneously deepens the intensity of personal relations while situating them within a realistically complicated social dynamic. But the crux of these complications is a direct challenge to a fundamental convention of the Western genre.

Cunningham's story makes much of Doane's arthritic hands, which the movie transfers to a new character not in the story, an old marshal (Lon Chaney, Jr.). The retired, because crippled, marshal, who has been Kane's mentor, can speak forthrightly (as Kane because he is the marshal cannot) of the sinister (but concealed) ambiguity of his communal role. Kane (unlike Doane) is not represented as a particularly wise man, nor a self-analytic one. The movie emphasizes how self-awareness is forced on him, a self-awareness inseparable from an increasingly painful consciousness of the moral dubiety of his social function. The pressure of this consciousness is dramatized by making the train central to the narrative—in Cunningham's story it pulls in for no particular reason at 4:15. Not only is the noon train made an impressive visual object in the film, but even by *not* being in sight though anxiously looked for it ratchets up tension, while reinforcing the relentless pressure of diminishing time on Kane to gather deputies—also dramatized by the pendulum clocks shown throughout the movie (a detail adapted from *The Gunfighter*). This focus on the train helps to upset the conventional "timelessness" of the Western genre even as it embodies *High Noon*'s representation of "progress" as exposing the traditional protagonist's contradictory moral situation. The train demonstrates Hadleyville's new linkage to other towns, but the brevity of its noon stop reveals how it threatens a social ethos which, like the genre itself, is dependent on slower moving horses. In *High Noon*, Western-saddled horses are ridden only by bad guys.

The most startling change in the original story is the revitalizing of Doane's dead wife—in "The Tin Star," Doane is at the cemetery putting flowers on her grave when the shooting breaks out in town. The old wife is not only transformed into a beautiful young bride but also a committed Quaker, adding an unusual religious dimension to the ethnic tensions the movie unconventionally foregrounds. Most important, however, is the movie's innovative emphasis on sexuality: no Western before *High Noon* had presented a male drama of revenge so entangled in intricate sexual relationships.

Sex may or may not be more important in movies than in novels, but movies cannot escape from confronting the hazards and possibilities offered by its medium for visual representation of sexuality. Pornography comes easily to visual make believe. Codes of "decency" censorship of movies are a social reflex to the fact that movies always have the potential to put explicit sexuality squarely in the viewer's embarrassed face. Kurosawa was neither facetious nor evasive when he suggested that *Rashomon*'s popularity was due in part to its story being of a rape. When a Cary Grant or Omar Sharif or Grace Kelly or Sophia Loren is put before the camera sexual implications are inevitably initiated—and require careful control by any artistically serious moviemaker (Stam, "Cinematic Eroticism," 157–186). The vulgarizations of both male and female movie stars' sex appeal should not blind us to the power of that appeal in making visual narratives uniquely enjoyable. That particular strength, however, was little exercised in conventional Westerns, and in none before *High Noon* had there been shown a significant social role for a variety of women—all of whom, however, can only act within the confines of a rigidly masculine ethos.

Despite its concentration on Kane's effort to gather deputies to help him against Miller, the primary context for the marshal's fruitless search is men's relations to women in Hadleyville. The young Quaker wife is so firm in her religious principles as to abandon her new husband less than an hour after their marriage. Mrs. Ramirez is ethnically disadvantaged in her commercial entrepreneurship (she must be a secret partner in the store, since she is unacceptable to the respectable women of the town), but her fear of Miller is sexually grounded—her contempt for the physicality of young Harvey making her fear of Miller especially sinister. One understands, moreover, why she "hates this town," yet she deserts Kane because he is no longer "her man," no longer her sexual property. Almost every male action in the film is illuminated by an ambivalent female response to it. Aside from the centrality of the ordeal of Kane's young wife, the cumulative effect of apparently subordinate details, such as the women in church, the old marshal's consort, and, perhaps most tellingly, the wife of Sam Ford, who must lie for him to the marshal's face when he and she know she is lying, offer a play of gender disequilibrium unparalleled in previous Western films—and illustrative of the unique capacity of visual narrative to represent directly the social significance of physical sexuality.

"The Tin Star's" young deputy Toby in the movie is divided unequally into Harvey and the anonymous boy who volunteers to help Kane when all the men have denied him. Harvey brings out the selfishness in Toby's first rejection of the life of a law-enforcer, while the boy embodies the immature foolishness of Toby's idealism. Such dividing is a form of simplifying that is the most efficient fashion for embodying moral ambiguity in visual make believe. "The Tin Star's" mayor is divided in the film into a range of public figures, including the judge and the minister, while the dead wife splits into new bride and old mistress, and old marshal Doane separates into a younger Kane and his crippled, retired mentor. Through this process of *analytical stylizing* the movie gives physical, visual form to psychological ambiguities and moral contradictions. *High Noon*, for instance, shows its audience visually what the old marshal tells Kane verbally, that the townspeople will fail to support him against Miller because they don't fully believe what they profess. Analytical stylizing takes advantage of film's unrivaled effectiveness at concentrating spectators' attention on minute details of behavior. It also exploits the stark contrasts essential to visual perception, an inherent oppositionalism most simply apparent in black and white photography. But color films, in subtler ways, are equally built on the opposition of light and dark, because our visual perceptual system depends on such contrasts. Visual antitheses are the means by which movies stimulate imaginative understanding of what is intellectually, emotionally, and ethically uncertain or confused.

High Noon's analytical stylizations reveal the "decency" and respect for law claimed by the responsible citizens of Hadleyville to be in fact the hypocrisy of moral cowardice. Yet, contradictorily, our sharpening recognition of this duplicity makes us reluctant to condemn Kane for having been—and continuing to be in the face of his discovery of this hypocrisy—a defender of his dishonest fellow citizens. This paradox is the problem the original story subverts by concluding with Doane's conventionally heroic death, whereupon his idealistic deputy assumes his mantle of dutiful service. "The Tin Star" affirms the redemptive power of some individual's mysterious personal virtue as transcendently superior to that of his social milieu. This blind hero-worship is what John Wayne and sentimentalizing critics like Robert Warshow wanted from Westerns (and apparently life), and they were correct in perceiving that *High Noon* disembowels their faith. *High Noon* became, and to a degree remains, controversial by calling into question the moral validity of the Western. It challenges what has been one of the most popular American forms for asserting a mystically transcendent virtue of individuality.

Adequately to develop this topic (which would carry one back at least as far as Ralph Waldo Emerson), one would need to analyze *High Noon* in terms of the movie Western's relation to the written Western, whose lineage originates in nineteenth-century cheap fiction (Slotkin). But even without becoming immersed in that history, it is easy to see some reasons why the movie genre was popular for so long—although moribund within a decade of *High Noon*'s release. Motion pictures are mass entertainments requiring a steady inflow of money to keep production going. Movie genres are patterns for manufacture, formulae for fabricating narrative artifacts rapidly and (relatively) economically. Genres generate. Which is why one must not push the factory analogy too far. An artistic genre is not merely a template. It is a formula for producing new works like, yet *different* (if only slightly) from, other works in the genre. Processes of genre-modification are best examined through manipulations of subgenres, the subordinate formulae nested within the major formula. The climactic "shoot-out" illustrates how the Western is constituted of subgenres, formulae of action, or character, or situation, gun slinger going straight, the schoolteacher as love interest, or social conflicts, ranchers against farmers, arid setting, finding water for cattle, the saloon, and so forth. These formulaic elements explain why historical accuracy needs to be of little significance to the artistic success of a Western. Ingenious and provocative organizing of the generic elements matters much more than historical verisimilitude. Every Western movie, however stereotypical, is in some ways unique, and it is the emergence of uniqueness out of stereotypical patterning that endows a superior Western with meaningfulness. A distinctive genre such as the Western (like the literary Pastoral) requires a formal structure produced by creators' acute self-awareness of the genre's form and functions. *High Noon* dramatizes the Western's most problematic elements, as, "to compare small things with great," *The Iliad* uses Achilles to challenge blind acceptance of a traditional heroic mode. I'm tempted toward this comparison, because Westerns characteristically tell a simple, physically violent story, one without great intricacies of plot, usually involving rather uncomplicated characters starkly opposed. Like the literary epic and pastoral, the Western accrues power through adroit manipulation of the stylizings of which it is constituted. *High Noon* focuses our imagination upon essentials of the Western by extreme simplifications, such as reducing the time of the story to the time taken to show the film.

This is a peculiarly effective device for visual narrative, because movie viewing is so integrally unified an experience. In *High Noon*, the place of the action, the small town, is restricted, yet not *too* limited, not too like a stage set. And this confinement intensifies the pressure created by the story of diminishing time. A movie can carry us around the world in eighty seconds with complete ease. It can (as in *2001*) race through millennia without causing spectators the least discomfort. But films can be equally effective through deliberate restrictions of time and setting, a concentration that is not (as with stage plays) enforced by the medium but a purposeful choice to reverse the form's "normal" modalities. As with *Rashomon*, which uses a minimal number of sets but is constructed of an extraordinary number of brief shots, in *High Noon* Fred Zinneman employs many short shots within the confined setting to encourage spectators' eyes into more-than-usual activity. And both films in distinct ways skillfully emphasize visual repetition. In *High Noon*, the building crisis is given physical reinforcement by Zinneman's skillful pacing of shot lengths, these in turn enriched by repetitions with variations of the musical score.

The limited time frame of *High Noon* reinforces the utter simplicity of the basic story line, embodied in the starkness of contrast between protagonist and villain, a contrast emphasized by the radical difference of screen-time given each. By focusing its analytical stylizations on these fundamental opposites, somewhat as a biologist with a powerful microscope examines tissue in which different constituents have been artificially colored, the movie presents troubling insight into the moral foundations of the Western. Of course the fierce political attacks on *High Noon* and its makers as "un-American" reflect the particular ideological climate in which the movie was produced and on which it comments. But the movie also, and more importantly, allows us to recognize beyond 1950s' "McCarthyism" a problem in the ideal of the Western in any era. The problem is the Western's hero. He differs strikingly from traditional heroes, not only Achilles but also Roland or Lancelot—warriors who seek glory and honor, and are heroic because they are adept at mashing other people's skulls or slicing them in half. The Western hero, who kills not *mano-a-mano* but neatly from a distance with a gun, acts only under compulsion. He is driven to violent deeds, reluctantly compelled publicly to assert his physical and moral courage. Being a hero is neither his occupation nor his *raison d'être*. And the Western hero is neither religiously nor ideologically motivated. Although he may finally act for the good of friend, family or community, he does not hold a position of prime authority. If, like Kane, he is a licensed lawman, by definition he is an agent of others. A difficulty in this position is exposed in *High Noon* when a respectable homeowner accuses Kane of weakness as marshal: he should simply arrest the members of the Miller gang who have gathered in town. Kane's reply, he can't arrest them because they haven't yet broken any law, defines the restrictive situation in which the Western hero operates. He is "heroic" because he tries to hold fast to rules not of his making, nor perhaps even to his liking. He does not claim the right to a preemptive strike (what made the Japanese attack on Pearl Harbor, "infamous," and has only become official American policy in the twenty-first century). Thus at the final shoot-out in *High Noon*, the first gun play comes when Kane steps out from a building behind Miller and his henchmen and, without drawing his gun, calls Miller's name. Only when the villains turn and draw their guns does Kane draw his and shoot. Until Miller tries to kill him, Kane has no grounds for shooting. Because Kane is supposed to embody the ideal coincidence of law and moral justice, he is prohibited from indulging in personal animosity, even at the risk of his life. Were he to plead the evilness of the villain as grounds for preemptive action he would violate with self-righteousness the modesty that gives him moral stature. Kane can only hope (against his more realistic assessment of the probabilities) that if he gathers together a large enough body of deputies Miller's gang will be intimidated from acting.

This passive and defensive, but not self-righteous hero, whose notorious inarticulateness is produced by both his constricted social situation as agent and the inhibition of personal emotion it enforces—especially when he has committed himself to dangerous action—emerges from deep layers in the American historical experience. There were, for example, many in this country who claimed that our foundational revolution was forced upon us; had the British Government acted more responsibly and generously, insurrection would have been unnecessary: in 1775 the "people of New England did not wish for war" (Fischer, 1994, 165). Americans pride themselves on being a society based on law, whose source is our constitution. That constitution, however, couldn't be clearer that the ultimate power to make and change laws is vested not in governmental bodies but in the people *as individuals*. The American ideal of individual independence leads to communal responsibility emerging in full strength only in circumstances of extreme crisis. Cincinnatus remained prototypical for Americans until the Bush/Ashcroft Patriot Act, even though for years not one in a million Americans has known the name of the Roman farmer-turned-fighter. Military conscription has always been unpopular, until the critical moment (as in *The General*) when suddenly everybody wants to enlist, while vigilantism is a constantly recurring problem on every level of American society. Such attitudes go far toward explaining American sympathy for the Western's protagonist as so reluctant, so temporary, so ad hoc a hero.

High Noon disturbs because it anatomizes the validity of this ideal. Kane fits his role in not desiring to be a hero, as he tells his wife when she foolishly accuses him of such ambition. He does not like what he finds himself having to do. It is difficult for him to explain why he is compelled to behave as he does because he is not motivated by private ambitions. And the movie displays a steady eroding of the communal commitment he serves, upon which his moral selflessness is founded. The one time Kane loses his temper and knocks down the saloon keeper, he accepts the justice of the man's rebuke—you got no right to do that, you wear a badge and carry gun (as I don't). Kane's increasing physical isolation accompanies a more terrifying ethical isolation. In the end, he fights the Miller gang on the basis of nothing more than self-survival, without a shred of moral justification. So far as he epitomizes the Western hero, Kane reveals the ethical bankruptcy upon which the entire genre is based. And so far as the genre is peculiarly American, then, *High Noon* may indeed seem anti-American.

But it is also an approved American tradition to challenge institutionalized ideas of social conformity. Our society until very recently celebrated the principle of the right of individuals to be critical of established concepts and persons. *High Noon* dramatizes this tradition in a fashion appropriate to a movie, that is, not overtly as the expression of a personal opinion nor of a publicly identifiable ideology. *High Noon* embeds its social commentary within the formulae of the Western. Were its message, as Foreman claimed, nothing more than a representation of the need for the United Nations in the early 1950s to support the United States in resisting North Korean aggression, the movie would have caused no controversy. But *High Noon* uses its popular genre to imply the traditional Western conceals through stereotypes of transcendently virtuous characters unresolved moral contradictions within American sociopolitical ideals.

Afternoon

High Noon is about hypocrisy. William Hogarth, the keen-sighted satiric painter of the 1700s, lamented that a visual artist was unable to expose hypocrisy, because a hypocrite by definition is one whose appearance is deceptive, and a painter can only represent appearances (137). The moviemaker, however, displays actions. And moviemakers love to show how actions belie visual appearances—the reverse of the enigmaticness of facial close-ups. Movies are the medium *par excellence* for revealing every nuance of human hypocrisy, which—let us be honest—constitutes a major part of all our lives. Hogarth, doing his splendid best as a narrative painter could show a man testifying in court with his left hand on the Bible and his right behind his back receiving from a court officer a bribe for giving false evidence. Actions alone can reveal the truth or falsity of appearances. To be a hypocrite one must act. One can smile and smile and not be hypocrite until one does something hypocritical. Dramatists have put many hypocrites on the stage. But the movies, with their command of concentrated visual detail (here close-ups are a terrific resource) can represent deceptiveness with far greater acuity and subtlety. And movies have delighted from their earliest days in exposing every shade and variety of conscious and unconscious duplicity. In so doing they exploit what seems a limitation of all visual arts, that they cannot directly represent ambiguity—as illustrated by the famous duck-rabbit.

We can *see* either a duck or a rabbit, not both simultaneously (Gombrich, 4). Because our eyes insist on registering either the duck or the rabbit, they are very effective in the right context at seeing *through* actions meant to confuse or disguise. We instantly spot the duck pretending to be a rabbit, and are not fooled by a false smile (Ekman, 2001, 158–160). The conjecturing imagination is perhaps stimulated most frequently by visual narrative toward estimating to what degree characters' appearance and intentions coincide. Movies are supremely effective in arousing suspicions about what we see, because they enable us to see so clearly: to what end is this guy trying to fake me out?

Good movies do lots of exposing of deceptions and hypocrisies, and *High Noon* is unusual only in its concentration on communal deceit at the core of a cultural ideal. The debate in the church (especially in contrast to highly deliberate personal actions of Sam, the judge, Mrs. Ramirez, the hotel clerk, etc.) dramatizes how efficacious communal hypocrisy can be. The implications in a conventional idea of Westerns, that Kane has made the town safe for decent women and children is illuminated by the anxiety of respectable townsfolk of both sexes to hustle their children out of church so as to debate

Figure 11.1   Duck-Rabbit. Reproduced from the nineteenth-century satirical Viennese Journal, *Die Fliegenden Blätter*.

whether to help Kane without the youngsters. Why? The result of this censorship is exposed when we see Kane outside the church encounter a group of children playing Kane and Miller shooting each other. And so far as we can tell, Harvey is strictly a local boy, perhaps all too representative of a community obsessed with "shielding" children from carefully unspoken truths about its "masculine" ethos.

All these hypocrisies bring us to *High Noon*'s final shoot-out, one of the most important subgenres within the Western, although as a movie climax historically relatively late to appear—only with the 1929 Gary Cooper film of Owen Wister's 1902 novel *The Virginian* did a climactic shoot-out become *de rigeur* for the genre. Decisive movie duels with swords came earlier. Sword-fighting is beautifully adapted to the visual medium, since it may be simultaneously realistic and balletic, whether in the savagely naturalistic mode of *Rob Roy* or the hilariously inventive (although also "realistic") extravaganzas of Lester's *Three Musketeers* and *Four Musketeers* (for anyone who has ever fenced, the sword-fight on the ice must be one of the great scenes in movie history). We see the sword "actually" going through the bad guy, and close-ups allow the pleasure of nose-to-nose sheering over crossed hilts—where even nostril flare could dramatize Rathbone's sheering villainy against Flynn's breezy virtue.

The Western shoot-out, however, provides better proof of the movie's appeal to conjectural imagining. The good guy shoots, the bad guy falls, and we *infer* he's been shot dead. That we only infer has sometimes been cleverly exploited, as in *Vera Cruz*, in which, because there is no visible evidence of a mortal wound, we wrongly believe at first the bad guy has won. One cannot see bullets. Even drawing the gun from the holster depends on a speed that defeats vision. The visual climax of the Western is something you can't see. It is notable, too, that in a gunfight the antagonists are usually apart, sometimes far apart. There is an absolute finality in the circumstances: two men face each other at a distance, visible separation embodying unmitigated opposition. The shoot-out as an event in itself is dramatic only as the culmination of other events. There is nothing inherently interesting in two men standing facing each other at a considerable distance. Sword-fighting can be interesting in itself—two good swordsmen going at it is fun to watch even if we care about neither. The concluding gun confrontation of the Western is effective only as the finalization of some complete impasse. The shoot-out embodies a knot in human relations that can only be cut, not disentangled.

Most Westerns, of course, do not advertise that the shoot-out resolves nothing. *High Noon* emphasizes just that troubling fact. The movies' opening credits show Miller's gang gathering and riding into town to kill Will Kane. Everything in the movie is oriented exclusively to bringing the shoot-out to pass shortly after noon, and it is this total "clarity" of narrative form that enables the film to arouse our imaginative perception of the genre's moral dubiousness. The choreography of the shoot-out in *High Noon* visually reinforces its critique of the Western's conventionalized morality even as it proves Kane's superiority and increases our desire to see Kane win. He has moved through the town (both physically and sociologically) in a manner that fuses disheartening visual and moral experiences. The sharpening distinctness of his physical predicament embodies the paradox of the situation in which he is trapped. He kills not only without any justification other than personal survival but even *against* the morality of the town he supposedly represents, which has demonstrated that it prefers, and deserves, Miller to Kane.

The significance of the gunfight in *High Noon* would not be so compelling, however, were its visual effects and implications not crafted with an adroitness that conceals its craftiness beneath what appears purely "realistic" action. What happens in *High Noon*'s shoot-out is totally intelligible as a series of self-contained causal sequences, but its actions *also* grow out of and reflect back upon the psychological/sociological significance of events that led up to the gunfight. This shootout, like those in other Westerns, is presented "objectively"—evidence that visual narrative's most "natural" mode of representation is not a subjective one. Verbal narration requires a speaker. But visual narrative does not require a "see-er." What is visible is *always* what more than one person could see. Any specific sight, of course, must be seen from some distinctive perspective, but that need not be one occupied by a particular subjective consciousness. Spectacular vista points, Ausable Chasm for example, are every day occupied by numbers of different people. And in looking at *High Noon*, however vigorously we are rooting for the marshal, we witness Kane in the gunfight with an objectivity made tense by our desire for his victory. This "emotionalized objectivity" makes it possible for the sequence of actions without freezing into rigid symbolism (everything seems to occur with natural "spontaneity") to embody the moral complexities that make *High Noon* a film of continuing interest.

We see the three gang members meet Miller as he gets off the train, hand him his guns, and stalk together into the empty streets of the silent town where Kane now walks alone. As the gang is about to turn into the main street, one of the four turns aside, breaks the window of a store and takes from it a woman's hat, while Miller says, "Can't you wait?" The act evokes the moral crisis Kane provoked trying to arouse the town to defend its claim to care about women's safety. The act—besides foretelling by dramatic contrast Amy's subsequent window-shattering murder of the window-breaker— advances the "physical logic" of the developing shoot-out. The sound alerts Kane to where the gang is. He retreats behind the corner of a building, lets them walk past, then challenges Miller, kills one member of the gang, and retreats safely down a side street. The marshal's first success comes not merely by chance or skillful shooting; it is made possible by his opponents' contempt for property: with Miller and his men Hadleyville isn't even safe for women's hats.

The robbery and the gang's carelessness in walking together prove the villains lack of intelligence. Ian MacDonald as Frank Miller presents a characterless, unimpressive face suited to his role. The specific crime for which he was jailed is never identified: he is a spirit of unjust retribution accurately represented by the empty chair in which he sat when promising vengeance. Miller embodies generalized fears and guilt of Hadleyville's property owners about "crime," which they condemn while refusing to recognize their unwillingness truly to resist it, and the hopes of others, such as saloon-keeper and hotel clerk, for a profitable unleashing of various personal indulgences by the less affluent. Kane takes advantage of his enemies' stupidity by retreating into the livery stable loft, which gives him an advantageous position from which to shoot. After killing another gang member, he is driven from the stable when Miller sets it on fire, displaying disregard for the horses that would be burned alive did Kane not free them, and, by clinging to the back of one, make his escape, although wounded and knocked from the horse half way down the street. Once again unpredictable physical details of the gun battle are shaped into a dramatic coherence that emphasizes the moral contrast between Miller's disregard for property and the marshal's sense of responsibility—even to dumb animals. It would be difficult not to root for Kane against such anarchic and insensitive opponents, but the simple appeal to our emotions comes as the climax of a story that has increasingly challenged any easy assumption that Kane represents a valid moral position.

Kane's wounding allows for an ingenious adaptation of "The Tin Star." In the story much is made of the marshal's crippled hands that limit his ability to fight. In the movie, Kane is unarthritic; he sometimes shoots with his left hand until wounded in the left arm, then shoots only with his right hand. Kane's ambidextrousness enables him to kill Miller, while reinforcing the point made throughout the shoot-out that he is more flexible and self-controlled than his enemies: he *deserves* to win on all counts—except maybe the moral one. Wounded Kane is apparently cornered by the last two of his enemies, when suddenly the third member of Miller's gang, standing in front of the marshal's office reloading his gun, is shot in the back through the office window by Kane's wife. The shattering of *this* glass is the moral climax of the movie, the first time in a Western that a hero's wife without warning ruthlessly shoots a man in the back. The nearest analog, significantly, is the 1945 self-spoofing *Along Came Jones*, produced by Cooper, in which he plays a clumsy cowpoke, inept with his gun, who is saved when the villain is gunned down by his former girl (Loretta Young). The unconventionality of Amy Kane's act is emphasized visually by its contrast with the beginning of the shootout, in which Kane, having heard the shattering of glass, comes up behind the gang, calls out Miller's name, and only shoots after the bad guys start to draw. Amy blows her man away without warning.

Although the act comes as a total surprise for us as spectators (as it does for both Miller and Kane *in* the picture), we instantly grasp what has happened and why, because the shooting climaxes an intercut sequence of Amy during the fight. On the train, ready to desert her husband, she hears the first gunshots (which in fact are Kane killing one of the gang); Amy leaps off the train, which we see pull out carrying Helen Ramirez away, and runs into the main street to see a body that she at first fears to be her husband. She then runs to the marshal's empty office, where she finds the will which Kane had written just as the noon train pulled in. The effect here illustrates what skillful visual narrating can achieve. We can be electrifyingly surprised by what we see, yet instantly comprehend the logic of the unanticipated event—if the moviemaker has taken care to make the unexpected simultaneously fit into both developing thematic and visual coherence. Our eyes, after all, have evolved for the express purpose of rapidly making sense of unexpected happenings. Our eyes can identify instantly the "meaningful coherence" or "intelligibility" in its context of an action we could not have foreseen. If we examine our behavior even in quiet modes of life we will find we are often taken by surprise, but our eyes adapt so swiftly that we usually overlook our having been startled. When there is a sudden sweep past us of a bird's shadow across sunlight, we immediately understand the event for which we could have had no preparation.

When we watch a movie our vision is continuously being controlled, directed, and focused by the fashion in which the film is organized. But we are not passive. We are aware that we are not really *in* the environment we watch: we know we are watching a movie, that we are engaged in making believe. What activates this making is that this artificial visual environment is consistently meaningful, densely coherent—as a natural environment seldom is. We see not merely a sequence of visual events but a sequence in which all parts are loaded with narrative meaning. Thus Amy's shooting the man in the back climaxes a sequential development begun from the moment she leaves the train. We are surprised by her act of killing in itself—we could not have foretold it—yet we instantaneously understand her act as a "logical" consequence of a series of preceding events. But the moment of surprise with simultaneous comprehension possesses a moral stinger.

What we see as the man falls to reveal Amy behind the shattered glass holding a gun is a moment of doubled moral significance. Amy's act is unpremeditated; we have seen but scarcely noticed the gun hanging by the window, left by Harvey when he deserts Kane. As the man she has shot falls showing Amy as his killer, we realize that she has snatched the accidentally "convenient" gun from its holster and fired—and simultaneously we recognize that in so doing she has shattered her commitment to the Quaker ideal of nonviolence, a commitment that led her to reject her husband within an hour of marrying him. In crises we do not thoughtfully adhere to logically thought-through moral precepts but behave in a fashion that simultaneously creates and reveals our fundamental ethical disposition. In this instance, Amy, the chief character in the film with strong religious convictions, violates a fundamental principle by which she has defined her personality. The film narrative is so arranged that we, the spectators, would condemn her for not killing the man; we are emotionally as pleased as startled when we realize what she has done. But immediately superimposed on that surprised pleasure is awareness that she has destroyed the moral foundation of her life. No wonder she sags weakly against the wall, totally debilitated.

The efficacy of such a movie event lies in its rapidity, its instantaneous fusing of the visual and the ethical. This fusion is not possible in a still photograph or a painting: their fixity eliminates the immediate context of the event that allows the movie viewer an *interactive* experience of it. We *see* what Amy does *as* a moral happening. In a fashion unequaled by any other visual art, movies by representing the immediate context of specific behavior can display the processes by which an action is endowed with ethical meaning. The profoundest power of visual make believe is this capacity for quick integration of psychological and moral into the coherence of a singular visual event.

One might think a stage play could present as successfully as a film the significance of Amy Kane's killing. But stage drama cannot engage us in the intricate articulation of the total experiential process as a movie can. A play cannot present, for example, the swift interruptive and itself interrupted intercut "sequence" of Amy's flight from the moving train to the empty marshal's office. The effectiveness of the sequence depends on its "broken" continuity, which evokes our conjectural imagining to give both physical and psychological order to the simultaneous unexpectedness and comprehensibility produced by the sudden sight of the man falling and Amy appearing behind him through the bullet-shattered window. There are, however, instances of fictional narrating parallel to the surprise evoked by Amy's act that fully highlight its fundamental contrast to any verbal make believe. An example is provided by Dounia, Raskolnikov's sister, when near the end of *Crime and Punishment* Svidrigailov traps her in an isolated room intending to rape her. Each event is a moral climax, but what happens in the movie exactly reverses the action in the novel. Dounia, the sister of a man who gratuitously murdered two women, throws away her revolver rather than kill the rapist threatening her. In opposite fashions impulsive acts epitomize a story's central moral problem. I cite from Dostoyevsky's novel at some length, even though my citations are only a small fraction of the entire scene, because the extensiveness, "extraneous" references, and "slow" pacing are characteristic of verbal storytelling even of such a sensational crisis.

> Suddenly she drew a revolver from her pocket, cocked it . . . Svidrigailov leapt up from his seat.
>
> "Aha! So that's it," he exclaimed, surprised, yet smiling ironically. . . . where did you get that revolver? Not from Mr. Razumihin, surely? Bah! It's my old friend! And I was looking everywhere for it! So the shooting lessons I gave you in the country were not wasted."
>
> "It's not your revolver. It's Martha Petrovna's—whom you murdered, you scoundrel. I took it when I began to suspect what you were capable of. Take one step, and I swear I'll kill you. . . ."
>
> "What about your brother?" Svidrigailov said, not moving. . . .

"Denounce him if you like! Don't move! . . . You poisoned your wife; you're a murderer yourself!"

"Are you sure I poisoned Martha Petrovna?"

"You did! You hinted as much to me. . . ."

"Even if it were true, it was your fault; you would have been my motive."

"You lie! I always hated you. Always!"

"Come, come, Avdotya Romanovna! You have forgotten how in the fire of your propaganda you began to melt. . . . Don't you remember that evening in the moonlight, when the nightingale was singing?"

"That's a lie. . . ."

"Lie? I lie? Very well, if you want to put it so, I told a lie. It won't do for women to remember feelings like that." He smiled ironically. "I know you will fire, you lovely little beast. All right. Shoot me."

Dounia raised the revolver, deathly pale, her lower lip trembling, her black eyes flashing fire. . . . He had never seen her so beautiful. It seemed as if the fire blazing from her eyes as she lifted the revolver seared him, and his heart contracted in pain. He took a step, and a shot rang out. The bullet grazed his hair and smacked into the wall. He stood still and laughed gently.

"A wasp stung me! Aimed straight for my head. . . . What? Blood!" He took out a handkerchief to wipe away the blood that ran in a slender stream down his right temple. . . . Dounia lowered the revolver and looked at Svidrigailov, not afraid but with a kind of wild bewilderment. She seemed not to understand what she had done or what was happening. "You missed! Fire again! I'm waiting," Svidrigailov said softly, still smiling, yet gloomily. "Or else I might grab hold of you. . . ."

Dounia shuddered, quickly cocked the revolver. . . . "I'll kill you."

"Of course . . . at three paces you can't miss." . . . he took two steps forward.

Dounia pulled the trigger and the gun misfired

"You didn't load it properly. Never mind! You've one bullet left. Fix it, I'll wait". . . .

He was looking at her with passionate determination, a feverishly serious look.

Dounia understood that he would die sooner than let her go. . . .

All of a sudden she threw away the revolver.

"She threw it away!" Svidrigailov said in surprise. He drew a deep breath. Something seem to lift from his heart, and it was not just his fear of death; he seemed at the moment scarcely aware of that. It was release from darker and grimmer feelings, which even he could not have defined. (Part 6, chapter 5)

To read the complete scene from which I have excerpted might take almost as long as watching the entire gun battle in *High Noon*. Verbal storytelling moves more slowly because it is more complicated than visual storytelling. Complexity in art, however, is not necessarily superior to simplicity—just different. In the movie, although we see Amy from different perspectives and a variety of camera angles and positions, relatively distant shots and closeups, our fashion of seeing her, because it is made possible by the camera, is always the same kind of vision. Our fashion of imagining Svidrigailov and Dounia is more varied because we share in the narrator's account, and also in Svidrigailov's subjective experience, as well as in Dounia's thoughts and feelings. As spectators of the movie we are by no means passive, but our psychic activity is more consistent because founded on our continuous detachment as witnesses, watchers in the shadows. But our imagining of the novel through entering into the psyche of Dounia with whom we are sympathetic is distinctively different from our entering into the psyche of Svidrigailov, whom we dislike and fear and yet who fascinates us. Furthermore, despite the intensity of the situation, our experience of it, like that of the characters themselves, extends beyond the limits of the immediate scene, especially in time. In reading, our imagination is as fully engaged with the past as with the present moment: the revolver is Svidrigailov's, he gave Dounia shooting lessons in the country, did he kill his wife? Did Dounia at one time have softer feelings for Svidrigailov? In imagining the scene we are drawn into imagining why Dounia might or might not shoot, which involves us in speculations on past events and Svidrigailov's dead wife. Simultaneously we are caught up in the strange subjectivity of a man whose motivations are puzzling, in part because of his odd mixing of rigorous logicality with powerful emotions partially repressed.

The writer of fiction enables us to enter into the turmoil and obscurity of his characters' elemental feelings and contradictory thoughts as they occur, simultaneously revealed, concealed, and distorted by their external manifestations. We imagine vividly the *strain* of Svidrigailov's controlling of his passion. Even when feelings are directly expressed, as when Dounia finally flings away the revolver, the act presents itself to us as the result also of thoughts and emotions other than those overtly expressed: she "grasped that he would sooner die than let her go." We experience Dounia's final moral decision as less sudden and "spontaneous" than Amy's. And in imagining what prompts Dounia to throw away the revolver we are simultaneously imagining Svidrigailov's tortured eagerness for her to shoot him. We imagine both sides of a paradoxical relationship.

A hyper-dramatic movie event such as Amy's shooting subsumes both past and future in its immediacy. The novelist's dramatic event inescapably resonates with our memories of what has gone before—which is why all the talk about the past and about other people by Dounia and Svidrigailov does not diminish the melodramatic quality of their confrontation. An imagined present is here constituted by our mind's ability to perceive any instant as interconnected to others, even those temporally distant. The witnessed present of a movie possesses a very different potency—the sensory integrity of the immediacy of an event. The forward impetus of visual storytelling is created by its concentration on distinct physical actions *as* they happen. Verbal storytelling may interweave imagining of different times and places even in moments of supreme crisis.

The contrast between our experiences of Amy's and Dounia's acts becomes more impressive when we reread or re-view. Rereading, we know that Dounia is going to throw away the revolver and that Svidrigailov will nevertheless allow her to escape, and these certainties enhance our awareness that the long-term and far from simple processes of their interrelationship can be brought into focus only by the weird logic of this hyper-melodramatic encounter. Belief in the possibility that once Dounia did have softer feelings for Svidrigailov enables us to imagine more painfully the ambivalences at play in her decisions to shoot or not to shoot. And on a second reading we feel the darker implications in the probable truth of Svidrigailov's claim that he seldom lies, especially to himself, even as we recognize Dounia's superior moral strength (unlike that of Sonia) in part arises from her robust sensuality. Seeing *High Noon* a second time we cannot recover our original amazement at Amy's action. But because we know it will happen we attend more carefully to her earlier behavior. We probably pay less attention to how her act saves Kane than to how her "hypocrisy" here contrasts to that of other characters—including Kane. The stunning immediacy of the original experience is forever lost, but there are substantial gains in reseeing the movie. Rereading *Crime and Punishment* involves less loss, but perhaps for very acute readers there is not quite so much gained.

Be that as it may, this contrast helps to explain why the effect of powerful movies is not simply cathartic. We leave the movie theater trying to recover patterns and orderings of scenes that have affected us most through their quick-moving continuousness. At the end of *High Noon*, Kane silently drops his badge in the dirt of the street and drives out of town, because (although physically surviving) ethically he has been isolated even from himself, with his only companion a Quaker killer. He has made apparent to himself and to us the ambiguity of the social and aesthetic traditions upon which he acted, and upon which the Western genre is founded. Of course our feelings are confused. Part of the troubling effect of this nonconclusion is further highlighted if we ask ourselves who we have been watching. Certainly most of the original audiences of *High Noon* saw primarily Gary Cooper, not Will Kane. In a movie, the character tends to disappear into the performer in exactly the opposite way from which on stage the performer loses himself in the character. This is a topic much discussed, by none more famously than Erwin Panofsky and Stanley Cavell, who begins his analysis by quoting Panofsky:

> Othello or Nora are definite substantial figures created by the playwright. They can be played well or badly, and they can be "interpreted" in one way or another; but they most definitely exist, no matter who plays them or even whether they are played at all. The character in a film, however, lives and dies with the actor.

Developing Panofsky's insight, Cavell says,

> For the stage an actor works himself into a role; for the screen, a performer takes the role into himself. The stage actor explores his potentialities and the possibilities of his role simultaneously; in performance these meet at a point in spiritual space—the better the performance, the deeper the point. . . . The screen performer explores his role like an attic; and takes stock of his physical and temperamental endowments; he lends his being to the role, and accepts only what fits; the rest is nonexistent. . . . A screen performance requires not so much training as planning. . . . the screen performer is essentially not an actor at all; a more accurate word [is] "star"; stars are only to gaze at. (89–91)

The judgment that movie actors don't truly act surfaced in objections to the award to Cooper of an Oscar for "Best Actor" for his performance in *High Noon*. The claim was that he didn't act—he just was himself. But so far as Cavell and Panofsky are right, that is exactly what Cooper should have done, because that constitutes "movie acting." Implicit in the distinctions drawn by Panofsky, Cavell, and many others is, perhaps, a judgment of stage acting as superior to movie acting: the latter is not quite the real thing. We need to understand fully the radicalness of the distinction Panofsky and Cavell insist upon, but we need not accept any devaluation of movie acting it may contain, as is eloquently elucidated by the best study (both theoretically and concretely) of the subject, James Naremore's *Acting in Cinema* 1988.

In *High Noon* even today most spectators probably do see first Gary Cooper, not Will Kane; but in so doing they use their eyes appropriately. Our visual perceptual system has evolved so as to permit us powers of rapid and complicated *recognition*. In Gibson's terms, our eyes perpetually seek invariants in a densely unstable environment. A simple-minded thought-experiment may dramatize the point. It would be impossible for us to follow any visual narrative, say that of *High Noon*, if we did not recognize that each of the characters remains the same person throughout the film, that we are always seeing the "same" Cooper/Kane. Of course, we have never seen "Will Kane" before, but we have seen Cooper often—so we recognize Cooper.

Useful for understanding this point are performances by fine "character" actors, perhaps supremely Alec Guinness (also an excellent stage actor). Guinness, despite the extreme range of his roles, seldom altered his physical appearance in any profound way (his appearance as Fagin being an exception), usually not so much as he altered his voice, which tends not to evoke so quick a response as the sight of a face (Ekman, 2003, 58–60). We always know we are seeing Alec Guinness, but subtle variations in makeup and behavior establish, as it were, the distinct identity of the character within the Guinness-form. His success illustrates what all intelligent actors have recognized as the primary requirement of movie acting: understatement. Because of the intensity and detailed precision with which we perceive figures on the movie screen, the tiniest nuance of gesture or expression is effective—indeed appeals exactly to a central pleasure of movie watching, using our eyes with enhanced efficacy. This is why an actor like Gary Cooper, who often comes very close to impassiveness, could often be an impressive movie presence, a figure *rewarding* to "gaze" at. In a movie, very often not changing one's expression is a powerfully meaningful act. As I observed with *La Strada*, movies emphasize the enigmaticness of other people by the very fact of visually displaying them with meticulous lucidity.

To me it seems true that outstanding movie actors depend on natural gifts, like swift runners, whereas stage acting is more of a craft in which learned skill is what counts. But just because a fast runner has been naturally gifted doesn't mean he may not be a fine sprinter—if he trains properly. Skill as a movie actor may exist even though it is a skill quite different from that required of a stage actor. And movie acting, like every other phase of moviemaking, is a collaborative enterprise. As stage actors making movies have frequently remarked, movie acting is constituted of small bits of performance, and involves a constant interaction not with just a director and other actors, but also many technical people on many occasions. The best actor in the world looks lousy if he is photographed by a bad cameraman, lighted poorly by a dumb electrician—and so on. Fred Zinnemann the director of *High Noon* has justly been praised for his skillful close-ups of Cooper's features in the film, but surely the actor had learned through long experience to control his features, and deserves at the least to share credit with the director and the cameraman for the extraordinary effectiveness with which he absorbs Will Kane into his star persona.

And that it is Gary Cooper who appears as Kane is of enormous value to *High Noon*. Cooper was then the epitome of the Western hero, and his appearance in this film gave complexity to spectators' visual recognition, for here Cooper appears older, more haggard than in earlier movies. His normal movie expression in repose had always suggested faint anxiousness, even hesitancy—a quality that rendered his rare smiles particularly beguiling. In *High Noon* he scarcely smiles, and his face vividly records the increasing tenseness, weariness, and loneliness of Will Kane—aided by the actual facts of Cooper's aging and recent illnesses. So far as *High Noon* challenges the underlying justification of the Western genre by dramatizing that the ethical grounds for the good guy killing the bad guys may be doubtful if not false, audiences seeing Cooper primarily rather than Kane deepens the film's moral critique. In Cooper we literally see the questionableness not merely of Hadleyville but of a whole tradition of storytelling to which we have been profoundly committed, through which, indeed, we have in part defined ourselves and our social aspirations. No wonder that the movie has caused anger and distress, as well as received acclaim. But whatever one's response, *High Noon*'s potency arises from its skillful exploitation of those features that give visual make believe its unique effectiveness.

CHAPTER 12

GREAT EXPECTATIONS: INSIGHTS FROM THE IMPOSSIBILITY OF ADAPTATION

I n contrasting verbal and visual make believe, I have said little about the adapting of fiction into movies, even though this has been a major topic in film criticism since the pioneering work of George Bluestone half a century ago. Leading critics now recognize that the key issue is not simple fidelity of movie to written text, but the effectiveness of transformation of forms appropriate to one mode of make believe into another (Naremore, 2001). Exemplary is Shakespeare's "adaptation" of Homer's *Iliad* into *Troilus and Cressida*, a transformation of Homer's story so complete that even a literary scholar watching the play scarcely thinks of its relation to the Mycenaean epic. But the idea of movie-adaptation-as-transmutation has had difficulty becoming established because the formal principles of verbal and visual make believe have not been adequately distinguished.

A recent adaptation of a nineteenth-century classic that demonstrates how necessary to success is the adapter's willingness to exploit differences between the media is Sergei Bodrov's *Prisoner of the Mountains* derived from Tolstoy's story written 120 years earlier, "Prisoner of the Caucasus." Bodrov adds many details and numerous characters and gives the story a contemporary (1990) setting visually to embody Tolstoy's enduring insights into ethnic war. Bodrov takes advantage of the obscene fact that, except for improvement in the deadliness of weaponry, the bitter struggle between Russians and "Tartars" (Chechens) has continued for over a century. Tolstoy's story depicts how antagonism between peoples is sustained by the use of linguistic terms that define others as hostile, starting simply with generic identifiers, "Russian" and "Tartar." This linguistic obliteration of the individuality of human beings is extended by each side's use of metaphors of wild beasts to misidentify their enemies. For such linguistic devices Bodrov's film substitutes visually startling displays of depersonalized physical hostility, while adding a variety of highly individualized characters, both Tartar and Russian. But Bodrov displays how recognition of a common humanity founded in respect for the individuality of others is annihilated by the technological impersonality of modern war. *Prisoner of the Mountains* by such historical transmutations recreates the essential thrust of Tolstoy's story through a scrupulous infidelity to the text.

Few moviemakers have dared to "distort" with such faithful purposefulness famous nineteenth-century fiction. This timorousness is visible in the adaptations of the novels of Charles Dickens, the novelist most popular with film adapters. When I last counted there had been, aside from television versions, over a 130 films made from his novels, all of which (along with "A Christmas Carol") have appeared in multiple versions (with more of *Oliver Twist* and *Tale of Two Cities* than any of the others). Most of these adaptations are best left forgotten in unvisited archives, but the one most artistically successful as a movie is also the most faithful to the original story line and even to its original illustrations: David Lean's *Oliver Twist*, with a visually perfect Oliver and bravura melodramatic performances by Robert Newton as Sikes and Alec Guinness as Fagin. Lean's first Dickens film, *Great Expectations* of 1947, however, has been more often praised by commentators. It is an intelligent reworking of a stage version—Lean claimed he had never read the novel. If *High Noon* demonstrates how a poor piece of writing may inspire an excellent movie, Dickens's novel illustrates fundamental problems of adapting a fictional classic, even one that speaks powerfully to contemporary obsessions with crime and money-worship.

The first difficulty for an adaptor is how to reduce into a two-hour visual experience the dense complexities of a novel published in installments over half a year. Movie narratives are emotionally evocative through clear definition of sharply conflicting forces, best attained through what I've called analytical stylizing. In most instances, as *High Noon* and *Prisoner of the Mountains* illustrate, this transformation creates *additional* characters to externalize internal conflicts—additions adapters understandably, but unwisely, avoid. Temporal considerations are not unimportant. Most movies run from eighty to one hundred and eighty minutes. That span reflects the optimum time for visual narrating, which, because so relentlessly continuous, makes severe demands on an audience's capacity for attention. There is no parallel of "appropriate" length for novels, which can be read equally well at various paces suited to the individual tastes, capacities, and circumstances of readers. Any novel will be of different "lengths" for different readers, but that variability the movie adapter must make uniform.

Like most adaptations of the novel, Lean's *Great Expectations* abbreviates by cutting the character of Dolge Orlick, Joe Gargery's assistant who strikes down his wife, Pip's sister, and very nearly succeeds in murdering Pip. But Orlick embodies the most sinister implications of Dickens's social commentary. Orlick "characterizes" Pip's repressed anger and frustration, as is made manifest in a melodramatic scene (that one might think particularly suited to movie presentation) in which Orlick stuns and ties up Pip and then taunts him before moving to murder him. Here Orlick claims that it was Pip, not Orlick, who smashed the skull of his "shrew sister." The seemingly bizarre accusation is true, so far as Orlick acted out Pip's repressed desire. Throughout the novel Orlick literally shadows Pip from place to place, suggesting ominous linkages between the two that Pip's first-person account will not overtly admit. Orlick, of course, also functions as foil to Magwitch, Pip's criminal benefactor: Orlick, the bad unidentified criminal psychologically inside Pip dramatically contrasts with the good but legally condemned criminal who must be physically concealed from public view. The full meaning of what happens to Pip (which is in part conveyed by *how* he tells, including mistelling, his story) is determined by Orlick's concealed presence. Without Orlick, Dickens' narrative could not provoke in readers the disturbing underawareness of a suppressed connection between "respectability" and murderous impulses.

So why would an intelligent movie director omit Orlick? Perhaps because Orlick is visually unrepresentable. Orlick is the *un*conscious, and movies cannot represent what is *un*, cannot show negatives. The character called "Dolge Orlick" (in the novel described as an "impossible" name) does not exist in quite the same fashion as characters who are "positive" fantasies of Dickens, Pip, Estella, Miss Havisham, and the rest. For the novel reader, Orlick is like these characters but also unlike them, so far as he represents an unadmittable part of Pip, the narrator of his own story. One might argue that a moviemaker should accept the difficulty posed by Orlick and make him part of the screenplay to sustain to the moral aim of Dickens's text. Yet perhaps

Orlick should be eliminated, on the grounds that any visual presentation of him will falsify the strange real-unreal duality of the figure in the novel.

It is virtually impossible, as I've observed, to imagine what one is actually perceiving. One imagines only what is *not* perceptible—not present, or not existent. What we call Dickens's "characters" are imaginings evoked in us by his language. An Orlick, who is partly a figment of the *imagined* Pip's psyche, perhaps must be left inside the book. Illustrative of this problem for a movie adapter is the film *A Beautiful Mind*, which shows people who are only fabrications of the protagonist's schizophrenic imagining. During the first part of the movie for first-time viewers these nonexistent character are as "real" as the other figures in the film. After John Nash's schizophrenia is revealed, viewers recognize these characters, who unlike other characters appear unchanging, are Nash's hallucinations. The device is successful, because the film is focused on Nash's schizophrenia—during which he did not in fact have hallucinations but heard voices, yet here the movie's "falsification" is entirely appropriate for its medium. And for him the hallucinations were real. So far as my experience goes, the most successful movie representations of ghosts, angels, or hallucinations employ some form of this technique of showing normal-appearing figures whose unusual condition, being invisible, for example, is established by cues to the audience's imagining rather than depending on ectoplasmic physical distortions of visual appearance. Orlick, however, poses a special difficulty, because in the novel he is *both* a "real" person *and* Pip's shadow self, a doubleness that causes no problem in a verbal story. The telling of a visual story, however, is consistently driven toward an either-or presentation, because that is in fact how we always try to see things. In *A Beautiful Mind*, for example, first-time viewers at the beginning will see Nash's roommate as an actual person, whereas for those who see the movie a second time, the roommate is from the beginning hallucinatory. In Dickens's novel, from the beginning with his "impossible" name of Dolge Orlick, the character is *both* a distinct person *and* Pip's psychic shadow.

Less complicated (because a camera is not a person) is the question of why there is no satisfactory visual equivalent for *Great Expectation*'s first-person or "autobiographical" narrative form. Sustained voice-over is rarely successful and usually advertises a failure fully to transmute verbal story into a visual one. One difficulty for movie adapters of personal memoirs is the temporal dimension within subjective self-depictions of verbal storytelling. A moviemaker, for an obvious example, needs two actors to represent the novel's protagonist, Pip as a very young boy and as an adult, because there is no visual equivalent for verbal self-retrospection. The audience for a verbal story without the slightest confusion can continually imagine backward and forward through diverse epochs of a teller's life. Pip changes but he has been continuously Pip—which of course like our own real identity is largely self-imagined—and that continuity a reader may readily enter into. Readers can even recover the effect of earlier false anticipations, because in a verbal telling *both* the current moment and the past appear retrospectively. This establishes a ground for readers' participation in what Pip says "now" as inflected by his understanding of his "former" self. These fluidities are exemplified in brief chapter 14 of *Great Expectations*.

It is a most miserable thing to feel ashamed of home. There may be black ingratitude in the thing, and the punishment may be retributive and well deserved. . . . Home had never been a very pleasant place to me, because of my sister's temper. But, Joe had sanctified it, and I believed in it. I had believed in the best parlor as a most elegant saloon. . . . I had believed in the kitchen as a chaste though not magnificent apartment. I had believed in the forge as the glowing road to manhood and independence. Within a single year all this was changed. Now it was all coarse and common, and I would not have had Miss Havisham and Estella see it on any account. . . . Once, it had seemed to me that when I should at last roll up my shirt-sleeves and go into the forge, Joe's' prentice, I should be distinguished and happy. Now the reality was in my hold, I only felt I was dusty with the dust of small coal, . . . I remember that at a later period of my "time," I used to stand about the churchyard on Sunday evenings, when night was falling, comparing my own perspective with the windy marsh view, and making out some likeness between them by thinking how flat and low both were, . . . I was quite as dejected on the first working-day of my apprenticeship as in that after-time, but I am glad to know that I never breathed a murmur to Joe while my indentures lasted. It is about the only thing I *am* glad to know of myself in that connection. It was not because I was faithful, but because Joe was faithful, that I never ran away. . . . It is not possible to know how far the influence of any amiable honest-hearted duty-doing man flies out into the world; but it is very possible to know how it has touched one's self in going by, and I know right well that any good that intermixed itself with my apprenticeship came of plain contented Joe, and not of restless aspiring discontented me. What I wanted, who can say? How can *I* say, when

I never knew? What I dreaded was, that in some unlucky hour I, being at my grimiest and commonest, should lift up my eyes and see Estella looking in at one of the wooden windows of the forge.... Often after dark, when I was pulling the bellows for Joe, and we were singing Old Clem, and when the thought of how we used to sing it at Miss Havisham's would seem to show me Estella's face in the fire, with her pretty hair fluttering in the wind and her eyes scorning me,—often at such a time I would look towards those panels of black night in the wall which the wooden windows then were, and would fancy that I saw her just drawing her face away, and would believe she had come at last.

If we contemplate this unspectacular passage from the point of view of someone thinking of making a film of *Great Expectations*, we recognize immediately that the chapter evokes imagining of *chronic* misery. But what is chronic is visually unrepresentable. Exacerbating our adapter's difficulty that visual narrative cannot represent the continuousness of the past in the present is the fact that Pip suffers from *loss* of belief in the specialness of his simple home. And the precise yet indeterminate nature of his feeling for a place secularly "sanctified" by familiarity is evoked for a reader in several nonvisual ways, as when Pip refers to the kitchen a "chaste" apartment. The adjective's very inappropriateness renders it imaginatively apt for the boy's mistaken (from a later perspective) yet not "ungracious" conviction of the indefinably admirable quality of his dwelling.

"Once it had seemed"—everything in this chapter comes to us through the temporal dynamics of fluctuating feeling within the chronic pain of lack of change: "I *used* to stand about . . . on Sunday evenings." Dickens here is representative of nineteenth-century novelists who (unlike contemporary authors) frequently exploit the subtleties of modulations in sequences and modalities of verb tenses. Before the development of Pip's dissatisfaction, he had anticipated the time to come with pleasure that contrasts bitterly with subsequent feelings *now* remembered as past, and defined as *more* severe than depressions *still later* in his life. At this point our movie adapter, already baffled by a "chaste" kitchen, may abandon his project, for there is no visual comparative, let alone any instantaneous visualization for the range of times the novelist effortlessly interweaves in a single sentence. Pip's dismal memories, moreover, are lightened only by his knowledge that he never revealed them to Joe. "Never"—the continuous negative—is another of the words for which visual storytellers have no satisfactory equivalent. In Dickens's novel, however, it defines something even more baffling to the camera—a relationship constituted of feelings withheld from one party over a long period of time.

Analogously, Joe's faithfulness is a persisting disposition, significant because it cannot adequately be embodied in any singular act. All these details lead to a generalizing judgment that concludes the chapter, a common progression in verbal narrative. Language is the means, and essentially the only means, by which we can articulate such *cumulative* judgments (Arendt, 1971, 92–96). And fictional discourse always carries the potentiality for evaluation. The language of "display," the language of verbal make believe, Mary Louise Pratt rightly insists, serves the primary purpose of offering topics for shared assessment (136–148). Dickens's passage appeals to his readers' capacity to recognize an ethical fact (like the physical facts of wine, bread, and stone discussed previously) that cannot be reduced to a singular visualization: how the quiet goodness of a simple person may over time powerfully affect others. The recognition is in one sense definite; there is nothing vague about affects of a pervasive goodness orienting our daily behavior over a course of years, but these affects are simultaneously indeterminate because they can be unreductively concretized only by imagining.

Although not as obviously "antivisual" as ambiguity and ambivalence (of which there is God's plenty in these few sentences from *Great Expectations*), the intrinsically evaluative mode of verbal storytelling as decisively differentiates it from visual storytelling. Linguistic communication necessarily carries evaluative implications: the efforts of, say, scientists and bureaucrats to write neutrally in fact manifest distinctly their ethical purposes. The critical concept of depersonalized language, "degree zero" writing, is a delusion whose source is revealed by the modernist fascination with photography. The visual as such is not inherently judgmental. Visual perception first registers what is, then what it means, what its value may be. Language, moreover, creates definite vagueness, distinct uncertainties. Pip can enable us clearly to imagine that he never—then or now—knew—or could have known—what he desired. Such decisive and continuing ignorance of specific feelings visual narrative may imply but cannot display, any more than it can show Pip's chronic fear of what *might* happen, especially his *fancy* of Estella (with whom he simultaneously makes *us* imaginatively "remember" he used to sing Old Clem in different circumstances) now seeing him in the grimy conditions of the forge. In our imagining of *his* imagining of what he claims to fear, the possibility of her face drawing away from the black window, we are enabled to imagine simultaneously what never happens as well as his unconscious ambivalence toward this non-event. Here in miniature is exemplified the intrinsic complexity of excellent novelistic make believe. The temporal unfolding of the verbal narrative is seldom unidirectional, being normally inflected by contradictory vectors of diverse feelings and competing moral judgments whose temporal development often run counter to sequences of physical actions. What happens in this chapter is infinitely complicated by countermovements of memory and fancies possible and impossible, factual and contrary to fact. But these complications we imaginatively comprehend with so little difficulty that in ordinary reading we scarcely notice their intricacies. This normal super-flexibility of our imaginative consciousness is astounding. We grasp at once, for example, the significance of the concluding ambivalence in Pip's phrase that he "would believe that she had come at last"—how he simultaneously wanted and didn't want to see Estella seeing him.

Novels are intrinsically self-complicating structures because their forward-moving plot runs counter to the retrospectiveness of the language through which it is articulated. This counteractive process sets up multiple associations unstably related and tending to upset commonplace orderings of both time and space. One effect of this continuous subversion is to intensify our awareness that we are exercising our consciousness. This helps account for the extraordinary addictiveness of reading fiction. Reading a first-rate novel is an unparalleled learning experience, not because of knowledge we acquire from its subject, but because the process of reading improves our imaginative competency. Verbal make believe enhances the efficacy of our self-consciousness.

Central to this enhancement is the intruding of moral considerations into processes of physical reality. By imagining we put ethics into the world, for we raise the possibility of new ways of conceiving both actions and their contexts. Practical choices are easily inflected morally—is it *better* to act this way or that? Story, whether fantasy or history, allows us to make right or wrong as important to a sequence of events as snow or sunshine. The remarkable achievements of nineteenth-century fiction in part reflect an advancement in human consciousness of its own historicity. Then, for the first time, creators of verbal make believe began to write under the pressure of developing "scientific" history, epitomized in the concept of "progress," which necessitated self-questioning as to worthwhileness of their imagining. This is why in one fashion or another all the finest nineteenth-century novels are "historical," some (led by Walter Scott) imagining the past, others (led by Jane Austen) imagining the present as a historical phenomenon. These novels are also *about* what historical awareness may mean for ordinary people carrying on the mundane businesses of daily life. The concurrence of such various dimensions of historical consciousness is almost paradigmatically illustrated by the first paragraph of one of the earliest great works of nineteenth-century fiction, Heinrich von Kleist's *Michael Kohlhaas.*

> On the banks of the Havel there lived, around the middle of the sixteenth century, a horse trader named Michael Kohlhaas, the son of a schoolmaster, one of the most upright and at the same time one of the most abominable persons of his time. Up to his thirtieth year this extraordinary man could have passed for the model of a good citizen. In the village that still bears him name he owned a farm on which he peacefully made his living by his trade. The children his wife bore him were raised in fear of the Lord and taught industriousness and loyalty. There was not a man among his neighbors who had not profited from his generosity and fairness. In short, the world would have blessed his memory if he had not carried one virtue to excess. His sense of justice turned him into a robber and murderer.

Kleist's famous paragraph is useful for reminding us how easy it is for verbal narrative (and how impossible for visual narrative) simultaneously to sweep forward and glide back in time, and as effortlessly to tell what might have happened but did not simultaneously with what did happen. In visual narrative even "flashbacks" are in themselves confined (as is not the case with verbal flashbacking) to the forward "arrow of time." In our actual vision of course there is no going back. While this strong directionality is a limitation in movie art, it is also a source of its peculiar strength. The unfolding movie plot we understand cognitively reinforces—as it is reinforced by—physiological eye processes. This helps to explain why we so frequently are persuaded a movie has portrayed "realistically" what we have in fact never before seen. We feel that this is how we *would* see the event. In normal vision, moreover, new information always supersedes what has already been received. The eye persistently seeks novelty. Nothing dims visual perception (and numbs the mind) quicker than an environment without anything new to look out for. This is why sustaining the forward pressure of visual narrative is commonly more effective than interruptive flashbacking. The movie plot attaches itself to normal sensory processes—as in its static fashion does sculpture, the greatest works of which require nothing more than ordinary vision to move us profoundly.

Some movies, of course, are simpler than others, and some novels are more complicated than others, but *Great Expectations* validly illustrates why *all* novelistic art may be characterized as intrinsically complex. Fictional art inevitably tends toward density of interrelations between *all* the different elements constituting its make believe. This intricacy in *Great Expectations* might perhaps first impress a potential moviemaker through its tonal variations, wherein humor and seriousness continuously interplay. It is not merely that there are funny episodes—such as Wopsle's hilarious appearance in *Hamlet* (surely among the most memorable performances of that classic), or absurd people, like Pumblechook or Waldengarver's rigorously artistic dresser ("I don't see them wafers"), or the many ludicrous brief descriptions, such as Joe formally dressed looking like a "scarecrow in good circumstances." Even within intensely serious and morally tense passages, humor often intrudes. The effects of such tonal upsets can be judged by contrasting the novel's opening scene with Lean's faithful rendering of Pip seized by the starving convict in the graveyard. The contrast is particularly revealing because the movie keeps something of the humor in the representation of Pip's fears, as is evidenced by the device of having the cattle speak What the movie cannot do, however, is reproduce the odd humorousness embedded in Dickens's opening paragraph by "irrelevant" details such as the gravestones of his five brothers, whom Pip thinks of as having been born with their hands in their pockets. Such absurdities contrastively highlight this frightening moment in the graveyard as giving Pip his first sense for "the identity of things," a sense inaccessible to direct visual manifestation.

After the movie's brilliantly startling appearance of Magwitch (unexpected appearances are a movie strong point, because our eyes have evolved specifically to enable us to register the unanticipated), the convict frightens Pip with his story of his fictitious murderer companion. Actor Peter Finlay conveys Magwitch's fantasy threat effectively, but it is not possible for any actor to evoke through visual representation—as the verbal rendering so easily does—the amusement a reader (in resonance with Pip's own *later* understanding of his childish naiveté) feels at the boy's fear of the absurdity of the imaginary "wicious" young man, a feeling strengthened by the convict's

Dickensian relish in his inventive power in making believe.

> I am a-keeping that young man from harming of you at the present moment with great difficulty. I find it very hard to hold that young man off of your insides. (Chapter 1)

This fiction within the novel is more effective because the enjoyment it arouses coincides with our appreciation as novel readers as to why Pip is more afraid of the fictitious companion than of the terrible convict physically gripping him. Even though directed with sensitivity to the nuances of the text, the movie's visualization is necessarily more simply frightening than the novel's verbal representation, because more consistent, less densely complicated by undercurrents of feeling deriving from Pip's retrospective evaluations of the experience. For instance, Pip notices a familiar sight in a way no moviemaker could hope to represent:

> a gibbet, with some chains hanging to it which had once held a pirate. The man was limping on towards this latter, as if he were the pirate come to life, and come down, and going back to hook himself up again. It gave me a terrible turn when I thought so, and as I saw the cattle lifting their heads to gaze after him, I wondered whether they thought so too. (Chapter 1)

Some movies have effectively juxtaposed contrastive tones and moods—*Fargo*, for a recent example, is a funny movie about seven brutal killings. But there is in it no true visual equivalent for the kind of continuous, minuscule verbal modulations operative on almost every page of *Great Expectations*, modulations characteristic of much of the best nineteenth-century fiction. In *Madame Bovary*, for instance, Flaubert continually shifts with smooth dexterity from declarative directness of description into vividly subtle metaphors and back into flat literalness. Some of the richest pleasures of associative imagining are evoked by such variations, because they encourage ever more intense imaginative activity. Language is polysemic, each word containing within itself meanings differing from, even contrary to, its primary meaning, and skilled novelists build their art upon that self-contradictoriness. Verbal make believe is at root auditory (why, thanks to Bakhtin, we now speak of "polyphonic" novels) and therefore possesses rhetorical devices unavailable in visual make believe. An extreme example although a revealing one, is the linear repetitions of narrative verse. Dactylic hexameter in *The Iliad* or iambic pentameter in *Paradise Lost*, for instance, offer a ground of continuous sensuous formal repetitions by which the sequentiality of the narratives is dramatized. This is a relation of texture to structure unavailable to visual storytellers.

The simplest rhetorical device possessed by novelists but not by moviemakers is the choice of who shall tell their story—a narrator, a single character, many characters, whether speaking or writing letters, and so on. That Dickens chose, against the grain of his usual practice, to tell *Great Expectations* in the first-person mode is of particular significance because Pip, although he becomes associated with criminals and criminality, unlike Raskolnikov, commits no criminal act (except harboring a transported convict). Yet he often feels, and is, "contaminated" by an ambience of criminality. Unlike Raskolnikov, who commits a sensationally public crime and to be redeemed must publicly confess and undergo officially sanctioned punishment, Pip has no specific means for redemption. He can only offer a personal memoir told in a fashion that leaves us in doubt as to how deeply he understands his moral culpability or its source. He cannot, like Raskolnikov, publicly kiss the earth as a manifestation of his desire for forgiveness founded in realization of the evil he has done. For Pip has "appropriately" internalized the ideals of his society, which were making any concept of evil-doing obsolete and replacing it with the concept of law-breaking. *Great Expectations* has in recent years become the most popular of Dickens's novels because it articulates modern uncertainty about what constitutes subjective morality when criminality increasingly infects traditionally responsible elements of our society, founded as it is on legality rather than ethical principles (Arendt, 1963, 120–122).

Pip's internalizing of his society's ideals is specifically focused by his desire to become a gentleman, which means having and spending for personal gratification wealth he did not earn. Pip's internalizations are revealed in his never asking himself why he is troubled by unknowingly having accepted financial support from Magwitch (who earned his money honestly by hard work), when he has had no qualm about believing he was taking Miss Havisham's inherited wealth. This failure in self-awareness is not an idiosyncratic defect of Pip's personality, but the common infection of a "normal" modern mind— everybody invests in the stock market hoping to gain money without effort. The consequences of this way of thinking are dramatized by the humor that keeps erupting in *Great Expectations*. A central function of comedy is to expose the reality underneath socially approved pretenses, and Dickens's novel shows us that in Pip's society an unselfish man like Joe Gargery can be neither a hero nor a saint—only a ludicrous joke. But it is Joe as a creature of language, either used by him or applied to him by Pip, that makes him funny. Joe uses language, and becomes the object of language, in a fashion that proves *he* has internalized almost nothing of his society's real, not pretended, values. He enjoys the newspaper in an unusual way (looking for Js), he is unashamed of earning a meager living by the dirty physical labor of blacksmithing, and his incredible tolerance of his wife's shrewishness arises from having seen his mother battered and maltreated in a manner not seriously condemned by his social superiors. As a figure whose attractiveness derives so largely from his comical engagements with language, Joe (without the faintest tinge of self-righteousness) offers a subjectivity against which Pip's acquired ambitions (contrary to some of his natural attributes revealed not only by Joe's affection but also by much of the language of his autobiography) appear as rotten as Miss Havisham's wedding cake.

Humor always involves the breaking up of preconceptions. So it is significant that the latter part of Dickens's novel provokes less laughter than its beginnings. The melancholy tone of the last third of *Great Expectations* arises principally from the loss of the freedom and vitality of Pip's language of which he is only dimly aware. This devolutionary process may help to explain Dickens's choice of the first-person form, and it makes *Great Expectations* probably the saddest of his fictions, as well as one of the most difficult to adapt into a successful movie. The power of visual storytelling is generated by compelling us to focus on a particular set of events for what it is "here and now" in itself—or at least what the moviemaker wants us to believe the set of events is in itself. Unique sights—distinct singularities—can build to a strongly affective total coherence of visual narrative, but not of the kind of narrative of incomplete and uncertain self-reflexiveness that distinguishes *Great Expectations*. A particular sight in a movie may recall, even repeat, an earlier sight—but in such cases what dominates the mind of a spectator is the phenomenon of recollection or repetition. Novelistic texts can be more subtly interpenetrative (and so be both self-deconstructive and self-reconstructive) in their self-allusiveness. Thus in Chapter 49 of *Great Expectations*, Pip, having journeyed to Satis House to condemn Miss Havisham for misleading him, revisits her room (he tells us) to assure himself that she is well, because walking in the abandoned brewery (the source of the money she didn't give him) he has just had a hallucinatory vision of her hanged—revealing the depth of his unconscious hostility.

> In the moment I was withdrawing my head to go quietly away, I saw a great flaming light spring up. In the same moment I saw her running at me, shrieking, with a whirl of fire blazing all about her, and soaring at least as many feet above her head as she was high. I had a double-caped great-coat on, and over my arm another thick coat. That I got them off, closed with her, threw her down, and got them over her; that I dragged the great cloth from the table for the same purpose, and with it dragged down the heap of rottenness in the midst, and all the ugly things that sheltered there; that we were on the ground struggling like desperate enemies, and that the closer I covered her, the more wildly she shrieked and tried to free herself; that this occurred I knew through the result, but not through anything I felt, or thought, or knew I did. I knew nothing until I knew that we were on the floor by the great table, and that patches of tinder yet alight were floating in the smoky air, which a moment ago had been her faded bridal dress.

This passage is, of course, dense with symbolic overtones, the literal flames, for example, reveal the consuming passion which Miss Havisham has repressed, enriched by the overt sexual implications of the bodily struggle in which Pip tries to "save" her by "covering" her. In narrating this action, Pip says he was unaware of what happened while it was happening. He regains the sense of where he is only as he sees black ashes of her "pure" white bridal dress drifting down upon them, still not even recognizing that his hands have been seriously burned. This telling of his unawareness has the effect of focusing readers' attention on the ambiguities hidden within Pip's claimed feelings and motives. The scene of course echoes Pip's first view of Miss Havisham (chapter 8), but phrases such as "like desperate enemies" and "holding her like a prisoner," trigger our imaginative memory of Magwitch and Compeyson struggling in the marshes. The subterranean allusion of Pip and his false benefactress wrestling ablaze to Pip's true benefactor fighting in the torch-lit marsh necessarily carries judgmental valences, which for the reader are in part determined by reminders of linkages to which Pip the narrator remains as unaware as he is to the implications of his wrestling with Miss Havisham. We read in his account as much what he does not tell as what he does, because we connect what is said here with what has been said—or significantly not said—before.

This internal multileveled self-referentiality does not, of course, exclude external, intertextual references. These are often most effective, however, when integrated into systems of internal allusiveness. But both kinds demonstrate verbal make believe's "openness" of form, its most salient characteristic being a capability for continuously reconfiguring itself. Sequentiality in superior novels is continually counteracted by self-referential feedback on every rhetorical level. It is this continual self-reorganizing that makes novels so satisfying a subject for the exercise of our imagination, especially in rereadings, when we are positioned more fully to appreciate the self-reflective dynamics of the story's linear progress.

Visual narrative is a less open form, less capable of self-reconfiguration. The difference is at the root of most difficulties in adapting nineteenth-century fiction into motion pictures, difficulties that sometimes evoke remarkable ingenuity from moviemakers—as is illustrated by the ending of Lean's movie, which derives from the "revised" version of the conclusion Dickens composed to replace his original. He did so at the suggestion of Edward Bulwer-Lytton, who argued a happier ending would better please a sentimental public. Lean's film comments with hidden sharpness on the change by concluding with a literal visualization of an important passage of fantasy earlier in the novel, when Pip tells us he thought that

> it could not fail to be her [Miss Havisham's] intention to bring us together. She had reserved it for me to restore the desolate house, admit the sunshine into the dark rooms, set the clocks a-going and the cold hearths a-blazing, tear down the cobwebs, destroy the vermin—in short, do all the shining deeds of the young knight of romance, and marry the princess. (Chapter 29)

The movie offers as a "realistic" concluding picture of what in the novel was presented as Pip's foolish *fantasy*. In the novel, Pip's imagining the melodramatic tearing down the shutters, letting in the light, getting rid of the decayed wedding feast and walking away with Estella exhibits his blindness to his complicity in the corruptions embodied in Miss Havisham's darkened rooms and rat-infested wedding cake. He fancies himself the hero of a conventional romance when in fact he is not only the puppet of a convicted criminal but also is trying his best to scorn the kindnesses bestowed on him by generous and decent people. The movie's "happy" ending thus ironically challenges any of its audience who know the novel to consider if they have shared in the blind internalizings of Pip at his least self-conscious. It sends the larger part of the audience, the Bulwer-Lytton part, out of the theater cheered by a conventionally upbeat ending, while in an appropriately visual fashion it evokes for others the unresolved uncertainties with which Dickens exposed how we conceal from ourselves the deadly corruption of our worship of Mammon.

CHAPTER 13

MAGNIFYING CRIMINALITY: *FARGO*, FILM NOIR, AND *A PERFECT WORLD*

Everyone recognizes that in the twentieth century movies have superseded fiction as the most successful form of popular entertainment. Less commented upon is the fact that after the 1930s crime has been increasingly a favored subject for motion pictures, and not just pot boilers but also films of high seriousness both ideologically and aesthetically—a preference less apparent in equivalently serious novels, even when one admits exceptions offered by authors such as Mailer. The difference is a bit surprising, because printed fiction from its picaresque beginnings in the Renaissance has featured criminals—who even play a considerable role in *Don Quixote*. More or less fictionalized biographies of celebrated criminals have always drawn a substantial readership, and in Britain in the eighteenth century both Daniel Defoe and Henry Fielding wrote lengthily of the first "master" criminal, Jonathan Wild. William Godwin at the beginning of the nineteenth century in *Caleb Williams* created what has good claim to being the first detective novel, although it was Poe and Conan Doyle, of course, who established the stereotype of the detective with more brains than police bureaucrats, while Dickens and Wilkie Collins popularized the figure of the sympathetic professional policeman (Miller). Despite this history, recent fiction has not significantly advanced this long tradition, although whodunits keep proliferating. It will help to define formal difference between visual and verbal make believe to investigate why movies may appear to be more effective than fiction in exploring the nature and social importance of modern criminality.

Fielding's and Defoe's works are especially interesting in relation to what has been called the progressive criminalization of industrialized societies, because they depict connections between ever more sophisticated economic structures and ever more systematically organized criminality. Gay's *Beggars Opera* neatly dramatizes this development, playing off Macheath the romantic highwayman against the "crime as business" practiced by Peachum and Lockit. Jonathan Wild was both a "thief taker," an agent of the law, and an organizer of diverse criminal activities. In *Oliver Twist*, Dickens represents Fagin as the mentor of a gang of young thieves who disturbingly resemble an extended family. Two decades later in *Little Dorrit* Dickens created the forger-financier he called (putting his knowledge of French to shrewd use) Merdle. Merdle, who until his suicide is lionized by good society, would have been quite at home in the Enron Corporation. Indeed, had Merdle lived in our own times, he surely would have retired with a golden parachute, or, if briefly sent to an minimum security prison, could have made another fortune on his release by peddling financial advice to suburban investors in southern California. *Great Expectations* offers not only Jaggers, a criminal lawyer who succeeds financially by breaking the law, but also his assistant Wemmick who profits from receiving the "portable property" of clients unsuccessfully defended against execution. Wemmick, though a charming character, lives off criminals and epitomizes the moral schizophrenia foreshadowed by Jonathan Wild. In a polity without social security, his ingenious suburban castle, complete with moat and cannon, is an admirable retirement home for his "Aged P," and a place where Wemmick can honorably court the chastely adroit dish washer, Miss Skiffins. Wemmick succeeds by absolutely segregating his private life from his professional one, but the humor of his arrangement is rooted in an ethical absurdity that isn't funny at all. One cannot bend the law between 9 and 5 Monday through Friday and be morally admirable after hours and on weekends—although millions of commuters give it their best shot.

Dickens's later fiction is driven by his perception that in a society dedicated to the acquisition of money and committed to the rule of law criminality will flourish under the guise of righteous respectability. Pip notices that Jaggers creates the impression of knowing some dark secret about everyone he meets. Jaggers plays on the fact that everyone in contemporary society *is* a potential law-breaker. "Honest" citizens, after all, regularly drive faster than the speed limit and cheat on their taxes—trivial matters in themselves perhaps, but revealing of how easily law-breaking becomes the norm in a society in which legality has more force than ethical commitments. All that matters is not getting caught. The institutionalizing of "law-abiding criminals" begins with the self-validating justification that "everybody does it." The paradox of legality producing criminality, prisons being built with stones of law in William Blake's words, took on special cogency at the end of the 1920s when the conjunction of worldwide economic depression, the disruptive effects of Prohibition in America, and the emergence of talking pictures began to produce movies depicting organized criminality penetrating into the fundamental structures of respectable society.

After the mid-nineteenth century, however, major novelists had largely abandoned subjects of criminality that had fascinated Dickens, Dostoyevsky, and Zola (among others); crime became principally the concern of commercialized fiction by sensationalist writers. There has been, of course, an unending stream of equivalently sensationalist movies, beginning with *The Great Train Robbery*, but the visual medium developed styles of presentation enabling it to make crime a subject of films of social significance and high artistic merit. Much of the fascination for motion pictures critics and historians of *film noir* (whose origins include 1930s gangster films and German expressionism) springs from its success at realizing some of the most powerful capacities peculiar to visual make believe (Naremore, 1998). Because traditional visual artists in the twentieth century tended to concentrate on aesthetic avant-gardism, with a bias toward abstraction, they seldom addressed the mundane passions and suffering and social circumstances of the impoverished, who are most familiar with crime, as victims if not as practitioners. A great many excellent movies, however, have vividly portrayed these conditions and sufferings and their relation to crime. There are, of course, many causes for this difference between modern novels and films (differences I do not wish to exaggerate), but the influence of some fundamental aspects of the form of visual narrative ought not to be disregarded.

The gigantic magnifications of a movie can render unmistakably distinct "microscopic" behavioral acts by which respectable lawfulness slides unobtrusively into criminality, while the enlargement does not destroy the commonplace triviality of these acts. The Coen brothers' Dickensian *Fargo* usefully exemplifies this potency of film because it develops personalities Dostoyevsky introduced with Luzhin and Svidrigailov (Terras, 51–72). In *Crime and Punishment*, however, Luzhin knows he is despicable, and Svidrigailov is aware of his difficulty in distinguishing between fantasy and reality. Lundgren, the car salesman of *Fargo*, is only conscious of the pain of not making lots of money. Luzhin's dirty little trick of planting money on Sonia becomes Lundgren's dirty little trick of having his wife kidnapped, then murdered. Svidrigailov is capable of letting Dounia escape and of killing himself; Lundgren can only run away under a disguised name and fail to commit suicide. There are other, even bleaker "developments." Dostoyevsky narrates a deliberately planned, horrific murder of two women followed by the torture of remorse and despair their murderer undergoes. Seven people are brutally, yet rather casually, murdered in *Fargo*—with not an iota of remorse, regret, or redemption.

Fargo's success at mixing tonalities, in being often as funny as brutal, may also remind us of Dickens's style in *Great Expectations*, particularly because there is some parallel between the two works' critique of "respectability." Lundgren, in fact, is an "advanced" Pip, his "Orlick" entirely internalized. And his resentment is generalized, less personally focused; he has no specific *need* for money, he just wants more. He is, consequently, more abstractly self-righteous than Pip, and is incapable of telling his own story. Although *Fargo*, like Dickens's novel, is sometimes very funny, there is little laughter *in* the movie, and there are no equivalents to the characters of Wopsle, Trabb's Boy, or Wemmick. Instead the movie concentrates on characters detached from any real human relationships solemnly following routines that facilitate the disconnectedness encouraged by contemporary life, while talking with an amusing accent. The linguistic and climatological localization helps us to laugh at truths that in actual life *we* don't find funny. An instance is the couple trying to buy their car without undercoating. In making us laugh at the performance of this widely practiced scam, the movie forces upon us the unpleasant recognition of a hidden connection between a man foisting the falsity of "Tru-Coat" on honest citizens and his responsibility for getting his wife murdered.

Luzhin and Svidrigailov are almost insanely ludicrous—in *Fargo* the "almost" is erased. In part this is achieved by the movie forcing viewers to confront hyper-visuality as a salient feature in the de-realizations of contemporary life. *Fargo*'s characters frequently appear absorbed in TV programs of consistent if diverse vacuity. Mike, Marge's high school classmate, seems to fantasize in a totally conventionalized, soap-opera fashion his marriage and then the death of his wife because he can't cope with the barrenness of his real experience. Repeatedly we are shown a spurious organization of "normal" contemporary life shaped by computers and television programming that creates detachment while pretending to offer "reality." By literally magnifying the ubiquity of electronically generated imagery, *Fargo* makes manifest the processes through which kinesthetic actualities of feeling and behavior are eroded by relentless substitutions for them of commercially fabricated images, a process perfectly suited to visual narrative display.

Fargo's vibrant satire should make us reconsider William Hogarth's distress that as a painter he could not portray a hypocrite, whose appearance falsely represents what he truly is (137). Hypocrisy becomes apparent only with action, which movies alone among the visual arts can enact. Hogarth's frustration as a satirist emerged from his acute perception that hypocrisy was becoming a significant *social* phenomenon, not merely a personal vice. He shrewdly observed that with the rise of modern urban, industrialized, mass societies hypocrisy enters more and more into the ordinary transactions of life. Hypocrisy becomes not only the regular idiom of everyday interpersonal relationships but consistently determines commercial success and one's ability to rise in the social hierarchy. In less populous, less industrialized, less mobile societies, hypocrisy cannot be so significant. An extreme illustration is provided by many of the aboriginal peoples of North America I happen to have studied. Their cultures functioned through small communities, in which everyone was reasonably familiar with everyone else and all shared in multiple communal roles. Exactly opposite conditions prevail in modern society whose emergence Hogarth perceived, and even assisted. He was responsible for the first effective copyright law, which by identifying acts of imagination as personal, not community property (as are myths), opened up make believe as a field for advanced criminal activity.

Many if not most of the people we encounter every day in the contemporary world are either strangers or people with whom our intimacy is limited—colleagues and fellow workers at the office, for example. In these circumstances the hypocrisy of superficial congeniality is almost a necessity. In our complex, technological, densely crowded existence simple sincerity, the antitheses of hypocrisy, is likely to disrupt the smooth functioning of both business and social life. These circumstances make it easy to slalom into slightly dishonest behavior, and from there the going is straight downhill. We are encouraged in this direction by some essential social formations of modern life, most importantly advertising. Advertisers ask only two questions, will it sell? and, is it legally safe? With two yes answers, truth vanishes as completely as in political campaigning. Almost as significant as these overt falsifications upon which all business now relies are the simplifications that technologically mechanized life propagates.

Because of our ignorance of the technology we use every day, we now depend heavily on models and diagrams. Most of us have no idea how lasers, computers, or cell phones work—we are concerned solely with what these artifacts can do and under what conditions they will function most effectively. Staring at the screen of a crashed computer, I feel not far ahead of James Thurber's mother, who cautioned him against driving the car without gasoline because it fried the valves. Our ignorance both provokes and is nurtured by hyper-visual forms of information, consisting largely of the display of reductive visualizations—diagrams and icons superseding written instruction. Good movies restore our natural power of precisely complex and highly individual perception of fully contextualized realities instead of simplified models, sometimes, as with *Fargo*, by exposing the disastrous effects of the commodified simplifications by which we now arrange our lives. Thus in *Fargo* we are shown the two kidnappers with such minute particularity and distinctness that we can't miss the significance of the whores in the movie being unable to distinguish between them beyond "big" and "funny looking." Since movies became possible only through the development of both physical machines and intricate socioeconomic mechanisms of distribution and exhibition, it is ironically heartening when they remind us how the wonders of natural vision are now often diminished by repetitions of simplified images.

Even more important, however, is the movies' success at making visible accelerating changes in social behavior that have become the salient feature of all industrialized cultures. The giant silver screen makes apparent the pressure of vast social forces being manifested in the most transient and superficially unremarkable acts, what Mariano Azuela described as "a host of silly, insignificant things that no one notices . . . even a change of expression . . . lips curled in a sneer" (71). *Fargo* illustrates how a fusing of "crime" movies and "domestic dramas" (e.g., *In the Bedroom*) facilitates this special potency of visual make believe. Lundgren is not a "conventional" criminal; he does not even fit the traditional pattern of the hirer of criminals any better than a pregnant police chief fits law-enforcement stereotypes. Lundgren and Marge Gunderson make obvious destabilizations of traditional social structures, some of which are hospitable to the quiet spread of criminality. These characters reinforce the tiny, local, incremental signs of sociological shifts movies can magnify into conspicuousness without violating their mundane triviality, because everything in a movie is "enlarged." Such significant insignificancies are more difficult to represent in verbal storytelling, because their very naming raises them from being embedded within unnoticed normality of behavior into conspicuousness. The movie *mise-en-scène* offers a context of things as they "naturally" are, only super-sized.

The idea of literary art as imitation, for the novel applied by Stendhal in the famous image of his work as a mirror in the roadway, has for good reasons fallen out of favor with literary critics. Yet "imitation," properly understood, may explain the effectiveness of the magnifications of visual storytelling—which, perhaps because of its obviousness, critics unanimously ignore. The movie imitation of what is familiar is successful because (in terms used by Coleridge) it combines *likeness* to what is represented with *unlikeness* (Coleridge, 1962, 256–269). The visual accuracy with which a film records ordinary behavior in a "natural" context we recognize as artifice for several reasons, the most important being its magnification with consequent hyper-clarity. The movie, to use Coleridge's apt phrasing, does not *compete* with ordinary vision because it so far exceeds it in distinctness and enlargement of details. These enhancements of perception apply as fully to sociological processes as to physical events. I don't denigrate movies' capacity to dazzle us with spectacular excitements, but these delights are flamboyant extensions of motion pictures' ability to enchant us by perspicuous displays of entirely ordinary experiences. Many fine films, such as *Umberto D, Brief Encounter*, and *Tender Mercies*, are founded on deliberately unspectacular imitations of what Wordsworth called "the simple produce of the common day," an old man holding a dog in his arms, a talkative acquaintance in a tea room, a father and young boy clumsily kicking a football back and forth in evening twilight.

Movie imitation is illuminated by the performances of probably the greatest of all mimes, Marcel Marceau, because the art of mime is silently visual and concentrates on movement. Marceau usually began his programs with his simplest miming, of walking. Although I had looked at people walking all my life, it was only on seeing Marceau's performances that I realized I had never truly *seen* a person walk. I was enabled to recognize what human walking *looks like* by Marceau's *not* actually walking, for he stayed in the same place on the stage. Marceau's skill was to imitate a human action in person as Pudovkin imitated the action of scything on film, his artifice of falsification allowing us to perceive the otherwise invisible reality of the rhythm of scything.

A complementary foundation of visual make believe is its singular capability for providing the context of a *complete* environment. Movies can simultaneously make vivid the most trivial behavioral acts while situating them within a limitlessness of what we *might* see. Such potential unboundedness is, in fact, the fundamental condition of all our seeing (Gibson, 206). And the evocation of a total environment most decisively differentiates the movie *mise-en-scène* from theatrical staging—even when the movie takes place entirely within doors in an urban location. But of course it is the scenes of the natural world in which the environmental imagining evoked by visual storytelling is sensationally apparent, and the blatant appeal of such scenes should not blind us to their significance. Motion pictures are the one art that can do justice to our perpetual if unrecognized engagements with all that is not human by which we are continuously surrounded. In *Fargo*, for example, our response to the human absurdities and horrors it unfolds is inflected from the very opening of the film, when the flatbed carrying the kidnap car slowly emerges out of a highway devoid of everything but blowing snow. This empty, anonymous roadway where the first murders are to be committed inaugurates the movie's development of human isolation as the price of technological success. The hilarious yet haunting climax of this theme is the bloodied kidnapper struggling to bury in frozen ground a money-filled suitcase, trying futilely to mark the spot with his windshield scraper next to a fence stretching across mile after mile of empty, frozen fields. Here we *feel* with a shiver how civilizational progress may be bleaker than nature's most brutal indifference. *Fargo* is not unusual but mainstream in thus contextualizing its story of interpersonal conflicts within implications of the vast and inhuman totality of nature. Among more recent films with the same kind of social and psychological foci that offer analogous contextualizing, one might cite *House of Sand and Fog*. Here the liminal impersonality of coastal California gives expanding resonances to a story centered on personal suffering arising from crime created by legalisms, as Terence Malick's *The Thin Red Line* contrasts military technology with the flora and fauna of the island.

Clint Eastwood's slightly older *A Perfect World*, however, presents a particularly useful illustration of how movies' attraction to narratives of criminality may be linked to their success at situating human dramas within a *mise-en-scène* at least implicitly evocative of an encompassing nonhuman environment. The foundation of the linkage is the simple fact that all legal systems are fictions, artificial constructs of some group of human beings. A criminal technically, therefore, is someone who has been convicted of violating a rule that has only local and temporary authority. An act judged criminal here may be perfectly legal in the country on the other side of the mountain, and an act judged this year to be criminal may be legal the next. In social conditions that prevail in the Western world today, legal systems stand free from dependence on any higher authority of religious or ethical sanctions. Legality therefore is whatever people decide it is at any given moment, and, because "crime" has no meaning except as current law defines it, what constitutes criminal behavior is perceived as fluid and arbitrary. One of the appeals of movies is their offering a physically visual rather than ideational context within which moviegoers may explore the ethical significance of actions whose conventional categorizations, most significantly as "crimes," are no longer certain. Moral assessment of such actions may thus be inflected by their display within a superhuman natural environment.

This effect is of course most obvious in movies that take place predominantly out of doors, as happens with all "road chase" movies, the genre to which *A Perfect World* belongs, although it gives unusual emphasis to goalessness. The escaped convict Butch's (Kevin Costner) putative destination is Alaska, where he knows he is not going, and is in his mind only because the one postcard from his father came from there—the father whose desertion he deeply if ambivalently resents. When he tells the boy he has kidnapped that their automobile is a time machine, one feels he describes his purposelessness as well as helping young Philip enjoy the ride. The pointlessness of their journey we perceive appropriately in a Texas landscape virtually without boundaries. Only a movie can present us with such limitlessness of open country, a *mise-en-scène* that simultaneously manifests and ironizes Butch's, and perhaps our own, aspiration for personal freedom. The natural setting serves another ironic purpose in allowing Butch to demonstrate how ill-suited he is for the role of mindless drifter, offering wide scope for the display of his agile intelligence, not only in improvising but also in planning ahead and accurately forecasting consequences. He consistently acts upon acute insight into the character of those he encounters, and he becomes genuinely interested in Philip as only an intelligent adult can be interested in a child. Meanwhile, a vehicular office serves to disorient (both literally and symbolically) the Sheriff Red Garret (Clint Eastwood) and reverses the conventionally linear relation of hunter and hunted, since finally the sheriff is trying to save Butch. Like Ahab after Moby Dick, the sheriff begins by trying to establish through "scientific" techniques where the criminal is to be located, but for the spectators the continuous flow of landscape increasingly compels viewers to regard both Butch's circling and the sheriff's pursuit (through which he is ever more entangled by the unexpected consequences of his earlier actions) as poignantly meaningless within the context of vast, enduring rhythms of the natural environment.

This making visible an ironic structure of futility is initiated by *Perfect World*'s opening credits, where we see Butch lying in the grass. Since we see only his face, we may think he is sleeping, and wonder why the dollar bills drift in the wind and the ghost mask and the post card lie in the grass. This scene is "repeated" at the conclusion of the movie; then we see the wind comes from the whirling blades of the rising helicopter. The detail prevents the natural scene from being frozen into mere symbolism even as it presents a final instance of circularities out of which the story is constructed, but which are consistently violated by the intrusion of contingent events. The unpredictable within the repeating circles of *A Perfect World* climaxes in the scene with the African American family. The episode (unusually lengthy in recent filmmaking) is constructed with a wide variety of shots, including some intricate manipulations of lenses and camera angles. We are not likely to notice such technical artistry because of the horror aroused at the apparent inevitability of a brutal murder. This "success," however, is probably a cause for the movie's relatively lack of popular appeal. A situation in which an attractive man (and a "heroic" movie star) reveals himself to be a psychopathic killer must provoke discomfort. And the color of the participants intensifies such anxiety. How many movies have shown a white man preparing gratuitously to murder a decent black man before the eyes of his wife and child? Worse, the killer is free of racial prejudice. The movie is unique in presenting a scene of personal violence involving people of different races, with the difference emphasized, but in which the violence has nothing to do with race. This challenge to our preconceptions about both prejudice and violence is peculiarly upsetting because it comes in visual form—which automatically compels us to respond to the distinction between "black" and "white," the very difference that made possible motion pictures. No verbal telling could so effortlessly keep this complex of contrasting preconceptions so continuously at the forefront of our awareness.

Butch is about to kill the African American farmer not because he is black but because he has displayed an attitude (abuse of a child) that Butch can't tolerate. Exemplified here is the very foundation of human intolerance: Butch cannot control the feelings of anger that rise up inside him. This is a scene to which Afro-Americans will respond differently from whites, but I assume that most spectators both favor racial tolerance and condemn child abuse. For such viewers, Butch is dismaying because his extreme hatred of child abuse undercuts his appeal as a parental figure. The movie has steadily provoked our admiration for his behavior as a surrogate for Philip's absconded father—not merely indulging the boy but consistently building his self-respect and self-confidence (especially in trusting him to control the runaway car) and treating him with forthrightness and honesty that should foster those virtues in the boy. A troubling awareness that must surface as Butch prepares to kill the black farmer is that we have been approving a psychologically damaged criminal as a good parental model.

A Perfect World here illustrates how visual narrative can extend the paradox of the close-up, wherein the clarity with which we see enhances the enigmaticness of what we see. The movie's plot forces upon our attention a puzzle of positive relations between a religiously inhibited child and a psychologically injured adult (how often movies are built around the stories of an odd couple!), which reaches its ironic climax in this scene. When Butch first breaks into Philip's house he persuades the terrified child to pick up the fallen revolver, point it at Butch, and say "Bang!" Seeing, rather than imagining, Butch thus trying to free the boy from his fear surprises us—how can a violent criminal behave in this fatherly fashion? And the further the story develops the more we (along with the sheriff) realize that we do not, and probably can never, entirely comprehend Butch. And as that realization strengthens, it surreptitiously prepares us for the reverse surprise of Philip, fulfilling what Butch desired for him, having the courage to shoot Butch.

Although the springs of personality and interior motives are always hidden, always only to be imagined, relations are embodied in visible behavior. *A Perfect World* illustrates the special efficacy of visual make believe to exhibit without oversimplifying relational ambivalences and ambiguities by displaying minuscule and fleeting behavioral acts without abstracting them from their environing circumstances, spatial, temporal, or social. Eastwood's movie exploits this capacity, not least in offering a respectful presentation of a preadolescent boy shaped by his family's religion. As a Jehovah's Witness, Philip is cut off from many "normal" activities, here specifically from Halloween trick-or-treating. The shot of him inside his house looking out the window at the other children derisively pelting him epitomizes the isolation to which his mother's faith condemns him. But the suburbanized Halloween proceedings, including an adult-chaperoned gang throwing debris at a lonely boy, suggest "normality" has its dark sides.

Although we see Philip's working mother doing her best, without a husband, to give her children full moral and physical support, the restrictions of Philip's family faith enable Butch to give the boy experiences he has been cut off from. In helping Philip to mature, Butch gives him freedom—spectacularly realized when he lets Philip, in lieu of a roller coaster, ride on the top of the speeding car (the ambiguity of course being that Philip has to be tied down). But the freedom includes stealing a Halloween mask, and their adventure together is no mere rejection of Philip's heritage—he wants (and Butch plans for him) to return to his mother, whom he insists is "good." Throughout their time together we see that Philip possesses strength to overcome induced inhibitions and the intelligence to learn what Butch teaches. And, despite our admiration for Butch's understanding of and respect for Philip, and his efforts to let the boy find himself, we recognize the depressing conventionality of Butch's ideas of god-given American rights to eat cotton candy and ride roller-coasters. That recognition, however, increases our awareness of how little social assistance Butch has had in developing his impressive natural gifts. As the story unfolds it steadily increases the complexity of the audience's ambivalences. Butch's "freedom" is taking him nowhere, and the personal independence of maturity he points Philip toward seems too much the freedom of someone who cannot be totally in control of himself. Yet Philip's decisive act of shooting Butch ironically strengthens our conviction that Butch is a far better man than the official representative of law-and-order (the other person who shoots him), the out-of-control FBI agent who successfully relies on social support for a buttoned-up and vicious selfishness. Through these inversions and reversals, *A Perfect World* troubles us by suggesting how perilously close to our society's ideals of individual maturity—and even of responsible fatherhood—are the criminal's rather than the licensed lawman's attributes.

That Butch understands the rightness of Philip's actually picking up the gun and shooting him as he had taught the boy underscores the ironies of the final scene in which Butch is gratuitously killed in the open field. Not the least of these ironies is Sheriff Garrett's recognition of his responsibility for having brought Butch into a situation where he can "justifiably" be killed. Garrett is like Butch: he will not let himself off the hook with easy excuses. Butch, for example, has been explicit to Philip that stealing is wrong, although sometimes one is so positioned that one has to steal. Butch never falsely justifies his actions, one reason he appears a good parental model. Analogously, Red Garrett did what he sincerely believed was the right thing for Butch as a boy. But that for him—and for any thoughtful spectator— is his problem, not its solution. So his final words (to be almost exactly echoed by Marge Gunderson at the close of *Fargo*) speak appropriately for the film's viewers as well as himself: "I don't understand a thing; I don't understand a damn thing." The moral resonance of the words arises from our having seen events posing unanswered questions not only with absolute lucidity but always within the context of a beautiful environment—"a perfect world."

My attention to the inconclusiveness of many fine movies is intended to emphasize how visual make believe is profoundly rooted in the normal processes of vision. In actual life, visual experience is continuous, and always an experience of possibilities—even on the dim-lit stair, is there another step here? As many experiments have proved, the quality of our vision declines if the visual array around us is too uniform and unexciting. Visual scanning is insatiably curious, and that curiosity visual storytelling enhances. Perhaps above all else it uncovers how much that is problematic is concealed by the transparently obvious. Implicitly or explicitly, visual make believe renders reciprocally relevant to each other our smallest, most commonplace acts and the encompassing boundlessness of our environment— without which there would be neither range nor enduring power to imagining of any kind. This is why it is reasonable to assert that "cinema . . . of its essence [is] a dramaturgy of Nature" (Bazin, 1997, 110). This fundamental orientation of movies is readily perceptible in a film such as *A Perfect World*, but, with Bazin, I believe it is, as implicitly effective even in films confined to dark interiors of ill-lit city streets, the most usual *mise-en-scène* for movies about crime, such as *film noir*.

Among good representatives of the diversity of films about criminals one might cite from different eras Lang's *M*, Huston's

Asphalt Jungle, and Leigh's *Vera Drake*. Surprisingly considering their settings, none makes one feel claustrophobic, although each emphasizes conditions painfully cramped, cribbed, and confined. Even watched in dark, stuffy, rather uncomfortable theaters these grim depictions of enclosed urban interiors seldom produce the suffocating effect one might expect. Partly the cause is the continuous movement in a narrative film. Mobility is the essential characteristic of life, and response to visible energies of life is the fundamental pleasure in every movie. And that pleasure implies the ultimate context of all terrestrial seeing, the ever-changing circumambience of light, displayed or implied. "Crime" is never "natural"—by definition it is a social construction. For spectators not profoundly committed to any religiously validating system, but who feel that not only murder, but many other kinds of inhumane behavior are "wrong," a movie's evocation, even if only by implication, of the natural context of all human behavior offers a nonsectarian, nonideological basis on which strong and complicated but personal emotionalized judgments may be created. The extensive commentary on *film noir* leads me to believe most moviegoers' responses to urban crime films are morally conflicted. These movies' dark concentration on constricted, oppressive city settings seem to evoke simultaneous condemnation of criminal acts *and* of the social conditions that make them possible, even inevitable. We do not forgive the "bad" people for their actions, but are made uncomfortable that we cannot do so. Such movies are peculiarly troubling—yet fascinating—in making us feel how fundamental circumstances of modern life (epitomized by the motion picture itself) pervert what we feel should be "natural" human relationships.

Movies are at their best when depicting violent action, plenty of which crime stories supply. The importance of this banal point is suggested by the relative rarity in literature of scenes like those of Raskolnikov's murders. Crime, after all, is essentially physical behavior. And crime is a behavioral act that in one fashion or another reveals practices of hypocrisy that movies are supreme among the arts at exposing. Critics have shown convincingly that *film noir* formally depends on hyper-dramatic visual, structural, and moral contrasts— thereby making direct use of the foundational formal opposition of black and white, light and dark, upon which every part of every movie is built. Substantively, every movie displays human actions occurring within a context of visible circumstances composed of physical phenomena embodying the nonhumanness of our environment. That is why to me modern crime appears unusually appropriate subject matter for a popular art which, as Parker Tyler suggested, recovers to carry forward the deeply rooted Western conception of the finest art as that which, without sinking into superficial verisimilitude, seeks to embody its most imaginative visions in representations scrupulously imitative of the world as it is—for good or ill.

Chapter 14

Innovative Lawfulness: Learning to Read

Visual make believe cannot directly represent the imagery of dreams. Dreams are involuntary imaginings and exteriorizing them falsifies their subjective nature. Subjective experience is sharable with others only through language. All nonlinguistic semiotic systems are efficacious only for "exterior" communications. For practical cooperation in external affairs, humans could get along with something close to the gesture-inflected pseudo-languages animals use. Human speech alone enables us to enter into one another's dreams, aspirations, ideas, memories, desires, all that is imagined. Through such communication of the subjective arise enduring creations of myth, history, religion, and literary art that are the essence of every civilization.

The successful communication of our subjectivity to others makes possible reciprocal intimacies unknown to any other creature. Storytelling nurtures this intimacy, because stories are the principal language form that facilitates sharing the emotional, aspirational, and moral orientations of consciousness. I call the psychic activity evoked by verbal make believe associative imagining, because psychoanalysis has familiarized us with the paradox that "free associating" may be simultaneously logical and a-logical. Words seemingly without rational connection to one another when spoken in the context of a whole set of terms may reveal fundamental psychic patterns. "Associating" means bringing together elements that remain disparate, establishing connections between items that stay independent. Associative imagining is an additive process that encourages the crossing of mental and linguistic boundaries. "Free association," as Freud perceived, calls attention to the perpetually dynamic interplay between mind and language. Our verbalizations affect how and what we imagine, even as how and what we imagine affects our verbalizations. We can articulate our subjective imaginings solely through the learned constructs of some common language. But by so communicating we can affect how these constructs function, thereby endowing them with the power to modify reality. Verbal make believe thus can shape and enrich the significance of involuntary imagining.

Crime and Punishment exemplifies different ways in which verbal storytelling can evoke the experience of dreaming. Svidrigailov's dreams shortly before he commits suicide follow the style of Lockwood's dreams at the opening of *Wuthering Heights*. Like Brontë, Dostoyevsky evokes the circumstance in which a dreamer is partially aware that he is dreaming. But Dostoyevsky ratchets up the hyper-reality of some unpleasant dream experiences, as when, trying to sleep in the dirty hotel room the night before his suicide, Svidrigailov tells himself to stop thinking about Dounia. Then—

> He was beginning to doze. His fevered shivering slackened a little. Suddenly he felt something run across his arm, then his leg, under the blanket. He shuddered. "Damn! A mouse . . . because I left the veal on the table." He resisted uncovering himself and getting up in the cold, but all at once something scrambled unpleasantly over his leg. He threw off the blanket and lit the candle. Shaking from the chill of his fever, he stooped, searching the bed. Nothing. He shook the blanket, and a mouse dashed onto the sheet. He tried to catch it, but the mouse zigzagged elusively, not leaving the bed, slithering under his fingers, then ran over his hand and his underneath the pillow. He flung the pillow on the floor, but at once felt something leap onto his chest, run under his shirt across his body, down his back. Shivering, he woke up. (6:6)

So vivid here is the evocation of the liminal processes by which our mind creates transitions between inner and outer realities that a reader is as startled as Svidrigailov at waking up. A dream of a mouse running over one's body may have a stronger affect than would the actual event, because the imaginer contributes to the sensations, rather than passively undergoing them. Less literal and more surreal transitions surface in Svidrigailov's subsequent dream of the rain-soaked little girl he finds in the hall, puts to bed, and before leaving checks to see if she is asleep. He notices an unnatural flush of her cheeks.

> She's feverish, Svidrigailov thought. Or perhaps wine. It seems as if somebody may have given her a glass full of wine. Her lips were scarlet, burning. What's this? Suddenly it seemed that her very long, dark

eyelashes flickered, then fluttered as if about to lift, and a sharp, sly eye peeked out. Her eye winked at him in an unchildish way, as if she were just pretending to be asleep. She *was* pretending. Her lips were parting in a smile. The tiny corners of her mouth quivered as though she was restraining herself — and then she let go — laughing, laughing openly at him. The unchildlike face became provocative, hard-bitten, shameless. It was a whore's expression . . . the total lewdness of the child's face was appalling. "What? A five-year old?" Svidrigailov whispered in horror. (6:6)

Here Dostoyevsky seizes on the narrative structuring of much dreaming to represent the fearful transformative potency of imagining, deliberate or involuntary. Dreaming or storytelling, we can make external reality malleable, modifying by the creative vitality of our self-reflective subjectivity any features of our environment. When awake, conscious of the limitations, material reality seems to impose upon our actions, we usually confine our imagining to the accomplishment of feasible tasks. But when we dream, our self-consciousness adventures into improbabilities, even impossibilities. The novelist deliberately fits such psychic adventuring into the coherence of his narrative to arouse in readers new insights into the reciprocal affects of mind and environment.

Crime and Punishment also includes a different kind of dream when Raskolnikov remembers the horse beaten to death by peasants (2:5). The narrator tells us that it is a dream of Raskolnikov's, but nothing ostentatiously distinguishes these paragraphs from other narrative portions of the novel. This "dream" could well be a literal memory of Raskolnikov's; most critics have treated it as an "actual" memory recalled in a dream. Dreaming, imagining, and remembering are intimately interconnected. Verbal storytelling always comes after the events it narrates, and so invariably involves some mnemonic *remaking*. In shared make believe diverse "memories" are a primary foundation for communicability of subjective "inventions" — memories of what has happened *in* the story, and perhaps what a character or narrator recalls as "preceding" the events being recounted, plus common memories of the actualities from the external context of reality of the story shared by teller and audience. As time passes the context of external reality changes, so the mode of sharing alters, and the "classic" story takes on fresh life through new meanings the teller could not have predicted.

However sensational, nothing in Raskolnikov's horse-beating dream contravenes how we commonly experience events in our waking life. The ghastliness of what happens in front of the tavern consists in what would be perfectly possible for us to remember had we been present. This dream has been triggered by a letter from Raskolnikov's mother, telling of Dounia's plan to sacrifice herself for him (an act which he has no way of preventing), and claiming to recall "good times" when his father was alive. The dream presents what could scarcely be called a good time, made worse by the father's timorous evasiveness, his words being "don't look," "come away," "it's none of our business." The dream, whether or not founded on an "actual" experience, embodies Raskolnikov's judgments on himself and his family that have brought him into his present terrible position. In a dream everything, all the people and all the events and objects, are created by the dreamer—as everything in the novel is the novelist's imagining. Raskolnikov is not only the boy in his dream, witnessing the killing, but also Mikolka, the killer, the other peasants (such as the one who shouts, "Get an ax!"), his father, even the horse. *In* the dream Raskolnikov runs to the horse to protect it; but Mikolka *in* the dream is also Raskolnikov, murderously battering a helpless creature (Raskolnikov as horse)—even as his father unable to confront reality is also Raskolnikov. The dream thus offers a second level of the processes of imagining experienced by a reader of *Crime and Punishment*. In sharing Dostoyevsky's make believe we take part in creating out of our psychic energies all the figures and actions of the story that, Dostoyevsky imagined out of himself, just as "Raskolnikov" created everything in his dream. The decisive difference, of course, is that Raskolnikov did not consciously control his dreaming, so it remains within the novel a purely private experience, unknown to anyone else. Dostoyevsky, however, constructed *Crime and Punishment* to be read by others, thereby making it a focus for creative imagining even by non-Russian readers a century and a half later.

Verbal storytelling is the transformation by a teller of thoughts, desires, fantasies, and memories, some vague and some hyper-specific, into an intensely organized linguistic structure. Language makes possible the mutual creativity of teller and audience because it is a system with almost unlimited powers of self-reconfiguring. Every language easily develops new words for new facts or ideas. Even more important, every human language readily articulates unresolvable contradictions. Such paradoxes mark the limit of a given mode of mental activity, thereby offering an opportunity for the development of a new way of thinking to overcome the limitation. Thus philosophers' traditional example of paradox, the Cretan who tells you all Cretans are liars, may be "resolved" by a tiny linguistic recategorizing, such as putting quotation marks around "liars." This power to reconstruct our mental capabilities is energized by verbal make believe. How this happens is explained by Coleridge's description of Shakespeare as the finest exemplar of the "genius" of human imagination, which "cannot be lawless; for it is even this that constitutes genius—the power of acting creatively under laws of its own origination." A common language allows all who share it to participate in such innovative lawfulness, so that *all* readers may benefit from the poet's private make believe that directs "self-consciously a power and an implicit wisdom deeper even than our consciousness" (Coleridge, 1960, 198).

The greatest power of verbal make believe is to change our mind's organization, above all its systems of categorizing. This is accomplished by a story's productive recursiveness—an exercising of our consciousness of being conscious. The exercise allows our mind to reconfigure itself, to modify preconceptions even physical time and space, as is illustrated by is the opening sentence of *A Hundred Years of Solitude* (as translated by Gregory Rabassa). Like the first sentence of *Pride and Prejudice*, this one's complexity has presented no difficulty to thousands of readers—proof that verbal make believe exploits elemental—not esoteric—qualities of language. "Many years later, as he faced the firing squad, Colonel Aureliano Buendia was to remember that distant afternoon when his father took him to discover ice." Readers' imaginations have no difficulty in accompanying the colonel's memory back across several decades, nor of at once entering the mind of a man facing (as they never have) a firing squad, or "recalling" a less violent but perhaps more meaningful experience they themselves may have forgotten of "discovering" ice. Neither do readers have difficulty accepting as a starting point the indeterminate comparative "later." This is the true "magical realism" of all verbal make believe that appeals first and foremost to the eager delight with which we exercise our imaginative powers. The exercise serves to strengthen our shaping engagement with reality, not merely assisting us to comprehend the actuality of firing squads that execute men who once were children for whom ice was an exciting discovery, but also increasing the power of our minds to unify disparate events unconnected in time or place into the super-organization of an individual consciousness. Embodied for readers in a single sentence is the process of imaginative reconfiguring by which we extend and enhance our emotionalized experiences (Kearny, 17) and thereby improve our ability to refashion nonsubjective realities.

Superior make believe of all kinds strengthens our capacities for dealing with new and unexpected situations in the real world, and also to change it, hopefully to make it a better, not a worse, place for the flourishing of individual self-consciousness. The make believe of excellent films and novels is the precise reverse of "escapist," for it teaches responsibly proactive engagement with both social and natural environments. But movies and fiction teach in decisively different ways. And probably the best way to appreciate the unique potency of verbal make believe is to examine the experience of rereading. Among novelists writing in English, Jane Austen best illustrates the rereadability of fiction. Her novels appear to be the most reread by the greatest number and variety of readers. Many of these, moreover, testify to being addicted to *frequent* rereadings. To speak only for myself, I have read, taught, and written about Jane Austen for more than fifty years, and I continue to reread her novels with undiminished pleasure and profit. A substantive cause is the subtle cogency with which her fiction demonstrates how and why relations of recognized mutual interdependence are indispensable to the success of both individuals and communities. But there is a deeper appeal.

The Greeks made memory the mother of all the muses, yet she is far more active in the experience of musical compositions and verbal storytelling than in any of the visual arts. The enjoyment of symphonies and novels demands continuous exercise of our mnemonic skills, about which most of us are ignorant, although we busy ourselves remembering things all the time. Plenty of psychologists and physiologists eagerly offer explanations, but unfortunately their disagreements recall a bad day in Bosnian history. Most of the combatants now concur, however, that memory is not composed of neat little images stored somewhere in our brain that we pull out from their pigeon hole when we want them. Agreement that this naive scenario can't be correct has led to growing attention to the presentness of remembering, memory as a current activity of the mind. But what is the mind doing now as it remembers? The most convincing neuroscientific explanation I have found is that the mind remembering is reorganizing itself (Edelman and Tononi, 93–101). This is peculiarly interesting because we use our memory vigorously all the time. We couldn't decide wisely what to avoid or what to pursue without our memory. It is astonishing how much we can bring to mind instantaneously and with what precision—our memory is so consistently efficient that we notice with irritation when we can't remember something. The process by which remembering reorganizes our mind may be described as the opposite of feedback. Feedback depends on prespecification—you preset the furnace thermostat for a certain temperature. Feedback is a corrective and responsive process: it responds to previously selected "information" (in the furnace thermostat, to air temperature changes) in a fixed way in order to return to a predefined condition—the temperature you desire. Memory, to the contrary, can function as part of an open selective system that chooses amongst "information" that has not been prespecified. We can choose to remember anything we wish. Nor is the consequence of the selection predetermined. What we do with memory may have little or nothing to do with what provoked it.

Remembering is not the reiterating of something fixed in the past but a recreating of previous psychic events under different conditions. Remembering, therefore, always transforms what is remembered. This is why the poet Wordsworth, who anticipated many modern conceptions of how our mind functions, insisted that memory was a creative power. The neuronal basis for this process of renewal seems to be that input to the brain, a visual perception, let us say, never affects only a single point but always affects different points in a network. How the brain categorizes the perception is determined by the patterning created by interchanges between different points in the particular brain network affected. When the next perception arrives, the brain has a pattern into which to fit it. But perception #2 arrives later than #1—and in that time, brief though it may be, both the brain-context and the environmental context have changed: we are vital, ever-changing organisms in a dynamically unstable world. Therefore the brain may fit #2 into its established pattern, thereby reinforcing #1, or it may modify the existent pattern to accommodate #2's inevitable "historical" difference from #1 (Edelman, 1989 209–212; 1992, 81–91).

Memory is an "open system" as defined by Mayr. Remembering is not an automatic response. It is active, a "choosing" what to do with the phenomena with which we are presented or which we discover, either outside or inside our body. The basis for our "choice" is presumably what seems best for us, the remembering organism, what will make us stronger, more effective, better able to cope. Memory thus becomes the foundation for learning, our means for putting both past and new experience to what we as individuals judge to be the most productive use. Exercising memory may enhance the effectiveness of our brain networking, sometimes by reinforcing an established pattern, but sometimes by revising to improve the pattern (which will alter the relation of that network to others). This understanding of memory appeals because it helps to explain the evolutionary success of the human species. Our power of reconfiguring our mental capacities would seem to make us an organism perfectly adapted to a dynamic environment. Viruses and similar tiny organisms of course do quite well by breeding very quickly, but their method remains confined within the mechanisms of genetics. That allows us, at least temporarily, to clobber bacteria we disapprove of with an invented antibiotic. Humans, that is, can deliberately choose to change themselves and their environment for what they judge to be their benefit—which almost invariably means some other species pays a price. But without ignoring the claims of spotted owls or Siberian tigers, we should recognize, first, that Mother Nature's economy runs on the brutal rule that anyone's success is at somebody else's expense, so that, second, the dangerous power of our self-consciousness in *no* way alienates us from the natural world. To the contrary, it makes us a species well fitted to survive in an environment operating on principles of purposeless evolution.

Language enables "collective memory," but remembering occurs only in single organisms; remembering establishes and sustains individuality. No other creatures of which we have knowledge are individualized as are human beings, because none of them possess the power consciously to reconfigure the systems by which they think, feel, perceive, and behave. Verbal storytelling is always promulgated by an individual, always begins in the expression of a single person's imagining. But, appropriately shaped and structured, my story can be imagined by others, for all humans possess mnemonic and imaginative powers. That the form of narrative provides access into it for someone not the narrator is proved by the amazing facility of stories, despite language barriers, in crossing cultural boundaries. In a relatively brief time, the story of Cinderella moved from its point of origin in South East Asia into Northern Europe. Stories have been described as the most transmissible of human artifacts. The structure of a story, one might say, offers a pattern for mental reconfiguring. And so far as that opportunity is seized by an audience, there emerges an amazing thing—a community of individuals. We should not be surprised, then, by the fact that, just as we know of no human society without language, so we know of no human society without stories. Verbal storytelling has been of the utmost importance in every human culture because it is a primary means for developing skills in exercising individual self-consciousness in a fashion that fosters communally profitable interpersonal relations—which in turn sustain the productive individuality of community members.

Here we need to recollect that psychic organization is an organization sensual and emotional as well as intellectual—and a good verbal story appeals strongly to all these powers. Building on the existence of a common language, the story's structuring permits an audience to enter into its *process of development*. The complexities involved in this are difficult truly to comprehend because it is so much easier to think of what is produced, the result of evolving activities, something determinate and completed, which allows us to conceive of the process in terms of an intention that is fulfilled. Such a conception distorts by oversimplifying. A story is created in and by every phase of its telling, its precise direction being *discovered* only as it is formed, rather in the manner of physical evolution by which, for instance, five-toed horses became the one-toed animals familiar to us. And, as we noticed before, storytelling is a process that audiences participate in making. This participation may not result, as Vygotsky observed, in immediate practical activity, yet it may be a significant mental learning experience—learning about one's capabilities, limitations, and possibilities as a sensual/emotional being blessed with self-understanding that permits modifying one's natural inheritance as well as previously learned psychic habits. This is true learning, not a passive reception of information, but a self-enhancing of one's competence in putting to fresh use sensory sensitivities, emotions, and reason.

The foregoing is an answer to the inquiry with which I began, why for thousands of years millions of people have enjoyed telling and attending to stories they recognize as make believe. It also allows us to escape from the modern presupposition that the deepest significance of a story is its plot, an essential meaning that can be abstracted from the particularity, and particular sequence, of events it recounts (Brooks). The plot is, indeed, the skeleton of story to which all its delightful flesh adheres. But if an abstractable plot were so dominant we would never reread a novel by Tolstoy or Jane Austen. We do reread good novels with pleasure and profit because their form consists of much more than their skeleton. What we like about novels is what we like about people, not the articulation of their bony structure (necessary though that is) but the vitally shifting complexities of relations between physical flesh and psychic activities that stimulate our imagination. It is our experience of a *historical process* that makes a verbal story enchanting. Even on a first reading, that history rewards us by more than mere satisfaction of curiosity about what will happen next. By moving our mind continuously backward as well as ahead, the story engages us in reshaping our consciousness. That reward may increase with rereading, because then we use what we've gained from the earlier experience to enter more deeply into the narrative's processes of imagining.

Self-reconfiguring is especially rewarding in Jane Austen's novels because even their simple plots are innovative. Though critics casually categorize them as "courtship" or "marriage" novels, the story of each is without significant literary predecessor, though each has become a model for subsequent popular fiction and film. *Pride and Prejudice* supplied the pattern for the earliest Harlequin romances, and *Emma* is the model for "Chick Lit" such as *Bridget Jones*. No novel before *Mansfield Park* had built its love story around an open-minded exploration into incestual inclinations: "Children of the same family, the same blood, with the same first associations and habits, have some means of enjoyment in their power, which no subsequent connection can supply . . . even the conjugal tie is beneath the fraternal" (*Mansfield Park*, 2:24). And the only precedent for the key plot element of *Persuasion*, the successful renewal of a rejected marriage proposal, is *Pride and Prejudice*. The repeated-proposal story in its original form develops from the chapter following the first proposal (2:12), when Darcy finds Elizabeth walking in grounds of Rosings and hands her the letter he wrote after she had dismissed him. The text of the letter constitutes the entire remainder of the chapter and marks a radical modification in the tradition of epistolary fiction, novels made up entirely of letters, which Samuel Richardson had made the favorite novelistic form in Britain. It seems likely that when first composed (in the 1790s) *Pride and Prejudice*, then entitled *First Impressions*, was written as a epistolary novel. Why Austen revised the traditional form appears in Volume 2, Chapter 13, of *Pride and Prejudice*, the first chapter in fiction narrating the experience and consequences of multiple *rereadings*.

Elizabeth interpreting and reinterpreting Darcy's account of his opinions and actions is unrepresentable in visual narrative, especially because Darcy's letter is analytically retrospective, rehearsing in minute detail, for example, his various encounters with Elizabeth over the past few months. This concentration on memories compels Elizabeth to reexamine and reevaluate their past relationships with equivalent mnemonic scrupulosity. When Darcy writes of his youth and events relating to his sister of which Elizabeth has no first-hand knowledge, she has no choice but thoughtfully to analyze the conflicting accounts of Darcy and Wickham to decide which appears more truthful on the basis of its formal coherence and logicality. The whole process of reinterpretive reading, of textual criticism, is an imaginative act, not mere recall. Elizabeth is compelled consciously to *reexamine* not merely what happened but why, how she felt and why, what she assumed Darcy's feelings were and why. She is forced to pass judgment on others and herself. And when we read, or reread, this chapter we necessarily become involved in Elizabeth's careful—and revisionary moral discriminating.

These pages are without physical action. They tell solely of a mind absorbed in self-reflective interpreting. They manifest the very processes by which we interpret verbal make believe, for example, *Pride and Prejudice*—and above all how our imagination is stimulated into evaluative reassessments of earlier judgments. Although there is no account of Elizabeth's bodily movements, the chapter conveys the effect of a tremendous exertion of mental energy as she reconstructs her moral position. When Elizabeth finally heads back to the Collins's house, her imagining provoked by Darcy's letter has radically altered her morally.

> How despicably I have acted. . . . I, who have prided myself on my discernment! . . . How humiliating is this discovery!—Yet how just a humiliation! Had I been in love, I could not have been more wretchedly blind. But vanity, not love, has been my folly. . . . I have courted prepossession and ignorance, and driven reason away, . . . till this moment I never knew myself.

One would seek in vain through the hundreds of earlier epistolary novels for an equivalent passage of such intensely interpretive response to a letter, such an evocation of the dynamics of rereading arousing stringent critical self-evaluation—"I have courted prepossession and ignorance." In reading we share in Elizabeth's reshaping of her response to the letter and through that process reconfiguring her understanding of all the events that provoked its writing. These acts of consciousness alter Elizabeth's ethical judgments, because she does not evade, dismiss, or ignore her past but applies her imagination to reevaluate it. That mental process empowers her to reverse, not just her view of the past but also her current manner of thinking and behaving: She is the same person self-fashioned into a different one by rereading. And by sharing in her self-reconfiguring, readers of

Pride and Prejudice partake of that self-reconstituting power. This is an activity to which any intelligent and morally serious person would be happy to return—indeed, which may become more addictive than jogging or pumping iron.

The story of Elizabeth's rereading embodies the way verbal make believe enables us to reconstruct the workings of our mind through attention to the processes by which our thinking and feeling and evaluating have arrived at their present condition. But *Pride and Prejudice* of course offers a second proposal scene that complicates and enriches by further developing the processes set in motion by the first proposal and Elizabeth's response to Darcy's letter. Her reading of the letter does not make Elizabeth love Darcy. She is clear and explicit about her feelings—she does not at all regret rejecting his proposal because she does not love him. She regrets only that she misjudged him through vanity and deliberate ignorance (which may remind us of how much of our ignorance is chosen, not inadvertent). Some months later, however, she walks alone with Darcy, the physical situation deserves notice, because three of the culminating proposals in Austen's novels are made while the couples walk (Darcy and Elizabeth for "several miles"), and in two others proposals are followed by confirmatory conversations on long walks. In a quiet way, expressive of Austen's trust in her readers' intelligence, she shows the union will be as active physically as it is emotionally vital. Here Elizabeth thanks Darcy for saving her sister Lydia, telling him that if the rest of her family knew, they would be as grateful. He replies that her family owes him nothing, that in his actions he had thought only of her.

> Elizabeth was too much embarrassed to say a word. After a short pause, her companion added, "You are too generous to trifle with me. If your feelings are still what they were last April, tell me so at once. *My* affections and wishes are unchanged, but one word from you will silence me on this subject for ever."
>
> Elizabeth feeling all the more than common awkwardness and anxiety of his situation, now forced herself to speak; and immediately, though not very fluently, gave him to understand that her sentiments has undergone so material a change, since the period to which he alluded, as to make her receive with gratitude and pleasure, his present assurances. The happiness which this reply produced, was such as he had probably never felt before; and he expressed himself on the occasion as sensibly and warmly as a man violently in love can be supposed to do. Had Elizabeth been able to encounter his eye, she might have

seen how well the expression of heart-felt delight, diffused over his face, became him; but, though she could not look, she could listen, and he told her of feelings, which, in proving of what importance she was to him, made his affection every moment more valuable. (3:16)

This is the climax of the novel, the point toward which more than 200 pages have been leading us, the moment of highest emotional intensity and satisfaction. Yet we are not allowed to hear the crucial words that are spoken—we must be satisfied with rather abstract and generalized descriptions of them. And Darcy, we are told, had *probably* never been so happy before, while Elizabeth *might* have seen how well his happiness made him look. At the moment of supreme intimacy, the prose backs us off—way off. Nevertheless this conclusion has for 200 years fully satisfied most readers and rereaders of the novel.

For one thing, by drawing back from dialogue into narration Austen evokes our awareness of the mutuality of interdependence that marks this proposal as properly successful. And the conditionally inflected, precisely formal writing demonstrates the value of authentically (not conventionally) good manners in making possible the realization of intensely subjective desires. The nature of the love of Darcy for Elizabeth, and hers for him, is such that it can *only* be truly fulfilled through the sacrament and social sanctioning of marriage. Most so-called love stories at their conclusion require nothing more than a firm bed. Genuine love not only makes two people better and happier people but also makes their community better and happier.

This is why respect for genuine mannerliness (not mere adherence to rules of etiquette) may facilitate individual fulfillment. Mannerliness allows one to extend and complicate and thereby enhance such personal virtues as sincerity and honesty. These, in turn, permit one's subjective desires to be reciprocated, realized in social interactions that manifest the social system is functioning productively. Darcy is honest in his first proposal but boorish in his failure to recognize what his honesty owes to Elizabeth's honesty—a failure in recognition that shrinks his sincerity into selfishness. Darcy must learn to assess how his feelings need to be articulated so as to assure their fullest efficacy, that is, to inspire in Elizabeth a reciprocal love for him. Until he learns this, he will be as ineffectual as Miss Bingley, who cannot use social conventions to fulfill her desires because she so quickly gives way to satisfying her narcissistic impulses. Darcy at first defeats himself in this way with Elizabeth. He does not attract her into loving him. At his second proposal (unlike the first) he is painfully embarrassed. He makes himself dependent on her generosity. And she is equally embarrassed, in part *for* him. Their mutual embarrassment expresses their increased awareness of how sensitive each is to the other's feelings; each has become fearful of behaving selfishly toward the other. Austen's task is to enable her readers to share in this sensitivity expressive of the pleasure in entire mutuality of affection that produces embarrassment. She succeeds by evoking our imagination of Elizabeth not able to look at (but to imagine, as we are doing) the transfiguration of Darcy's features expressing that extraordinary delight that wells up when one's embarrassment is relieved through another person's affectionateness—a pleasure enhanced when one senses, as Darcy does here, that one's expressions of affection will equivalently relieve the embarrassment of one's partner.

Embarrassment is for many of us shy persons a too-familiar experience, yet it is an exceedingly complex one that has rarely been adequately analyzed (Ricks, 9–11). It involves self-consciousness in both common meanings of that term, our awareness of our own consciousness and our awareness of somebody else being very conscious of us. Embarrassment epitomizes human beings' capability for socializing their subjectivities. The painfulness of being embarrassed arises from its bringing to the sharpest emotional focus awareness of our dependence on other people. This explains the apparent paradox, as is dramatized by Darcy and Elizabeth, that a very high valuation of us by another can be embarrassing because it provokes the humility of gratitude. It is no accident that Darcy speaks of being "humbled" by Elizabeth's reproofs, as she has spoken of being "humiliated" by his letter. Such humility is the basis for a socially validated self-esteem that makes possible genuine reciprocity of affection. Elizabeth learns from Darcy's words "of feelings, which, in proving of what importance she was to him, made his affections every moment more valuable." Realization of her subjective desires occurs because Darcy is reciprocating the transformation she worked in his personality by teaching him, as he says, "How insufficient were all my pretensions to please a woman worthy of being pleased." Mutual love has never been better articulated.

The unusual degree of embarrassment felt by Darcy and Elizabeth in part arises, of course, from this being a second proposal, and Austen's manner of presentation keeps us subterraneously reminded of the former disaster, aware that the original proposal is being continued but transformed within the second. Indeed, the second really evolves from the first, as is emphasized by Darcy's opening words, which explicitly renew it. This reference allows us to perceive that Darcy's wishes although unchanged are different, because he has come to value them and their object in a new fashion. So he speaks of his affections and wishes differently, although one assumes that, since the vocabulary of courtship has its limits, he probably uses some of the same words. This assumption is reinforced by the most startling phrase in the passage, when the narrator describes Darcy as expressing himself "as sensibly and as warmly as a man violently in love can be supposed to do." What is startling here is not the narrator's refusal to reproduce directly the language of his passion, nor her funny appeal to supposition, but that she describes Darcy with a phrase, "violently in love," which intelligent Mrs. Gardiner has explicitly condemned as a meaningless cliché—"hackneyed, so doubtful, so indefinite, that it gives very little idea" (1:25). The trouble with the cliché is that in fact a very few people are ever, as Darcy is, violently in love. Most of us, like Mr. Bingley or Mr. Wickham, are—alas—incapable of genuinely powerful feeling for another. *Pride and Prejudice* is about a man who is unusual because he does fall violently in love, and Austen persuades us of that violence by explicitly calling our attention to the tendency of language to debase the very feelings it alone is capable of imaginatively evoking. Most novels of courtship do not convey firm belief in the reality of the love they narrate, in good measure because they evade, as Jane Austen does not, confronting the limitations of language for expressing profound feelings. Clichés are verbal structures that come into being because in their origin they effectively expressed some truth. The problem is to recapture the truth that falsifying repetitions of the expression conceal. All words and phrases are potential clichés, because everybody keeps using them—and a good expression of, say, true love, is terribly attractive to someone who thinks himself, or who wants to be *thought* of, as deeply in love. Very swiftly the once-effective phrase blocks convincing expression of the authentic emotion. By subtly reminding us that Darcy for all the truth of his emotional commitment can only propose in hackneyed terms, but not putting those words in his mouth, Austen persuades us of his deep affection for Elizabeth.

In part she succeeds because she's established good reasons for quietly recalling Mrs. Gardiner to her readers' minds (as I hope I have been doing). It is with the Gardiners that Elizabeth first reencounters Darcy after his original proposal. At that unexpected meeting at Pemberly we are told that the Gardiners observe with much surprise but equal pleasure that Darcy is "overflowing" with love for Elizabeth. The Gardiners's approval of Darcy as a husband for Elizabeth reinforces the rightness of his preference by providing disinterested evidence that he responds to Elizabeth's most admirable qualities, qualities Mrs. Gardiner in particular has long appreciated, as she shows when she warns Elizabeth not to be attracted by Wickam's admiration. These features of Austen's writing help to explain why most readers find her account of the second proposal satisfying, and, more significantly, why so many people reread *Pride and Prejudice* with a pleasure, finding no diminution in their enjoyment of Darcy's success at his second attempt. The proposal is presented in a manner that provokes imagining of what is required for a mutually rewarding marriage, chiefly an intensity of interdependence deriving from unsparing evaluations of self and partner, accompanying the energetic willingness to build the present on honest confrontations of the past. All of Austen's readers have participated in a real social transformation that was beginning to gather force during her lifetime, the development of preferences for companionate marriages based on personal choice over traditions of arranged matches. Arranged marriages were probably in most cases economically, socially, and politically useful— and not infrequently led to love. But once we commit ourselves to the idea that every human being, of whatever class, economic position, or gender, possesses an inalienable right to life, liberty, and the pursuit of happiness, the responsibility for making a good marriage becomes more personal—and much more difficult. In an arranged marriage, one's personal responsibilities are limited and can be rather distinctly defined. To make a good marriage under conditions of more-or-less free choice and subjective preference is a demanding a task, and its rate of success, as is shown in *Pride and Prejudice*, has never been high. Darcy and Elizabeth embody what we all hope for when we marry. And those lucky and skillful enough to have had successful marriages may see in Darcy and Elizabeth's behavior the promise of that continuing mutuality of respect, the ready admissions of interdependence, and the capacity to accept new responsibilities in a relationship never static and continually subjected to unexpected pressures, the behavior necessary to make "a good marriage" endure.

Beneath this sociological cogency of Darcy and Elizabeth's courtship, however, there is a deeper appeal of Austen's writing—a specific imaginative realization of which verbal make believe alone is capable of evoking. What her novel exemplifies almost paradigmatically is verbal make believe's power to excite a reader's consciousness of how awareness of a present moment at its most intense connects itself to the experiences out of which it has evolved. That exercise improves the quality of our genetically derived self-awareness, making it more efficacious in enhancing our capacities as individuals who can only fully realize individuality through social interactions. Self-consciousness is above all else of our continuity of being, both personally and communally. We can understand and evaluate what we are thinking and feeling only because we can connect current thoughts and feelings to those out of which they have developed. Such understanding enables us to intensify or transform what heretofore we have been capable of thinking or feeling. Verbal make believe by fostering consciousness of the continuousness by which our past productively enters into present experience endows us with more power to determine what will happen next, helping to free us from the control of mechanical processes and external pressures.

Our socialization is far more complicated and rewarding than that of other social animals because our processes of socializing are dependent on imagination, not merely physiological, automatic mechanisms. Contrary to bees and ants, our individuality may be sustained and enhanced by the social structures in which we participate. It is this intricate and dynamically ever-changing interrelation that superior verbal make believe enables us imaginatively to comprehend and to profit from — to the advantage of our particular community as well as ourselves.

Even with the help of a novelist as fine as Jane Austen, I know that I have only feebly sketched the tremendous cultural significance of make believe, especially why verbal storytelling has been essential rather than peripheral to all that is best in the diverse civilizational achievements of humankind. As excuse, I offer the testimony of Goethe, who in conversation with Eckerman on January 22, 1830 (Eden, 133) identified the source of my difficulty: "Folks don't realize how much time and effort it takes to learn to read. I've been at it for eighty years, and I still can't say I've completely got the hang of it."

SELECT BIBLIOGRAPHY

Adorno, Theodore W. *Aesthetic theory*, trans. and ed. Robert Herblot. Minneapolis: U of Minnesota P, 1997.

Alexandrov, Vladimir E. *Limits to interpretation: the meanings of* Anna Karenina. Madison: U of Wisconsin P, 2004.

Anderson, Joseph D. *The reality of illusion: an ecological approach to cognitive film theory*. Carbondale: Southern Illinois UP, 1996.

Anderson, Joseph, and Barbara Anderson. "The Case for Ecological Metatheory," *Post-theory*, ed. David Bordwell and Noël Carroll. Madison U of Wisconsin P, 1996, 346–367.

— — —. "Motion Perception in Motion Pictures," *The cinematic apparatus*, ed. Teresa deLaurentis and Stephen Heath. London: Macmillan, 1988, 76–96.

Arendt, Hannah. *Eichmann in Jerusalem: a report on the banality of evil*. New York: Harcourt Brace Jovanovich, 1963.

— — —. *The life of the mind: thinking*. New York: Harcourt Brace Jovanovich, 1971.

Armstrong, Nancy. "Emily Brontë In and Out of Her Time," *Genre* 15 (1982), 243–264.

Arnheim, Rudolph. *Film essays and criticism*, trans. Brenda Bentheim Madison: U of Wisconsin P, 1997.

Austen, Jane. *Pride and prejudice. The novels of Jane Austen*, 3rd ed., 5 vols., vol. 2, ed. R. W. Chapman. Oxford: Clarendon Press, 1966.

Azuela, Mariano. *The underdogs*, trans. E. Munguia, Jr. New York: New American Library, 1963.

Baetens, Jan. "Novelization, A Contaminated Genre?" *Critical inquiry* 32 (Autumn 2005), 43–60.

Bakhtin, Mikhail. *Art and answerability: early philosophical essays*, ed. Michael Holquist and Vadim Liopunov, trans. Vadim Laopunov. Austin: Texas U of Texas P, 1990.

— — —. *The dialogic imagination: four essays*, ed. Michael Holquist, trans. Caryl Emerson and Michael Holquist. Austin: U of Texas P, 1981.

— — —. *Problems of Dostoyevsky's poetics*, ed. and trans. Caryl Emerson. Minneapolis: U of Minnesota P, 1984.

— — —. *Speech acts and other essays*, ed. Caryl Emerson and Michael Holquist, trans. Vern W. McGee. Austin: U of Texas P, 1980.

Balázs, Bela. *Theory of the film*, trans. Edith Bone. New York: Arno Press, 1972 (1942).

Barfield, Owen. *The rediscovery of meaning*. Middletown, CT: Wesleyan UP, 1977.

Barthes, Roland. *Image/ music/ text*, trans. Stephen Heath. New York: Hill and Wang, 1977.

Bazin, Andre. *Bazin at work: major essays and reviews*, trans. Alain Piette and Bert Cardullo. New York: Routledge, 1997.

———. *What is cinema?* 2 vols., Selected and translated by Hugh Gray. Berkeley: U of California P, 1967.

Bergman, Ingmar. "Introduction: Film Has Nothing to Do with Literature," *Four screenplays of Ingmar Bergman*, trans. Lars Malmstrom and David Kushner. New York: Simon and Schuster, 1960.

Bernstein, Michael André. *Foregone conclusions: against apocalyptic history*. Berkeley: U of California P, 1994.

Biancorosso, Giorgio. "Beginning Credits and Beyond Music and the Cinematic Imagination," *Echo* 3:1 (2001), <www.humnet@ucla.edu/echo>.

———. "Film, Music, and the Redemption of the Mundane," *Bad music*, ed. M. Darno and C. Washburne. New York: Routledge, 2004.

Birkerts, Sven. *The Gutenberg elegies: the fate of reading in an electronic age*. London: Faber and Faber, 1994.

Bluestone, George. *Novels into film*. Berkeley: U of California P, 1957.

Booth, Wayne. "Distance and Point of View: An Essay in Classification," *Twentieth century literary theory: an introductory anthology*, ed. Vissilis Lambropoulos and David N. Mill. Albany: State U of New York P, 1987, 269–284.

———. *The company we keep: an ethics of fiction*. Berkeley: U of California P, 1988.

Bordwell, David. *Making meaning*. Cambridge, MA: Harvard UP, 1989.

———. *Narration in the fiction film*. Madison: U of Wisconsin P, 1985. "The Viewer's Activity," 29–47.

Bordwell, David, and Kristin Thompson, eds. *Film art: an introduction*, 2nd ed. New York: Knopf, 1986.

Bordwell, David, and Noël Carroll, eds. *Post-theory: reconstructing film theory*. Wisconsin: U of Wisconsin P, 1996.

Braudy, Leo. *The frenzy of renown: fame and its history*. Oxford: Oxford UP, 1986.

———. *The world in a frame*. Chicago: U of Chicago P, 1984.

Brontë, Emily. *Wuthering Heights*, ed. Richard J. Dunn. New York: Norton, 2003.

Brooks, Peter. *Reading for the plot: design and intention in narrative*. New York: Knopf, 1984.

Bruner, Jerome. *Acts of meaning*. Cambridge, MA: Harvard UP, 1998 (1990).

Cameron, Ian, and Douglas Pye, eds. *The book of westerns*. New York: Continuum, 1996.

Carpenter, Edmund, and McLuhan, Marshall. *Explorations in communication*. Boston: Houghton-Mifflin, 1970.

Carroll, Noël. *Engaging the moving image.* New Haven: Yale UP, 2003.

———. *Interpreting the moving image.* Cambridge: Cambridge UP, 1998.

———. *Mystifying movies.* New York: Columbia UP, 1980.

———. "The Power of Movies," *Daedalus* 114 (1984), 79–104.

———. *Theorizing the moving image.* Cambridge, MA: Harvard UP, 1996.

Casey, Edward S. *Imagining: a phenomenological study.* Bloomington: Indiana UP, 1976.

Cavell, Stanley. *The world viewed: reflections on the ontology of film.* Cambridge, MA: Harvard UP, enlarged ed. 1979.

Chatman, Seymour. *Coming to terms: the rhetoric of narrative in fiction and film.* Ithaca: Cornell UP, 1990.

———. *Story and discourse: narrative structure in fiction and film.* Ithaca: Cornell UP, 1978.

Chion, Michel. *The voice in cinema,* trans. and ed. Claudia Grobman. New York: Columbia UP, 1999.

Cocteau, Jean. *Beauty and the beast: diary of a film,* trans. Ronald Duncan-Devereux. New York: Dover, 1972.

Coleridge, Samuel Taylor. "Lecture," *Coleridge: Shakespearian criticism,* 2 vols., 2nd ed., ed. Thomas Raysor, London: Dent, 1960, 1:197–198.

———. "On Poesy and Art," *Biographia literaria,* 2 vols., ed. John Shawcross. London: Oxford UP, 1962, 2:254–269.

Crary, Jonathan. *Suspensions of perception: attention, spectacle, and modern culture.* Cambridge, MA: MIT Press, 1996. "Modernity and the Problem of Attention."

Currie, Gregory. *Image and mind: film, philosophy and cognitive science.* Cambridge: Cambridge UP, 1996.

———. "Making Believe," *Dialogue* 32:4 (1993), 359–374.

———. *The nature of fiction.* Cambridge: Cambridge UP, 1990.

Danto, Arthur C. *The end of art: contemporary art and the pale of history.* Princeton: Princeton UP, 1997.

Darnton, Robert. "First Steps Toward a History of Reading," *The kiss of Lamourette: reflections on cultural history.* New York: W. W. Norton, 1990, 154–190.

Darwin, Charles. *The expression of emotions in man and animals.* 3rd ed. New York: Oxford UP, 1998, 43.

DePryck, Koen *Knowledge, evolution, paradox.* Albany: State U of New York P, 1993.

Dickens, Charles. Great expectations. *The Works of Charles Dickens: The Authentic Edition,* vol. 13. London: Chapman and Hall, 1901.

Dostoyevsky, F. M. *Crime and punishment. Complete works,* 30 vols., vols. 6 & 7. Leningrad: Science Publishers, 1973.

———. *Crime and punishment,* 2nd ed., trans. Jesse Coulson. Norton Critical Edition, ed. George Gibian. New York: Norton, 1975.

Drummond, Philip. *High noon.* London: British Film Institute, 1997.

Eagleton, Terry. *Myths of power: a Marxist study of the Brontës*. London: Macmillan, 1975.

Eco, Umberto. "*Casablanca:* Cult Movies and Intertextual Collage," *Travels in hyperreality*. trans. William Weaver. New York: Harcourt Brace Jovanovich, 1986, 197–212.

Edelman, Gerald. *Neural Darwinism*. New York: Basic Books, 1989.

———. *Wider than the sky: the gift of consciousness*. New Haven: Yale UP, 2004.

Edelman, Gerald, and Giulio Tononi. *A universe of consciousness*. New York: Basic Books, 2000.

Eden, Kathy. "Great Books and the Undergraduate Curriculum," *Literary Imagination* 2:2 (Spring 2000), 125–133.

Ekman, Paul. *Emotions revealed*. New York: Henry Holt and Co, 2003.

———. *Telling lies: clues to deceit in the marketplace, politics, and marriage*. New York: W. W. Norton, 2001 (1985).

Eliot George. *The mill on the floss*, ed. Carol T. Christ. New York: Norton, 1996.

Erb, Cynthia. *Tracking King Kong: a Hollywood icon in world culture*. Detroit: Wayne State UP, 1998.

Fischer, David Hackett. *Paul Revere's ride* New York: Oxford UP, 1994.

———. *Washington's crossing*. New York and Oxford: Oxford UP, 2004.

Flaubert, Gustave. *Madame Bovary*, ed. Thiery Laget. Paris: Gallimard, Folio Classique, 2001.

———. *Madame Bovary*, 3rd ed., ed. Margaret Cohen, trans. Eleanor Marx Aveling, rev. Paul de Man. New York: Norton, 2004.

Foreman, Carl. "On the Wayne," *Punch* 14 (August 1974), 240–242.

Foster, Gwendolyn. "The Women in *High Noon:* A Metanarrative of Difference," *Film Criticism* 18:3 (1994), 72–81.

Frank, Joseph. *Dostoyevsky: the miraculous years, 1865–1871*. Princeton: Princeton UP, 1995.

French, Philip. *Westerns*, rev ed. London: Secker and Warburg, 1977.

Frye, Northrop. *Fearful symmetry*. Boston: Beacon Press, 1947.

Gallie, W. B. *Philosophy and the philosophical understanding*, 2nd ed. New York: Shocken, 1968.

Gay, Penny. *Jane Austen and the theatre*. Cambridge: Cambridge UP, 2002.

Gay, Peter. *Savage reprisals: Bleak House, Madame Bovary, Buddenbrooks*. New York: Norton, 2002.

Gaylin, Ann Elizabeth. *Eavesdropping in the novel from Austen to Proust*. Cambridge: Cambridge UP, 2002.

Gianetti, Louis. "Fred Zinneman's *High Noon*," *Film Criticism* 1:3 (1976–77), 2–12.

Gibson, James J. *The ecological approach to visual perception*. Hillsdale, NJ: Lawrence Erlbaum, 1986 (1979).

Ginsburg, Michael Peled. "Pseudonym, Epigraphs, and Narrative Voice: *Middlemarch* and the Problem of Authorship," *ELH* 47 (1980), 542–558.

Goldner, Oroville. *The making of King Kong*. New York: Ballantine, 1976.

Gombrich, Ernest H. *Art and illusion*. London: Phaidon, 1960.

Goodwin, James, ed. *Perspectives on Kurosawa*. New York: G. K. Hall, 1994.

Gorbman, Claudia. *Unheard melodies: narrative film music*. Bloomington: Indiana UP, 1987.

Gray, Francine Du Plessix. "Dirty Dancing," *The New Yorker*, February 28, 2005, 86–89.

Grene, Marjorie. "Perception and Human Reality," *Harré and his critics*, ed. Roy Bhoska. Oxford: Blackwell, 1990, 17–25.

Harding, D. W. "The Role of the Onlooker," *Scrutiny* 6:3 (December 1937), 247–258.

Harré, Rom. *Great scientific experiments*. London: Phaidon, 1981.

Hitchcock, Alfred. "Directing," *Footnotes to the film*, ed. Charles Davy. London: Lovat Dickson and Thompson, 1937.

Hogarth, William. *The analysis of beauty* (1753), ed. Joseph Burke. Oxford: Clarendon Press, 1955.

Holland, Norman. "Film Response from Eye to I: The Kuleshov Experiment," *Classical Hollywood narrative*, ed. Jane Gains. Durham: Duke UP, 1991, 79–86.

Iser, Wolfgang. *The act of reading: a theory of aesthetic response*. Baltimore: Johns Hopkins UP, 1978.

Jacobs, Carol. *Unattainable romanticism: Shelley, Brontë, and Kleist*. Baltimore: Johns Hopkins UP, 1989.

Kaufman, Stanley. *Living images*. New York: Harper, 1975.

Kearney, Richard. "Paul Ricoeur and the Hermeneutic Imagination," *The narrative path: the later works of Paul Ricoeur*, ed. T. Peter Kemp and David Rasmussen. Cambridge, MA: MIT Press, 1989, 1–23.

Kurosawa, Akira. "Notes on Filmmaking," in Goodwin, 63–64.

Lesser, Simon. *Fiction and the unconscious*. New York: Vintage, 1962.

Levinson, Jerrold. "Seeing Imaginatively at the Movies," *Philosophical Quarterly* 170 (1992), 70–78.

Lindsay, Vachel. "Moving Sculpture," *The art of the moving picture*. New York: Macmillan, 1922 (1915), 84–96.

Llosa, Mario Vargas. *The perpetual orgy: Flaubert and Madame Bovary*, trans. Helen Lane. New York: Farrar Staus Giroux, 1975.

Lombardo, Thomas J. *The reciprocity of perceiver and environment: the evolution of James J. Gibson's ecological psychology*. Hillsdale, NJ: L. Erlbaum, 1987.

Lukács, Georg. *Writer and critic and other essay*, trans. and ed. Arthur D. Khan. New York: Grosset and Dunlap, 1970.

MacAndrew, Elizabeth. *The gothic tradition in fiction*. New York: Columbia UP, 1979.

Mast, Gerald. *Film/cinema/movie: a theory of experience*. New York: Harper and Row, 1977.

— — —. "On Framing," *Critical inquiry* 11 (September 1984), 82–109.

Mayr, Ernst. "Behavior Programs and Evolutionary Strategies," *American scientist* 62 (1974), 650–658.

McGurl, Mark. "Making it Big: Picturing the Radio Age in *King Kong*," *Critical inquiry* 22:3 (Spring 1996), 415–445.

Meisel, Martin. *Realizations*. Princeton: Princeton UP, 1983.

———. *Shaw and the nineteenth century theater*. Princeton: Princeton UP, 1963.

Meister, Marcus. "Retinal Ennui," *Harvard Magazine* 108 (November 2005), 11–12.

Miller, D. A. *The novel and the police*. Berkeley: U of California P, 1992.

Mink, Louis O. "History and Fiction as Modes of Comprehension," *Historical understanding*, ed. Brian Fay, Eugene O. Cobb, and Richard T. Vann. Ithaca: Cornell UP, 1987, 42–60.

Mitchell, W. J. T. *Picture theory: essays on verbal and visual representation*. Chicago: U of Chicago P, 1994.

Moran, Richard. "The Expression of Feeling in Imagination," *Philosophical review* 103 (1994), 75–108.

Morson, Gary Saul. "Sideshadowing and Its Possibilities," *Narrative and freedom: the shadows of time*. New Haven: Yale UP, 1994, 117–174.

———. "Prosaic Bakhtin," *Common Knowledge* 2:1 (1993), 35–42.

———. "Sideshadowing and Tempics," *New literary history* 29:4 (1998), 599–624.

———. "Theory of Parody." *Rethinking Bakhtin: extensions and challenges*, ed. Gary Saul Morson and Caryl Emerson. Evanston: Northwestern UP, 1989, 63–86.

Nabokov, Vladimir. *Lolita*. New York: Putnam, 1955.

Naremore, James O. *Acting in the cinema*. Berkeley: U of California P, 1988.

———. *More than the night*. Berkeley: U of California P, 1998.

———, ed. *Film adaptation*. New Brunswick: Rutgers UP, 2001.

Neisser, Ulric. *Cognition and reality*. New York: W. H. Freeman, 1976.

Nichols, Dudley. "The Writer and the Film," *Great film plays*, ed. John Gassner and Dudley Nichols. New York: Crown, 1959.

Nussbaum, Martha C. *Love's knowledge: essays on philosophy and literature*. New York: Oxford UP, 1990.

———. *Poetic justice*. New York: Oxford UP, 1995.

Okrent, Peter, "The Public Editor," *New York Times*, Sunday, January 2, 2005, B2.

Ong, Walter J. *Interfaces of the word*. Ithaca: Cornell UP, 1977.

———. *Orality and literacy: the technologizing of the word*. London: Methuen, 1982.

———. *The Presence of the word*. New Haven: Yale UP, 1967.

Peacock, John. "Depiction," *The Philosophical Review* 96:3 (1977), 383–410.

Pittenger, William. *Capturing a locomotive: a history of the secret service*. Washington, DC: National Tribune, 1905 (1881).

Poulet, Georges. "Phenomenology of Reading," *New Literary History* 1:1 (1969), 53–68.

Pratt, Mary Louise. *Toward a speech act theory of literary discourse.* Bloomington: Indiana UP, 1977.

Pudovkin, V. I. *Film technique and film acting,* trans. Ivor Montague. London: Vision, 1958.

Ramachandran, V., and Antis, Stuart M. "The Perception of Apparent Motion," *Scientific American* 254 (June 1986), 102–109.

Ranier, Peter. "Blood Sport," *New York Magazine,* April 25, 2004, 64–65.

Read, Herbert. "Toward a Film Aesthetic," *Cinema Quarterly* 1:1 (Autumn 1932), 1–8.

Ricks, Christopher. *Keats and embarrassment.* Oxford: Clarendon Press, 1974.

Ricoeur, Paul. *Time and narrative.* 3 vol., trans. Kathleen McLaughlin and David Pellauer. Chicago: UP, 1984–1988.

Ritchie, Donald. *The films of Akira Kurosawa,* 3rd ed., expanded and updated, additional material by Joan Mellen. Berkeley: U of California P, 1996.

Ruskin, John. "The Lamp of Truth," *The seven lamps of architecture, works of John Ruskin,* vol. 8., ed. Cook and Weddeburn. Library Edition. London: George Allen, 1903–1912.

Ryle, Gilbert. *The concept of mind.* London: Hutchinson, 1963.

Sanders, Thomas, Ernest Tucker, and Gary Hamburg, eds. *Russian-Muslim confrontations in the Caucasus.* London: Routledge Curzon, 2004.

Sankovitch, Natasha. *Creating and recovering experience: repetition in Tolstoy.* Stanford: Stanford UP, 1998.

Scruton, Roger. *The aesthetics of music.* New York: Oxford UP, 1999.

Sedgewick, Eve Kosofsky. *The coherence of gothic convention,* 2nd ed. London: Atheneum, 1996.

Sennett, Mack. *King of comedy* (as told to Cameron Shipp). Garden City: Doubleday, 1954.

Shannon, Edgar F. "Lockwood's Dream and the Exegesis of *Wuthering Heights,*" *Nineteenth Century Fiction* 14 (1959), 95–109.

Shaw, Harry E. *Narrating reality: Austen, Scott, Eliot.* Ithaca: Cornell UP, 1999.

Siebers, Tobin. *Morals and stories.* New York: Columbia UP, 1992.

Slotkin, Richard. *Gunfighter nation.* New York: Atheneum, 1992.

Smith, Murray. "Human Expression," *Times Literary Supplement,* February 7, 2003, 13–15.

Sparshott, F. E. "Basic Film Aesthetics." *Film theory and criticism,* ed. Gerald Mast and Marshall Cohen. London: Oxford UP, 1974, 209–222.

St. Clair, William. *The reading nation in the romantic period.* Cambridge: Cambridge UP, 2004.

Stam, Robert. *Subversive pleasures: Bakhtin, cultural criticism, and film.* Baltimore: Johns Hopkins UP, 1989.

Stewart, Garrett. *Dear reader: the conscripted audience in nineteenth-century British fiction.* Baltimore: Johns Hopkins UP, 1996.

Stoneman, Patsy. *Brontë transformations.* New York: Prentice Hall, 1996.

— — —, ed. *Emily Bronte: Wuthering Heights.* New York: Columbia UP, 1998.

Stoppard, Tom. *Arcadia*. London: Faber and Faber, 1993.

Tandon, Bharat. *Jane Austen and the morality of conversation*. London: Anthem, 2003.

Tanner, Tony. *Adultery in the novel*. Baltimore: Johns Hopkins UP, 1979.

Terras, Victor. *Reading Dostoyevsky*. Madison: U of Wisconsin P, 1998.

Tolkien, J. R. R. "On Fairy Stories," *The Tolkien reader*. New York: Ballantine, 1966, 31–99.

Tolstoy, Leo. *Anna Karenina*, ed. V. A. Zhdanov and Z. E. Zaidenshnur. Moscow: Science Publishers, 1970.

———. *Anna Karenina*, trans. Richard Pevear and Larissa Volokhonsky. New York: Viking Penguin, 2001.

———. *Hadji Murad*, trans. Aylmer Maude. New York: Dodd, Mead, Co., 1912.

Trahair, Lisa. "Short-circuiting the Dialectic: Narrative and Slapstick in the Cinema of Buster Keaton," *Narrative* 10:3 (October 2002), 307–323.

Turner, Frederick. "The Neural Lyre: Poetic Meter, the Brain, and Time," *Natural classicism*. New York: Paragon House, 1985, 61–108.

Turvey, Malcolm. "Seeing Theory," *Film theory and philosophy*, ed. Richard Allen and Michael Smith. Oxford, Oxford UP, 1997, 431–457.

Tyler, Parker. "Movies and the Human Image," *The three faces of the film*. Rev. ed. London: Thomas Yoseloff, 1967, 137–141.

Vardac, A. Nicholas. *Stage to screen: rhetorical method Garrick to Griffith*. Cambridge MA: Harvard UP, 1949.

Vygotsky, L. S. *The psychology of art*. Cambridge, MA: MIT Press, 1971.

Walton, Kenneth. *Mimesis as make-believe*. Cambridge, MA: Harvard UP, 1990.

Warshow, Robert. "The Westerner" (1954), *Film: an anthology*, ed. Daniel Talbot. Berkeley: U of California P, 1954, 148–162.

Williams, Raymond. *The long revolution*. New York: Columbia UP, 1961.

Wolfe, Glenn Joseph. *Vachel Lindsay: the poet as film critic*. New York: Arno Press, 1973.

Wollen, Peter. "Cinema and Technology: An Overview," *The cinematic apparatus*, ed. Teresa deLauretis and Stephen Heath. London: Macmillan, 1988, 14–22.

Wood, Gillen D'Arcy. *The shock of the real*. New York: Palgrave, 2001.

Wood, Graham. "Re-reading Robert Louis Stevenson," *Dalhousie Review* 62 (1982), 44–59.

Woodring, Carl. R "The Narrator of *Wuthering Heights*," *Nineteenth Century Fiction* 11 (1957), 298–305.

Worth, Sol. "Pictures Can't Say Ain't," *Film/Culture: explorations of cinema in its social context*, ed. Sari Thomas. Methuen, NJ: Scarecrow Press, 1982, 97–110.

Young, Kay. "Word-Work, Word Play, and the Making of Intimacy in *Pride and Prejudice*," *The talk of Jane Austen*, ed. Bruce Stovel and Lynn Wemlos Gregg. Edmonton: U of Alberta P, 2002, 57–72.

Zinneman, Fred. *An autobiography*. London: Bloomsbury Publishing, 1992.

INDEX